DAM Jahrbuch 2006

DAM **Jahrbuch 2006**

Architektur in Deutschland
Architecture in Germany

Thematischer Schwerpunkt: Wohnen in der Stadt
Key Topic: Living in the City

Herausgegeben von Edited by
Deutsches Architekturmuseum, Frankfurt am Main
Annette Becker, Anna Hesse, Peter Cachola Schmal

Mit Beiträgen von With Contributions from
Yorck Förster, Falk Jaeger, Claus Käpplinger, Hanno Rauterberg, Inge Wolf

Mit Baukritiken von With Reviews by
Hubertus Adam, Matthias Alexander, Paul Andreas, Ursula Baus, Jörg Brauns,
Hans-Jürgen Breuning, Sabine Brinitzer, Michaela Busenkell, Christina Gräwe,
Oliver G. Hamm, Anna Hesse, Ulrich Höhns, Falk Jaeger, Karl Kiem,
Ursula Kleefisch-Jobst, Karin Leydecker, Sebastian Redecke, Peter Cachola Schmal,
Sabine Schneider, Christian Thomas

Prestel Verlag
München · Berlin · London · New York

Deutsches Architekturmuseum
Frankfurt am Main

INHALT
CONTENTS

VORWORT
FOREWORD

Die Strategie kommt ausgerechnet aus dem Land Baden-Württemberg, traditionell eine Gegend mit vielen Einfamilienhäusern... Mittels der rätselhaften Buchstaben MELAP, was für *Modellvorhaben zur Eindämmung des Landschaftsverbrauchs durch Aktivierung des innerörtlichen Potenzials* steht, werden dort Entwicklungskonzepte gefördert, die durch Umnutzung, Baulückenschließung und Wohnumfeldmaßnahmen der Stärkung von Ortskernen dienen. Die Strategie stimmt hoffnungsvoll und ist ein Zeichen dafür, dass ein Prozess des Umdenkens begonnen hat.

Übertragen in den größeren Maßstab der Stadt, entspricht sie dem heute gerne verwendeten Begriff der neuen Urbanität. Wir haben ihn in diesem Jahr fokussiert und die Renaissance des *Wohnens in der Stadt* zum Leitthema unseres Jahrbuches gewählt.

Der Begriff Urban Renaissance dient seit 1999 als Schlagwort, nachdem Richard Rogers in »Towards an Urban Renaissance« einen Bericht zur Stadterneuerung in England vorgelegt hatte. 2001 werden auf dem internationalen Kongress *Urban Renewal* in Barcelona ähnliche Ziele für Städte weltweit diskutiert. Während in England und Spanien mit einer schon in der Begrifflichkeit ausgedrückten Euphorie an die neuen Aufgaben herangegangen wird, spricht man in Deutschland medienwirksam von ›schrumpfenden Städten‹; erfolgreiche Initiativen wie das Stadtentwicklungskonzept *Perspektive München*, das die Münchner Innenstadt ›kompakt, urban und grün‹ gestaltet, dringen weitaus weniger ins öffentliche Bewusstsein.

Über Jahrzehnte waren die Menschen in die Vororte gezogen, in die Reihen- und Einfamilienhäuser, so dass die Städte ihre Konturen verloren. Diese Stadt-Umland-Wanderung hat sich inzwischen umgekehrt, denn die neuen Lebens- und Wohnformen lassen sich besser in den Innenstädten realisieren. Die Gruppe der Stadtfreunde wächst und sie findet in den Zentren plötzlich eine Vielfalt an Wohnformen, die zu ihrem individuellen Lebensstil passt. Wir zeigen dieses neue Raumangebot, legen die Situation in wichtigen deutschen Großstädten dar und verfolgen die Auswirkungen auf die Raumplanung.

So beschreibt Hanno Rauterberg in seinem Essay die Gruppe jener ›neuen Urbaniten‹, ihre Wohngeschichte und die Erwartungen, die sie an das Leben in der Stadt richten. Er stellt dar, wie sich ihr Lebensstil viel einfacher in der Infrastruktur einer Innenstadtlage realisieren lässt. Und er kommt zu dem Fazit, dass – allen Veränderungen des virtuellen Zeitalters trotzend – die Stadt mit ihren *Plätzen des Austauschs* und *Straßen der Begegnung* notwendig ist und bleibt.

Leipzig hat es in den vergangenen Jahren vermocht, mit den Themen »perforierte Stadt« und Olympia-Kandidatur, als Handelszentrum, mit gründerzeitlichen Stadtquartieren und spektakulären, mehrhöfigen Blockrandbauten mit weitläufigen

Of all places, it is the state of Baden-Württemberg, traditionally associated with one-family houses, that has come up with a new pilot project to stem land use by activating inner-city potential, under the acronym MELAP *(Modellvorhaben zur Eindämmung des Landschaftsverbrauchs durch Aktivierung des innerörtlichen Potenzials)*. The project supports development concepts that strengthen inner cities and smaller towns by means of conversions, gap-site developments and other housing measures. It is a welcome sign of changing attitudes. Applied on a wider scale to large cities, the strategy corresponds to what is now widely known as New Urbanity. This year's annual focuses on new urbanity and the renaissance of Living in the City.

Since 1999 and the publication of Richard Rogers' *Towards an Urban Renaissance*, describing the regeneration of Britain's cities, urban renaissance has become something of a buzzword. In 2001, similar aims were put on a worldwide agenda at the international congress Urban Renewal in Barcelona. But whereas Britain and Spain have enthusiastically set about tackling this new challenge and the very discourse itself is peppered with positively charged terminology there, the German media has tended to speak sombrely of our "shrinking cities", while even such success stories as *Perspektive München* – Munich's "compact, urban and green" inner-city regeneration project – have barely filtered through to the public consciousness.

Over decades, the exodus to the terraced houses and semis of the suburbs undermined the cohesion of our inner cities. Now the tables have turned, and it is the inner cities that are appealing to the way people want to live today. Increasing numbers of people favour an urban lifestyle and find that the city centres offer a range and variety of housing to suit their individual lifestyles. We look at the new spaces available, outline the situation in Germany's major cities and examine the effects on urban planning.

In his essay about the Germans' latest love affair with urban life, Hanno Rauterberg describes the history and aspirations of living in the city. He shows how the urban infrastructure caters to today's lifestyles and comes to the conclusion that, in spite of all the changes wrought by the digital media and the internet, the city with its "open places for communication" and "streets of communication" is still as necessary as ever.

Leipzig has drawn a lot of attention in recent years with its concept of the "perforated city" and its Olympic bid, as a centre of trade and commerce with fine nineteenth-century architecture, spectacular blocks punctuated by spacious arcades. Leipzig's vibrant cultural scene is attracting young people and investors like no other eastern German city, apart from Berlin. But a declining population and urban density call for a different approach to

Passagen Aufmerksamkeit auf sich zu ziehen. Die sächsische Metropole vermag als vielfältiger Kulturraum wie keine andere nach Berlin junge Leute und Investitionen im Osten anzuziehen. Gesunkene Bevölkerungszahlen und Baudichten erfordern allerdings andere Wege zur Urbanität. Stadthäuser, Wohneigentum mit geringeren Dichten auf Brachen, ist daher eine der Leipziger Initiativen. Claus Käpplinger beschreibt einige dieser Rückbau-Projekte und skizziert darüber hinaus die wichtigsten jüngsten Planungen in der Stadt.

An vielen Berliner Bauten spürt Falk Jaeger dem Charme der Stadt des 19. Jahrhunderts nach und kommt zu dem Ergebnis, dass es den gänzlich neuen Quartieren nirgends recht gelingt, ihn emotional zu berühren. Man sähe die europäische Stadt deutlich, doch erreiche man sie nicht mehr. Bemerkenswert an seinen Ausführungen sind auch die Erinnerungen an die IBA 1984/87 mit dem Thema ›Die Innenstadt als Wohnort‹ und an den Stadthaus-Typus von Laage, die die heutigen Diskussionen im deutlichen Licht einer sich wiederholenden Baudiskussion zeigen.

Beispiele von Projekten neuen innerstädtischen Wohnens aus Berlin, Hamburg, Frankfurt und München zeigen die Bandbreite aktueller Wohnformen vom Reihenhaus bis zum Mehrfamilienhaus und Loft. Aus Weimar schließlich stammt der Entwurf für eine komplette Quartiersplanung. Die Bauten stehen erst für einen Anfang, viele weitere Projekte sind im Entstehen, und so scheint es tatsächlich, dass die Renaissance der Stadt ein Versprechen ist, das vielerorts noch eingelöst werden muss.

14 Projekte schließlich zeigen eindrucksvolle Neubauten des vergangenen Jahres in Deutschland. Unvermindert attraktiv ist die Eröffnung neuer Museen, ob privater Bauherren wie Marli Hoppe-Ritter und ihr Museum von Max Dudler, Daimler Chrysler und sein Neues Mercedes Benz Museum von UN Studio oder das mit öffentlichen Geldern errichtete Phæno Science Center von Zaha Hadid für die Stadt Wolfsburg und David Chipperfields LiMo für das Deutsche Literaturarchiv in Marbach.

In der Nachbarschaft zu historischen Ensembles stehen der Neubau der Bibliothek der Freien Universität in Berlin von Norman Foster und das Servicezentrum von Staab Architekten für die Theresienwiese in München. Das japanische Architekturbüro SANAA von Kazuyo Sejima und Ryue Nishizawa ist mit seinem Bau Zollverein School of Management and Design in Essen die sicherlich spektakulärste Großform dieses Jahres.

Das Archiv des DAM zeigt seine Zukunftsfähigkeit und erklärt, wie die spannende Aufgabe der Archivierung im digitalen Zeitalter zu lösen ist. Mit dem Archiv von Peter Kulka, das der Kölner Architekt dem DAM großzügig überlassen hat, kann das Museum seine Sammlung wesentlich bereichern.

Annette Becker, Anna Hesse, Peter Cachola Schmal

urbanity here. And so Leipzig has set its sights on townhouses and low-density residential property on urban wastelands. Claus Käpplinger describes some of the city's projects and outlines some of its most important urban planning measures.

Falk Jaeger goes in search of Berlin's nineteenth-century charm and finds that none of the city's new-build districts really touch him emotionally. While conceding that the notion of the European city is clearly evident, he feels something is missing. Interestingly, in recalling the 1984/87 IBA, held under the motto "The City Centre as a Place to Live", and in looking to Gerhard Laage's ideas of the ideal townhouse, Jaeger sheds new light on today's debates about urban development as a recurrent theme in urban planning.

Examples of new city-centre developments in Berlin, Hamburg, Frankfurt and Munich cover a spectrum of contemporary housing from terraced house to apartment block to loft, including plans for an entire new district in Weimar. With many more projects in the pipeline, these buildings are just the beginning. The much-vaunted urban renaissance, it seems, is a promise that is still far from reality in many places.

Finally, 14 of last year's most impressive new buildings in Germany are individually showcased. New museums are still high on the agenda – from private collector Marli Hoppe-Ritter's museum by Max Dudler, to corporate client Daimler Chrysler's New Mercedes Benz Museum by UN Studio, to the publicly funded Phæno Science Center in Wolfsburg by Zaha Hadid and David Chipperfield's LiMo for the Deutsches Literaturarchiv in Marbach.

Examples of new buildings that dovetail with historic ensembles are also featured: the New Library of the Freie Universität in Berlin by Norman Foster and the Service Centre by Staab Architekten for the Theresienwiese in Munich. Probably the most spectacular large-scale building of the year is the Zollverein School of Management and Design in Essen by Japanese architectural team SANAA, headed by Kazuyo Sejima and Ryue Nishizawa.

The DAM Archives ring in the changes, outlining the challenges of archiving material in the digital age. Cologne architect Peter Kulka has generously donated his own archive to the museum, thereby greatly enhancing the DAM collection.

Annette Becker, Anna Hesse, Peter Cachola Schmal

ESSAYS
ESSAYS

DAS GLÜCK DER STADT – WARUM DIE DEUTSCHEN DAS URBANE LEBEN WIEDERENTDECKEN
URBAN BLISS – GERMANY REDISCOVERS URBAN LIVING

Hanno Rauterberg

Es gab eine Zeit, da schrieben große Wissenschaftler große Bücher über das Ende. Über das Ende der Geschichte, das Ende der Kunst, das Ende der Moderne und natürlich auch über das Ende der Stadt. »The city is dead«, so lautete die knappe Diagnose des amerikanischen Theoretikers John Friedmann, damals im Jahr 2002. Zum Glück kam dann bald das Ende fürs Ende.

Heute jedenfalls ist viel von einer Wiederkehr des Städtischen die Rede, von einer neuen Lust am urbanen Wohnen und Arbeiten. Über Jahrzehnte hatten die Menschen die Flucht hinaus in die Vororte angetreten. Jetzt aber beginnt sich der Drang nach draußen offenbar abzuschwächen. Erstmals wächst die Gruppe derer, die mitten im Geschehen und nicht irgendwo im Grünen leben möchten. Und viele Menschen zieht es zurück in die Stadtkerne, vor allem im Osten Deutschlands. Allein im Umkreis von Leipzig entschlossen sich 30 000 Menschen binnen weniger Jahre für einen Umzug ins Zentrum.

Nicht überall ist diese Bewegung zurück in die Stadt so stark, nicht überall wurde die Zersiedelung gestoppt. Und doch ist offenkundig, dass die Stadt vor einer Art Gezeitenwechsel steht, und die alten Standards, die alten Gewissheiten der Bundesrepublik ins Rutschen geraten.

Spätestens seit den sechziger Jahren hatte es im Wirtschaftswunder-Deutschland zum großen Lebensglück einfach dazugehört: das Häuschen im Grünen. Für Konrad Adenauer war es ein »Bollwerk gegen den Bolschewismus«; der Kunsthistoriker Heinrich Klotz sprach vom »röhrenden Hirschen der Architektur«. Die große Mehrheit der Deutschen wünschte sich eine eigene Scholle, eine Immobilie fürs Alter, etwas, das Dauer und Halt versprach und eine solide Hinterlassenschaft für die Kinder.

Doch mittlerweile haben sich die Lebensträume und die Lebenswirklichkeit vieler Menschen gewandelt. Und so wandelt sich auch die Stadt. Die eigentlichen, die ursprünglichen Qualitäten des urbanen Lebens werden wieder entdeckt. Im Moment ist das noch eine Entwicklung, deren Größenordnung sich nicht genau beziffern lässt. Eindeutig ist nur, dass die Gruppe der Stadtfreunde wächst, und dass sie stärker wächst als alle anderen gesellschaftlichen Gruppen. So sagt es der Bundesverband für Wohneigentum und Stadtentwicklung. Schon jetzt bilden diejenigen, die von Milieuforschern als Hedonisten, als Experimentelle und als Performer bezeichnet werden, rund ein Drittel der Bevölkerung. Sie sind maßgeblich daran beteiligt, gesellschaftliche Wohn-, Konsum- und Verhaltensweisen mitzuprägen und zu verändern. Sie sind in aller Regel gebildet, gut verdienend und sympathisieren mit einem städtischen, abwechslungsreichen Leben. Es ist ja auch nicht neu, dass die Gründerzeitquartiere gerade bei den Mode- und Lifestyle-Bewussten ebenso beliebt sind wie im eher studentischen und bürgerlichen Milieu; schon in den achtziger

There was a time when authoritative figures wrote authoritative books about The End. They wrote about the end of history, the end of art, the end of modernism and, of course, the end of the city. "The city is dead," was the laconic pronouncement of American theorist John Friedmann in 2002. Fortunately, soon afterwards, there was an end to all the ends.

Today, at any rate, there is a lot of talk about the return of urbanity, about a newfound delight in living and working in the city. For decades, people had fled to the suburbs. But now the lure of the great outdoors seems to be wearing off. For the first time, the number of people choosing to live in the midst of things, rather than in leafy suburbia, is actually on the increase. And many of them, especially in eastern Germany, are moving back to the inner cities. In Leipzig alone, 30,000 people have moved into the city centre in recent years.

This "back to the city" trend is stronger in some places than in others. Urban sprawl has not come to a halt everywhere. Yet the tide is quite evidently turning. The old habits and certainties of life in Germany are beginning to undergo a sea change. At the latest, since the 1960s – the heyday of Germany's miraculous post-war economic recovery – happiness has been a house with a garden. For the country's first post-war chancellor, Konrad Adenauer, who presided over the *Wirtschaftswunder*, it represented a bulwark against bolshevism. Art historian Heinrich Klotz spoke of it as the architectural equivalent of painting's "monarch of the glen". The overwhelming majority of Germans wanted their own little plot of land, a house for their old age, something that promised security and permanence and a decent inheritance for their children.

Since then, the dreams and reality of many people's lives have changed. And the city is changing with them. People are now beginning to rediscover the inherent qualities of life in the city. While it is still too early to tell just how widespread this phenomenon is, it is already clear that increasing numbers of people are embracing urban life and that this demographic group is growing faster than any other. Official statistics tell us so. Already, the segment of the population described by social analysts as hedonists, experimentalists and performers makes up about one third of the population. These are the people who are changing the face of society, its consumer behaviour and lifestyles. They are, for the most part, educated, high-income individuals with a varied and urban lifestyle. It does not come as news that the traditional urban quarters with their turn-of-the-century buildings are as popular with trendy fashionistas as they are with students and

Bolles + Wilson, Münster, Turm Falkenried, Hamburg
Bolles + Wilson, Münster, Falkenried Tower, Hamburg

Baumschlager Eberle Architekten, Lochau (A), Geschosswohnungen
Falkenried, Hamburg
*Baumschlager Eberle Architekten, Lochau (A), Falkenried apartment house,
Hamburg*

Jahren war viel von den ›neuen Urbaniten‹ die Rede. Doch ist
diese Gruppe in den vergangenen Jahren überproportional kräftig
gewachsen, und sie wird weiterhin wachsen, weil es immer mehr
Singles gibt und in immer weniger Haushalten Kinder wohnen.

Doch auch die ›Woopis‹ drängen verstärkt in die Stadt, die
›Well-off-older-people‹. Das sind Menschen Mitte 50, Anfang 60,
deren Kinder aus dem Haus sind, und die rund dreißig Lebens-
jahre bei derzeit noch guter Rente vor sich haben. Sie wollen noch
einmal etwas Neues beginnen, wollen nicht nur Rosen züchten,
Rasen schneiden, mit den Nachbarn plauschen. Sie fühlen sich fit,
sind aktiv, sie wollen etwas erleben. Und gerade diese Gruppe der
alten Hungrigen wird in den kommenden Jahren stark anwachsen.
Von den über Fünfzigjährigen, so die Prognosen, wird es 2020 bereits 10 Millionen mehr geben als heute. Viele von ihnen entstam-
men der Generation der 68-er, die damals mit ihren Kindern ins
Grüne verzogen waren, sich aber nun ihrer lebendigen Jugend-
und Studententage erinnern und in gewisser Weise dort anknüpfen
wollen, wo sie einst die Zelte abgebrochen haben: in der Stadt.
Weil dort das Leben ist, es dort Theater und Kunst gibt, Restaurants
gleich um die Ecke und die beste ärztliche Versorgung.

Gründe für die neue Bewegung zurück in die Stadt gibt es also
viele, der wichtigste ist aber wohl: das Geld. Während viele Ban-
ken über Jahrzehnte zum Bauen und Kaufen rieten, weil das
eigene Haus finanzielle Sicherheit und Unabhängigkeit und steten
Wertzuwachs versprach, raten sie neuerdings ab, sie warnen
sogar. Seit einiger Zeit schon, so rechnen manche vor, ist mit
Wohnimmobilien kaum noch Gewinn zu machen, real haben viele
Häuser und Wohnungen sogar an Wert verloren, vor allem jene
Häuser und Wohnungen, die nicht in den gefragten Stadtteilen liegen. Die Preisrückgänge für Einfamilienhäuser belaufen sich pro
Jahr auf bis zu 4,8 Prozent, in Offenbach fiel beispielsweise der
Durchschnittspreis sogar von 397 000 Euro 1994 auf 269 000 Euro
2004. Noch ein extremeres Beispiel: Im selben Zeitraum fiel der
Quadratmeterpreis für eine Eigentumswohnung in Kassel von
2559 Euro auf nur noch 822. Und diese Entwicklung, so lauten
jetzt die Vorhersagen, dürfte sich verschärfen. Im Jahr 2050 wird
es nur noch 65 statt 80 Millionen Deutsche geben, sagen viele
Prognostiker. Und sie sagen weiter, dass spätestens im Jahr 2015
die große Leerstandswelle, die den Osten der Republik längst

middle-class intellectuals. Even in the 1980s there was talk of
"new urbanites". But this group has grown disproportionately in
recent years and it looks set to keep on growing because there
are more and more singletons and because there are fewer households with children.

Woopis (well-off older people) are also moving back to the city.
These are the empty-nesters in their mid-50s to early 60s who can
look forward to another thirty years or so on a comfortable pen-
sion and who want to do more with their lives than just tend
roses, mow the lawn and have the occasional neighbourly chat
over the garden fence. They are fit and active and eager to live
their lives to the full. This group of ageing adventurers is set to
grow considerably in the next few years. By 2020, it is estimated
that there will be ten million more of them than there are now.
Many of them belong to the generation that was involved in the
student revolts of '68 and who moved out to more rural areas to
bring up their children. Now, as they recall the vitality and excite-
ment of their youth and student days, they feel drawn to the
very place they once turned their backs on: the city, because that
is where it is all happening; there are theatres and art galleries,
good restaurants within easy reach and, of course, the best
medical care.

There are many reasons for the new trend towards urban living. But the most important of all is money. For decades, banks
encouraged people to invest in real estate, assuring them that
home ownership would provide financial security and independ-
ence and a guaranteed increase in value. Today, they advise –
even warn – against it. Some have calculated that property is no

Spengler Wiescholek, Hamburg, Town Houses Falkenried, Hamburg
Spengler Wiescholek, Hamburg, Falkenried Townhouses, Hamburg

überrollt hat, auch die Kommunen im Westen erreichen wird. Natürlich, begehrte Ballungszentren wie München oder Frankfurt wird es weniger schwer oder auch gar nicht treffen. Auch die wachsende Zahl von Haushalten und die immer noch steigende Wohnfläche pro Kopf mögen ein wenig von dem Leerstand kompensieren. Doch kleinere, schwache Städte wie Bremerhaven spüren die Auszehrung schon heute; und auch wenig attraktive Wohnlagen wie Trabantenstädte dürften sich sehr bald schon zu Geisterstädten entwickeln. Spätestens also in zehn Jahren, wenn die Zahl der Haushalte nicht mehr wächst, werden sich viele Bungalows und Krüppelwalmhäuschen nur noch schwerlich verkaufen lassen; und manche, vor allem die mittelmäßigen Objekte in mittelmäßiger Lage, dürften gar keinen Käufer mehr finden. Das sagt eine Studie der Vereins- und Westbank.

Außerdem ist vor kurzem die Eigenheimzulage weggefallen, auch das erhöht die Realkosten für alle Käufer und macht für viele das Wohnen im Grünen unerschwinglich. Und die Pendlerpauschale sinkt, während zugleich die Benzinpreise drastisch gestiegen sind. Der Durchschnittspendler zahlt schon jetzt pro Jahr 740 Euro Sprit für seine Arbeitsfahrten. Weitere Steigerungen werden aller Wahrscheinlichkeit nach nicht ausbleiben. Auch aus diesem Grund überlegen sich viele potenzielle Käufer, ob sie tatsächlich hinaus ins so genannte Grüne ziehen sollen. In ökologischer Hinsicht ist so ein Umzug in jedem Fall problematisch: Jede Familie, die aus der innerstädtischen Etagenwohnung in das Giebelhäuschen im Grünen zieht, verdreifacht ihren Energieverbrauch. Und zu Recht weist das Worldwatch-Institut darauf hin, dass eine Reduzierung der industriellen Treibhausgase völlig wirkungslos bliebe,

spine2 architects, Hamburg, Dachausbau Juliusstraße, Hamburg
spine2 architects, Hamburg, Attic-story extension Juliusstrasse, Hamburg

Stadtvillen, Hamburg-Rotherbaum
Town villas, Hamburg-Rotherbaum

longer a reliable source of profit, and that many houses and flats have actually fallen in value – especially those that are not located in the most popular parts of town. The price of the average family home is falling by about 4.8 per cent a year. In the town of Offenbach, for instance, the average price fell from 397,000 Euros in 1994 to just 269,000 Euros in 2004. In Kassel, the situation is even more extreme: during the same period, property prices fell from an average 2,559 Euros per square metre to just 822. Analysts predict that this downward spiral will continue, forecasting that the population of Germany will have fallen from 80 million to 65 million by the year 2050 and that the wave of empty properties that has swamped eastern Germany will have reached the western German communities by 2015 at the latest. Of course, popular urban conglomerations such as Munich or Frankfurt are unlikely to be as badly affected, if at all. Rising numbers of individual households and the increasing demand for more space per capita is likely to compensate the property oversupply to some degree. But smaller, less economically robust towns such as Bremerhaven are already beginning to feel the pinch, and less attractive locations such as suburban housing estates could soon become ghost towns. Within ten years, according to a study by the Vereins- und Westbank, unless the number of households continues to grow, many bungalows and cottages will prove very difficult to sell or may not find any buyers at all.

The recent abolition of tax incentives for homebuyers has increased the cost to buyers in real terms, making rural and suburban life unaffordable. What is more, tax-deductible allowances for commuting have been cut, while petrol prices have rocketed. Already, the average commuter spends 740 Euros a year on fuel. Further price increases look more than likely. This is another reason for many potential buyers to think twice about living on the outskirts. Every family that moves from a flat in town to a house in the country trebles their energy consumption. As the Worldwatch Institute quite rightly points out, a reduction in the industrial emissions that contribute to global warming will be ineffective unless there is a reduction in road traffic at the same time. But every commuter from the country to the city adds to the number of car users on our roads. Indeed, two out of three employees today go to work by car, producing the very noise, pollution and congestion that makes city life so unappealing to some. This is hardly a new insight. Until now, very few people chose to live in the city on

wenn nicht gleichzeitig der Autoverkehr eingedämmt würde. Dieser aber erhöht sich mit jedem, der vom Land in die Stadt pendelt; zwei von drei Arbeitnehmern fahren schon heute mit dem Auto zur Arbeit. Und produzieren dabei jenen Lärm, jenen Gestank, jene Verstopfung unserer Straßen, die dann noch mehr Leuten das Leben in der Stadt vergällt. Diese Erkenntnis ist nicht gerade neu, und bislang waren es nur wenige, die aus diesen ökologischen Gründen ein Leben in der Stadt bevorzugten. Doch je stärker Energie- und Benzinkosten steigen, je stärker also ein jeder am Inhalt seines Portemonnaies feststellen kann, wie teuer ein Leben auf dem Lande eigentlich ist, desto attraktiver wird umgekehrt die Stadt.

Der zweite wichtige Grund für die wachsende Beliebtheit des städtischen Wohnens, Arbeitens und Einkaufens ist das verbesserte Angebot an Wohnungen. Keineswegs war es bislang so, dass alle, die aus der Stadt ins Umland zogen, dies freiwillig getan hätten. Im Gegenteil, man könnte fast von einer Stadtvertreibung sprechen. Denn die zentrumsnahen Lagen waren teuer, oft viel zu teuer, um dort eine entsprechend großzügige Immobilie etwa für eine Familie zu erwerben. Also entschlossen sich viele Bauwillige zum Verlassen der Stadt, weil die Grundstücke und Baupreise auf dem Land und in den Randlagen der Stadt günstiger waren. Das sind sie in den meisten Fällen zwar noch immer. Doch gerade dort, wo es hohen Leerstand gibt, vor allem in den ostdeutschen Städten, beginnt sich das Blatt zu wenden, das bisherige Kostengefälle zwischen Stadt und Land löst sich auf. Dort sind die Mieten und die Grundstückspreise auch in den städtischen Lagen derart gesunken, dass es für Familien wieder erschwinglich wird, in der Stadt zu leben und zu bauen. Mit anderen Worten: Die Städte sind

Bothe Richter Teherani, Hamburg, Elbberg-Campus, Hamburg
Bothe Richter Teherani, Hamburg, Elbberg campus, Hamburg

ecological grounds. But the more our fuel and energy costs rise, the more obviously we notice the effect on our wallets. And the more expensive country life becomes, the more attractive the city becomes.

Another important reason for the growing appeal of living, working and shopping in the city is that the housing situation has improved. Until now, not everyone who moved from the city to the suburbs did so willingly. On the contrary, many were forced out because they were unable to afford the necessary space for, say, a family, in the city centre. This meant that many of those seeking a foothold on the property ladder had to look further afield, where property prices were within their grasp. In most cases, that still holds true. But in areas where a lot of property is lying empty, especially in eastern German cities, the tables are starting to turn and, as a result, the price gap is narrowing. In those areas, rents and property prices in urban locations have fallen so much that families are now finding they can afford to live in the city after all. In other words, the cities have become competitive again. Or, in the case of western Germany, demographic developments are beginning to make them competitive again. Cities are now able to offer a more affordable life. With that, more and more people in future are likely to choose to stay in the city. And it is not just the cost that is changing – the quality and variety of housing too, has improved considerably in recent years.

For many people, the housing market was quite simply too unimaginative in the past. It could hardly even be called a market, given that most developers were simply churning out the same old 2.5-kids family accommodation. For a while, they were getting away with it because demand so consistently outstripped supply. More recently, however, falling demand has forced them to take their customers' needs more seriously and to broaden their product range: terraced housing, lofts, rooftop gardens – suddenly there is a variety of accommodation to an extent previously available only to those willing to have their own designs built outside town. The demand for unusual, individualistic housing is huge. Living space has become an integral part of the way people make a statement about their lifestyle. According to a study by the German Federation of Housing and Urban Development, more than 50 per cent of all Germans want houses and apartments that are special, different, and preferably tailored to their own needs. Some of these are now being built, albeit too few, and mostly on inner city gap sites vacated by old industrial, military, post office or railway premises. This is the big opportunity, the second chance, for many cities to offer an urban location to those people who would otherwise have moved out to the country. Gap sites and potential conversions in Germany's cities account for some 44,000 hectares – an area twice the size of Hanover.

Ironically, it is only since too much housing has become available in many places that the price situation has improved and the range on offer has become more varied. There is movement coming into the property market. But apart from the factors already mentioned, there is a third reason for this, which is socially determined. Lifestyles are becoming more and more individual. Age-old conventions are being broken. People are no longer tied for life to one place, one job, one partner. This increased flexibility that has become the norm for so many people simply does not fit in with a life in leafy suburbia. The suburbs have always been a place for families. As soon as children were on the way, couples used to look for a quiet life in greener surroundings. Today, with fewer couples having children, even those who do choose to

erneut konkurrenzfähig geworden. Oder für den Westen Deutschlands formuliert: Durch die demographische Entwicklung werden sie wieder konkurrenzfähig werden. Sie können ihren Bewohnern günstigere Angebote unterbreiten. Und so dürften sich in Zukunft noch mehr Menschen für ein Verbleiben in der Stadt entscheiden. Zumal sich nicht nur die Kostenseite des Angebots verändert. Es verändert sich auch das qualitative Angebot, die Vielfalt hat in den letzten Jahren deutlich zugenommen.

Vielen war das Angebot an Wohnungen in der Vergangenheit schlicht zu einfallslos. Der Immobilienmarkt war in Wahrheit gar keiner, denn etliche Baufirmen produzierten einfallslos immer dieselbe Zweikind-Familienware, schließlich war die Nachfrage stets so groß, dass sie alles loswurden. Erst in jüngster Zeit sind sie durch die schwindende Nachfrage gezwungen, ihre Kunden ernster zu nehmen und das Angebot zu erweitern: gestapelte Reihenhäuser, Lofts, Dachgärten – plötzlich gibt es eine Vielfalt an Wohnformen, die sich bisher nur in Eigenregie am Stadtrand erbauen ließ. Der Wunsch nach dem Ungewöhnlichen und Individuellen ist groß, denn längst ist die Wohnung ein Teil der Lebensstilgestaltung geworden. Mehr als 50 Prozent aller Deutschen wünschen sich besondere, möglichst auf ihre eigenen Bedürfnisse zugeschnittene Häuser und Wohnungen, ergab eine Untersuchung des Bundesverbandes für Wohneigentum und Stadtentwicklung. Zumindest einige davon entstehen nun, wenn auch meist noch zu wenige, und zwar oftmals dort, wo innenstadtnahe Bauflächen frei werden, weil die Bundeswehr abzieht, weil Bahn, Post oder alte Industriebetriebe ihre Grundstücke freigeben. Es ist die große, die zweite Chance vieler Städte: dass sie denjenigen, die sonst ins Grüne verzogen wären, einen eigenen, urbanen Raum bieten können. Rund 44 000 Hektar solcher Brach- und Konversionsflächen gibt es in den deutschen Städten – eine Fläche doppelt so groß wie Hannover.

Paradoxerweise haben sich also erst dadurch, dass es vielerorts zu viel Wohnraum gibt, die Kosten verbessert und hat sich das Angebot verbreitert. Der Markt ist in Bewegung geraten. Doch außer diesen beiden Gründen gibt es noch einen dritten, einen gesellschaftlichen. Das individualisierte Leben, ein Leben jenseits der alten Raster, ohne eine lebenslange Bindung an einen Ort, an einen Beruf, an einen Partner, an einen Verein, dieses flexibilisierte Leben ist für immer mehr Menschen zur Normalität geworden. Und dieses Leben will für viele nicht in die beschauliche Vorstadt hineinpassen. Die Vorstadt war immer ein Ort der Familien. Wenn sich Kinder ankündigten, dann hieß es: Hinaus ins Grüne und Ruhige. Doch heute bekommen immer weniger Paare Kinder, und auch die, die Kinder bekommen, begreifen das Häuschen im Grünen allenfalls noch als ›Lebensabschnittsimmobilie‹, wie es der Soziologe Walter Siebel bezeichnet. Oder sie wählen gleich das urbane Leben, denn auch das klassische Muster – der Mann geht zur Arbeit, die Frau bleibt daheim bei den Kindern – ist längst für die meisten Familien überholt. 59 Prozent aller erwerbsfähigen Frauen arbeiten, und ganz selbstverständlich wollen viele Mütter bald nach der Geburt der Kinder wieder berufstätig sein; viele müssen auch arbeiten, um der Familie das Auskommen zu sichern. Und gerade ein flexibleres Arbeiten lässt sich in zentrumsnahen Wohnlagen weit besser verwirklichen: ohne lange Anfahrtszeiten, ohne lange Einkaufswege und mit der Kindertagesstätte oder der Tagesmutter gleich in der Nebenstraße. Da erweist sich das Leben in der kompakten Stadt nicht nur als kostengünstiger, es ist auch zeitsparender und damit familienfreundlicher. Der Durchschnittspendler ist im Jahr umgerechnet 30 Tage lang auf

Hübbotter + Stürken, Hannover, Gilde Carré, Hannover Linden
Hübbotter + Stürken, Hanover, Gilde Carré, Hanover Linden

become parents tend to regard suburban living as a temporary phase, as sociologist Walter Siebel puts it. With the classic family structure of the man going to work and the woman staying at home with the kids already a thing of the past for most people, many couples with children now choose to live in the city anyway. As it is, 59 per cent of women work, and many mothers are eager to return to their jobs as soon as possible after their children are born. In order to support their families, many of them have no choice. In such cases, the flexible opportunities afforded by a central location are far more practicable: no lengthy commutes, no major shopping expeditions, and childcare facilities on tap. Life in the compact surroundings of the city can be not only less expensive but also less time-consuming and far more compatible with family life. The average commuter spends the equivalent of thirty days on trains or in cars. For both men and women, the city makes it easier to combine children and career, and have thirty more days of family time.

Even beyond the classic family structure, however, the aspirations of great swathes of the community have undergone a sea change. As have consumer demands: we want to be able to order a quick pizza, nip into a coffee shop for breakfast and have all the benefits of round-the-clock services on our doorstep. Yet the further we live from the centre of things, the more effort is involved and the wider the gaps in the network become. City life, on the other hand, offers high-density choice and variety. It is no

Schiene und Straße unterwegs. Wer also Kind und Karriere verein-
baren will – ob Frau oder Mann –, für den ist die Stadt der bessere
Ort. Er hat 30 Tage mehr Zeit für seine Familie.

Auch jenseits der klassischen Familienkonstellationen haben
sich viele Lebensvorstellungen in weiten Teilen der Gesellschaft
verändert: Die Konsumbedürfnisse sind andere geworden, man
will sich mal eben schnell eine Pizza bestellen können, man
möchte seinen Coffee-Shop um die Ecke haben fürs Frühstück im
Vorübergehen, man setzt immer selbstverständlicher voraus, alle
Vorteile der Dienstleistungsgesellschaft jederzeit verfügbar zu
haben. Doch je weiter draußen der moderne Mensch wohnt, desto
mühsamer und lückenhafter wird diese Allzeitversorgung. Die
Stadt hingegen bietet eine hohe Dichte an Abwechslung und Ein-
kaufsmöglichkeiten. Nicht zufällig bedienen sich daher etliche
Einkaufszentren in ihrer Namensgebung städtischer Begriffe und
nennen sich Forum oder Arkaden. Doch nur wenige vermögen
das zu bieten, was vielen Konsumenten wichtig ist: ein stärker
individualisiertes Angebot anstelle der großen Discounter und ein
Umfeld, das authentisch wirkt. Die Stadt ist ein solcher Ort, sie
steht für das Unverfälschte, das historisch Gewachsene. Und auch
das trägt dazu bei, dass sich das Städtische einer neuen Beliebtheit erfreut.

Doch so erstaunlich diese neue Beliebtheit sein mag, sie birgt
für die Städte auch einige Gefahren. Es ist zumindest nicht ausge-
schlossen, dass gerade die attraktiven Lagen einer Stadt verstärkt
für Wohlhabende erschlossen werden und die Ärmeren, die Alten
und Migranten weichen müssen. Denn obwohl immer mehr Menschen vom bunten, vielfältigen Stadtleben träumen, von den
spannenden Gegensätzen, den unterschiedlichsten Ethnien und
Lebensstilen, die sich dort auf engstem Raum vereinen – in Wahrheit sind die Grenzen der Toleranz oft eng gezogen. Viele schwär-
men zwar von dem Trubel, den Kneipen, den Cafés. Doch natürlich
wollen sie nicht über einem Café wohnen, wollen nicht den Lärm
vor ihrem Schlafzimmer, nicht den Fixer im Hausflur und für ihre
Kinder keine Schule mit vielen Ausländern. Sie wollen das Beste
aus beiden Welten: die Angebote der Stadt, ihre Dienstleistungen
und kulturellen Reize, zugleich aber auch die Beschaulichkeit der
Vorstadt, ihre Geborgenheit und Ruhe. Und so entstehen man-
cherorts bereits Einfamilienhausquartiere mitten in der Stadt, etwa
in Hannover auf dem Gelände der einstigen Gilde-Brauerei.

Die neuen Bau- und Wohnformen verheißen also keineswegs
automatisch ein vielfältigeres städtisches Leben. Und so erfüllt
sich die Hoffnung so mancher Soziologen und Planer nur teilweise: Sie preisen nicht selten das Stadtleben als die bessere
Daseinsform, weil es Toleranz lehre, weil es kulturelle Mischung
erlaube, weil es den Sinn für den Gemeinsinn schule. Vielen Urbaniten hingegen bedeutet Stadt vor allem Lifestyle, und sie scheren
sich nicht weiter um die Visionen der bürgerlichen Aufklärer.

Die Rückkehr in die Stadt ist nicht zwangsläufig eine Rückkehr
zu einer besseren Gesellschaft. Und doch ist es für eine schrump-
fende Gesellschaft durchaus sinnvoll, das urbane Leben stärker zu
fördern als bislang. Noch suchen die meisten Städte unbeirrt ihr
Heil allein in der Gewerbeansiedlungspolitik. Sie begreifen nicht,
dass auch das Wohnen und vor allem das familienfreundliche
Wohnen ein bedeutender Standort- und Überlebensfaktor für sie
ist. Natürlich soll, wer weiterhin sein Häuschen im Speckgürtel
bauen will, dies tun; doch er muss dazu nicht noch ermuntert
werden, auch nicht durch eine Entfernungspauschale. Solche
Formen der Bezuschussung gehören reformiert – erstens. Zweitens
müsste geprüft werden, ob das System der Steuererhebung

coincidence that so many shopping malls take names that echo
urban structures, such as Forum or Arcade. But only a few of
them actually offer what so many consumers really want: a highly
individual range of consumer services in an authentic setting
instead of just a motley collection of cut-price stores. The city is
just such an authentic setting. It still stands for something real and
authentic that has grown over the years. That in itself has con-
tributed to the renewed appeal of urban life.

Astonishing as this renewed appeal may seem, it also harbours
certain risks for the city. There is still the possibility that the most
attractive urban locations will increasingly become the preserve of
the well-heeled and that the less affluent members of society will
be pushed out. For even though ever more people are dreaming
the dream of a vibrant and exciting urban life teeming with ethnic
diversity and individual lifestyles, the truth of the matter is that the
boundaries of tolerance are often strictly drawn. People may
enthuse about the buzz of the pubs and cafés. But of course they
don't want to live directly above a bar. They don't want the noise
right outside their bedroom windows. They don't want the junkies
shooting up in their stairwells. They don't want their children to go
to multi-ethnic schools. They want the best of both worlds: all the
entertainment, culture and service the city can provide, but with
all the peace and privacy of the suburbs. And so developments
with one-family houses are already springing up in the middle of
the city, as on the former Gilde Brewery site in Hanover, for
instance.

The new diversity in building developments and housing does
not necessarily promise more diversity in urban life. With that, the
hopes of many a sociologist and urban planner are only partially
fulfilled. They frequently praise urban living as the better way of
life that teaches tolerance, that makes possible a blend of cultures
and develops a sense of commonality. But many urbanites see
the city only as a place that offers a certain lifestyle. They couldn't
care less about the visions of the enlightened bourgeoisie.

The return to the city is not necessarily a return to a better
society. And yet, in a shrinking society, it makes sense to promote
urban life. As yet, most cities still seek salvation in building industrial estates. They have not realised that housing – especially fam-
ily-oriented housing – is an important factor in their appeal as a
location and even in their survival. Of course, those who prefer to
build a home in the well-heeled suburbs should continue to do so
if they want – but they need not be encouraged, especially not by
granting them allowances for commuting. These forms of subsidy
need to be revised. First of all, we have to determine whether our
taxation system is the right one. Until now, people have paid their
income tax to their local councils at their place of residence. This
has prompted many outlying communities to offer cheap building
land in a bid to compete with the cities, thereby gaining additional
income. Thirdly, real estate legislation needs to be reconsidered.
Until now, cities with serious financial problems, such as those
faced recently by Dresden and Hamburg, needed to sell a lot of
real estate in order to fill their coffers. Needless to say, they sell to
the investors who offer the best price. And the best prices are
offered by the developers of office space. In the end, then the city
councils are left wondering at the number of families leaving the
city. Surely it would be smarter to intervene in the free market by
helping the very people who are indispensable: by subsidising
housing and small businesses.

Until now, many cities have seemed almost paralysed; they
have failed to see the new opportunities arising and have simply

Jan Störmer Architekten, Hamburg, Stadtlagerhaus, Hamburg
Jan Störmer Architekten, Hamburg, City storage house, Hamburg

noch das richtige ist. Bislang zahlen die Bürger ihre Lohn- und
Einkommenssteuer am Wohnort, und so werden immer mehr
Randgemeinden dazu verführt, billiges Bauland auszuschreiben,
mit den Städten zu konkurrieren und ihnen die Steuereinnahmen
abspenstig zu machen. Drittens gehören auch das Bodenrecht und
die Bodenpolitik auf den Prüfstand. Bislang ist es so, dass Städte,
denen die Geldnot mächtig zusetzt, wie jüngst Dresden oder Hamburg, viele ihrer Grundstücke verkaufen, um den Haushalt aufzu-
bessern. Und natürlich verkaufen sie an Investoren, die das meiste
dafür bieten. Und am meisten bieten diejenigen, die Büros bauen.
Anschließend wundern sich die Städte, dass immer mehr Familien
die Stadt verlassen. Viel klüger wäre es da, in den freien Markt
einzugreifen und just jene zu begünstigen, die für ein lebendiges
Stadtleben unverzichtbar sind, zum Beispiel Wohnprojekte oder
das Kleingewerbe.

Bislang allerdings wirken viele Städte wie gelähmt, sie sehen
nicht die neuen Chancen, die sich bieten, sondern scheinen ihr
eigenes Ende zu erwarten. Vor zehn Jahren hieß es ja noch, die Da-
tenströme des digitalen Zeitalters würden die Stadt hinfortspülen,
dank Internet werde alles überall möglich sein und der reale Ort
ganz und gar unbedeutend. Heute sieht es so aus, als brauchte
gerade der vernetzte Mensch eben jene Stadt, die es seit vielen tausend Jahren gibt: dicht, öffentlich und ganz unvirtuell, mit Plätzen
des Austauschs und Straßen der Begegnung. Das Leben verflüssigt
sich, wird flexibler, flüchtiger. Was aber bleibt, ist die Stadt.

watched and waited as the end drew nigh. Ten years ago, there
was talk of the data flow of the digital age sweeping the city away,
and of the internet making anything possible anywhere so actual
location would become irrelevant. Today, it looks as though the
very people who rely on the internet are the ones who really need
the kind of urban life that has existed for thousands of years:
dense and public and anything but virtual, with all its open places
for communication and all its streets of communication. Life
becomes more liquid, more fluid. What remains is the city.

DER OSTEN LEUCHTET NICHT GROSS, ABER WAHRNEHMBAR
LEIPZIG IM JAHRE 16 NACH DER WIEDERVEREINIGUNG
A WAN LIGHT IN THE EAST
LEIPZIG SIXTEEN YEARS AFTER REUNIFICATION

Claus Käpplinger

Wenn heute von Ostdeutschland die Rede ist, dann oft nur als Krisenregion. Arbeits- und Perspektivlosigkeit, Abwanderung und Fremdenfeindlichkeit, Bevölkerungsschwund und zerfallende Städte dominieren weiterhin die Vorstellung vieler Westdeutscher über die Realität Ostdeutschlands. Unvertraut ist das andere Deutschland, dessen alte Kulturlandschaften bewundert werden, aber dessen Gegenwart fremd erscheint. Positive Nachrichten kommen oft nur aus zwei Bereichen im Westen an. Einerseits stellen die Medien die Leistungen weniger Hochtechnologie-Unternehmen und -Institute im Osten immer wieder heraus. Andererseits fokussiert sich ihr Blick fast nur auf die Rekonstruktionen von Bauwerken der vor-sozialistischen Vergangenheit. Ihre Botschaft? Grau ist die Gegenwart im Osten zwischen den Zukunftsverheißungen der Technologie und den sentimentalen Rückbindungen an die Vergangenheit.

So fand kein anderes Ereignis seit 1989 eine derart vorbehaltlos positive Resonanz wie der Wiederaufbau der Dresdner Frauenkirche. Ihre Eröffnung wurde geradezu hymnisch gefeiert als die Wiederkehr eines Symbols der alten Zeit und einer neuen Gemeinschaft von West und Ost, ehemaliger und heutiger Dresdner. Ähnliche Beachtung und Euphorie konnte in den letzten Jahren nur die Renaissance der alten Ostseebäder oder alte Stadtzentren wie das mittelalterliche Quedlinburg und das preußische Potsdam auslösen, wo man bislang noch erfolglos eine Rekonstruktion des alten Stadtschlosses anstrebt. Dafür wurde aber bereits das Projekt eines brandenburgischen Parlamentsneubaus aufgegeben.

Zeitgenössische Architektur hat es zwischen Erzgebirge und Ostsee schwer, Anerkennung zu finden, sowohl vor Ort als auch überregional. Nur wenige Städte vermochten es im Osten, mit zeitgenössischer Architektur Furore zu machen. Wo kapitalkräftige Akteure vor Ort fehlen, bestimmen zumeist nur wenige auswärtige Investoren die neuen Stadtbilder mit ihrer Architektur der Camouflage und des geringsten Widerstandes. Dabei dominiert ihre Architektur längst auch den Bereich des öffentlichen Bauens, da nicht mehr selbst gebaut, sondern immer häufiger nur geleast wird.

Der einzige Bereich, der bislang davon verschont blieb, ist der Hochschulbau. Weshalb die bedeutendsten Bauten und häufig die einzig nennenswerten Bauten zeitgenössischer Architektur in ostdeutschen Städten zumeist Hochschulgebäude sind. Wo sich mehr als nur zwei, drei zeitgenössische Gebäude von Rang in einer ostdeutschen Stadt finden, waren es zumeist die Stadtbauräte und Planungsdezernenten, die sich gegen alle Widerstände der Politik und Brachialökonomie leidenschaftlich für eine zeitgenössische Architektur eingesetzt haben. Leipzig, Halle, Meiningen, Weimar, Chemnitz oder Cottbus setzten so offensiv und erfolgreich auf das Instrument des Architekturwettbewerbs.

These days, most talk of Germany's formerly communist eastern states is talk of a region in crisis. West Germans tend to associate the east with high unemployment, gloomy economic prospects, racism, a dwindling population and urban dilapidation. They may admire its cultural heritage, but they know little of its present-day reality. As often as not, the only good news reported about the east is either about its high-tech industries and research institutes or about the reconstruction of its historic pre-communist architecture. The media message is this: eastern Germany is a bleak place where the promise of future technology meets nostalgia for the past.

No event since 1989 has been hailed with such unanimous enthusiasm as the reconstruction of the Frauenkirche in Dresden. It was celebrated as the resurrection of a symbol of the city's proud cultural heritage, forging new links between the generations and between east and west. The only other things to unleash any comparable outpouring of euphoria in recent years have been the renaissance of eastern Germany's historic spas and the restoration of its historic city centres such as medieval Quedlinburg or Prussian Potsdam. Admittedly, in Potsdam's case, plans to reconstruct the old city palace have yet to come to fruition, while the planned new Brandenburg regional parliament building has been put on ice.

From the Erzgebirge mountains to the shores of the Baltic, contemporary architecture finds little acceptance and few eastern German cities can boast acclaimed new architectural projects. A dearth of heavyweight investors locally has left the market open to investors from outside who are more likely to play it safe with bland new buildings. These have now crept into the public sector as well, as authorities are choosing to lease rather than build their own premises.

The only field that has remained unscathed by this trend so far is the tertiary education sector. This explains why the most significant buildings and, for the most part, the only examples of quality contemporary architecture are university buildings. In any eastern German city with more than just a handful of fine contemporary buildings it has generally been the municipal building and planning authorities that have been the driving force behind the contemporary architecture. Leipzig, Halle, Meiningen, Weimar, Chemnitz and Cottbus have successfully implemented architectural design competitions.

Leipzig, in particular, enjoys as high a profile in the field of contemporary architecture as it does in the arts and culture and has attracted more new investment and young blood than any other

Ingo Andreas Wolf, Wohnhaus Schillerweg, 2004
Ingo Andreas Wolf, Residential building on Schillerweg, 2004

Besonders Leipzig profilierte sich damit wie auch kulturell in den letzten Jahren, es zieht wie keine andere Stadt nach Berlin im Osten Deutschlands junge Leute und Investitionen an und besitzt eine breit gefächerte Einwohnerschaft. Die frühere Industrie- und Handelsstadt, die mit 530 000 Einwohnern (1989) zweitgrößte Stadt der DDR, ist wieder aktuell im Gesprächsfokus und dies nicht allein mit Hochtechnologie oder Gebäuderekonstruktionen. Explizit gegenwartsgewandt gibt sich die Stadt, die vor allem mit ihrer zeitgenössischen Stadtkultur für sich wirbt und auch werben kann. Die so genannte Neue Leipziger Malerschule mit Künstlern wie Neo Rauch, Isabelle Dutoit oder Tim Eitel, aber auch die Photographen Ulrich Wüst, Thomas Schlink, Max Baumann oder Frank-Heinrich Müller werden längst nicht mehr nur national, sondern intensiv international wahrgenommen. In ihrem Schatten entstanden viele neue Galerien von Ortsansässigen oder Zugewanderten an abenteuerlichen Orten industrieller Vergangenheit, die sich nun zu Inseln einer neuen urbanen Lebenskultur entwickeln.

Sehr erstaunlich sind das neu erwachte Renommee und Interesse für Leipzig, das Anfang der Neunziger einen unvergleichlichen Immobilienboom mit folgendem Immobiliencrash erlebte. Unvergessen ist der Zusammenbruch des Immobilienmoguls Dr. Jürgen Schneider, der sogar die Deutsche Bank erschütterte und Leipzig für viele Jahre in ein tiefes Tal fallen ließ. Schneider hatte sich mit seinen 1a-Immobilien im Leipziger Zentrum schlicht verspekuliert. Seine Modernisierungen der alten Messehäuser jedoch waren überaus qualitätvoll, die bis zum Auszug der Leipziger Messe an den nördlichen Stadtrand das Herz der Stadt einnahmen.

Wolfgang Felder und Weis & Volkmann, GaraGe Technologiezentrum für Jugendliche, 2001
Wolfgang Felder und Weis & Volkmann, GaraGe Youth technology centre, 2001

Weis & Volkmann, Dienstleistungs- und Gastronomie-Ensemble Stelzenhaus, Fabrikumbau, 2003
Weis & Volkmann, Stelzenhaus factory conversion as service and gastronomy ensemble, 2003

eastern German city apart from Berlin. With a demographically diverse population of 530,000, this former industrial city and centre of commerce 1989 is the second largest in the former GDR. It is very much in the public eye at the moment – and not just for its high-tech industries or historic reconstructions. As a city that is so unashamedly forward-looking, it has every reason to trumpet its contemporary urban image as it does.

The so-called New Leipzig School, which includes such artists as Neo Rauch, Isabelle Dutoit and Tim Eitel, as well as photographers Ulrich Wüst, Thomas Schlink, Max Baumann and Frank-Heinrich Müller are not only recognised nationwide, but increasingly internationally as well. The reputation of this art movement has brought on a ripple effect, with many new galleries run by locals and incomers alike opening up in exciting venues housed in converted buildings from the city's industrial past, creating a vibrant urban culture.

The revival of interest in Leipzig and the city's renewed buoyancy are quite remarkable. This was, after all, the scene of an unparalleled property boom in the early 1990s followed by a devastating crash. The bankruptcy of property magnate Dr. Jürgen Schneider, whose collapsing empire shook even the mighty Deutsche Bank and sent Leipzig into a downward spiral for years, is still fresh in the memory. Schneider had quite simply overstepped himself in his property speculations with a portfolio of prime real estate in the centre of Leipzig. But his refurbishment of the magnificent old trade fair halls, the heart of the city till the trade fair moved to the northern outskirts, was of the highest quality.

His demise may have brought the property market to its knees, but ten years on, these historic trade fair halls, built in typical Leipzig style as deep blocks with several internal courtyards are now a bustling complex of commercial and office premises full of secluded and fascinating niches, whereas in their original form they were used only on a temporary basis for trade fairs. Interestingly enough, this revival was actually triggered by the well conceived redevelopment of Leipzig's huge main station to create a "department store with a railway connection", undertaken by Dusseldorf-based architects HPP Hentrich-Petschnigg & Partner, which attracted retailers back from the outskirts into the inner city.

Mit der Insolvenz brach der Immobilienmarkt zusammen, aber ein Jahrzehnt später tragen seine alten Messehäuser mit ihrer spezifischen Leipziger Typologie der ›Durchhäuser‹ – sehr tiefe, mehrhöfige Blockrandbauten – zur Wiederbelebung des Zentrums entscheidend bei. Damals oft nur temporär genutzt, sind sie heute belebte Geschäfts- und Bürohäuser mit vielen verschwiegenen Orten. Interessanterweise war der Startschuss zu dieser Wiederbelebung der solide Umbau des großen Leipziger Hauptbahnhofes zu einem ›Kaufhaus mit Bahnanschluss‹ durch das Düsseldorfer Architekturbüro HPP Hentrich-Petschnigg & Partner, das wieder den Einzelhandel von der grünen Wiese in die Innenstadt ziehen ließ.

Doch erst seit 2005 verzeichnet Leipzig leichte Bevölkerungsgewinne und wird wohl die Marke von 500 000 Einwohnern wieder überschreiten. Zuvor war die Bevölkerungszahl beständig gesunken. Anfang der dreißiger Jahre lebten 713 000 Menschen in Leipzig, 2004 hingegen nur noch 495 000 in einer Stadt, deren Grundfläche sich durch zahlreiche spätere Eingemeindungen nahezu verdoppelt hatte. Jenseits der relativ kleinen Leipziger City sind die Folgen dieser Entwicklung allerorten zu sehen. Nicht nur in den Plattenbauvierteln, sondern auch in großen Teilen der gründerzeitlichen Stadtquartiere, besonders im Osten und Nordwesten Leipzigs, stehen ganze Straßenzüge leer.

Die »Neue Leipziger Messe« und neue Industrieansiedlungen am Nordrand Leipzigs wie ein BMW-Werk, ein Porsche-Werk, die europäische Logistikzentrale von DHL sowie die neu entdeckte Attraktivität der Stadt haben viele Zuwanderer aus Ost wie West nach Leipzig ziehen lassen. Eine lebendige Zivilgesellschaft ist entstanden, die anlässlich der Kandidatur Leipzigs für die Olympischen Spiele 2012 unter dem Begriff »Leipziger Freiheit« verkauft wurde.

Leipzig schwelgt heute wieder in Wachstumsphantasien. Das Anfang 2005 politisch abgesegnete »Planwerk Stadtraum Leipzig« des damaligen Stadtbaurats und heutigen Staatssekretärs im Bundesministerium für Verkehr, Bau und Stadtentwicklung Engelbert Lütke Daldrup sieht neue großflächige Gewerbeareale im Norden vor, um den Flughafen Leipzig-Halle, wo Mitte der neunziger Jahre schon die »Neue Messe« von von Gerkan, Marg und Partner entstand, deren Werk mit der Glastechnologie des britischen Ingenieurs Ian Richie weltweit Anerkennung fand. Neue Wohnquartiere sind hingegen im Süden, im nie wirklich genutzten Hafengelände aus der NS-Zeit sowie den Eingemeindungen nahe den gefluteten Kohletagebaugebieten im »Südraum Leipzig« anvisiert.

Die frühere Mondlandschaft des Tagebaus wandelt sich rasant und verschafft der sonst topografisch reizlosen Stadt ein neues Umland, ein ausgedehntes, renaturiertes Seengebiet. Der erste Freizeithafen in Cospuden entfaltet bereits seine Wirkung, wenn auch im Südraum sonst wenig architektonisch Interessantes zu finden ist. Das 1999 aus seriellen Container-Modulen erstellte Teleport-Center des Leipziger Architekten Ingo Andreas Wolf am nahen Kraftwerkstandort Espenhain ist eine Ausnahme, die weit mehr räumliche Qualitäten besitzt als viele andere Gewerbebauten des Leipziger Umlands, die heute in großer Zahl verfallen.

Skepsis ist gegenüber den neuen Leipziger Entwicklungsphantasien angebracht. Nahezu unverändert liegen seit Jahren die Arbeitslosen- und Wohnungsleerstandsquoten über 20 Prozent. Doch beginnt Leipzigs neue Verkehrswegesituation Früchte zu tragen. Vom internationalen Drehkreuz Mitteldeutschlands spricht man heute beim neuen Flughafen der Stuttgarter Architekten

Lützow 7, Stadtteilpark Rabet, 2004, 1. Bauabschnitt
Lützow 7, Rabet urban park, 2004, first construction phase

It is only since 2005, however, that the population of Leipzig has started to increase and is now projected to pass the 500,000 mark again. Before that, the population was in constant decline. In the 1930s, 713,000 people lived here. By 2004 there were only 495,000 left in a city whose actual surface area had almost doubled due to the amalgamation of outlying suburbs. Beyond Leipzig's relatively small inner city, the effects of this trend are still clearly evident. Not only in the communist era prefab developments, but also in large swathes of the nineteenth-century districts, especially in the eastern and north-western areas, entire streets lie empty.

The New Leipzig Trade Fair and the new industrial estates on the northern edge of town, including a BMW plant, a Porsche plant and DHL's European logistics headquarters, coupled with the rediscovery of Leipzig as a city with real appeal have attracted many incomers from both east and west. The result is a vibrant social mix that the city has been quick to turn into a marketing strategy, as in its 2012 Olympic bid under the motto "Leipzig Freedom". Though the bid may have failed on the international stage, in national terms Leipzig managed to wrest the Olympic candidacy from the much bigger city of Hamburg.

Today, Leipzig is once again basking in its prospects for further growth. A redevelopment master plan drawn up in early 2005 by the then municipal building officer Dr. Engelbert Lütke Daldrup, who is now secretary of state for transport, building and urban development, envisages large new commercial districts in the north, around the airport of Leipzig-Halle, where the New Trade Fair by von Gerkan, Marg & Partner in collaboration with British architect Ian Ritchie, responsible for the glass technology engineering design, won international acclaim. A major new housing development is planned for the south of the city on the hitherto little-used river port docklands dating from the Nazi era, near the flooded former open-face coal mines.

What was once the almost lunar landscape of the former open-face mines is now rapidly metamorphosing into an extensive lake district that adds a whole new dimension to a city whose surrounding landscape has previously had little to offer. Cospuden, the first marina and lakeside leisure complex to open here, is already proving popular, even if this southern district so far has little in the way of architectural interest. The Teleport-Centre in

Hentrich-Petschnigg & Partner, Leipzig, Wohnen für junge Leute Pfeffingerstraße, 2000
Hentrich-Petschnigg & Partner, Leipzig, Residence for young people on Pfeffingerstrasse, 2000

Brunnert und Partner zwar nur noch selten, doch ihr Flughafen ist eine faszinierende technoide ›Landmark‹ mit einer höchst effizienten Organisation der Verkehrswege. In der Endbaustufe wird sie sich vollständig über die Autobahn- wie die Bahntrassen spannen, die noch beide Flugfelder voneinander trennen.

Die Nähe zum Flughafen und zu zwei wichtigen Nord-Süd- und Ost-West-Autobahnen dürfte entscheidend zur Neuansiedlung von BMW, Porsche und DHL beigetragen haben. Trotz des großen internationalen Lobs überzeugt aber das neue BMW-Werk von Zaha Hadid (2005) nicht ganz. Weitab von der Stadt und völlig introvertiert steht es nun auf der grünen Wiese. Die große Eintrittsgeste ihres viel gerühmten Eingangsgebäudes verpufft in der freien Landschaft, zu der es allein ausgerichtet ist. Zur Stadt, Autobahn und Anfahrt steht es mit seinem kaum sichtbaren Rücken, der in der Masse des gewaltigen, von den BMW-Ingenieuren geplanten Fabrikkomplexes nahezu untergeht. Gekonnt ist jedoch ihre Simulation postindustrieller Teamarbeitsverhältnisse, die Dynamik ihrer Innenräume. Ein seltener Gewinn an internationaler architektonischer Avantgarde ist es für Leipzig auf jeden Fall, das darüber noch mehr mediale Beachtung fand. Der silbern glänzende Pilzpavillon der Porsche-Fabrik von von Gerkan, Marg und Partner ist zwar von der Autobahn sichtbar und erregt Neugier, doch wurde er überregional ignoriert.

Weniger glücklich erging es den Projekten anderer international renommierter Architekten wie Kees Christiaanse, Peter Kulka, Peter Eisenman oder Barkow-Leibinger, die nach der verlorenen

nearby Espenhain, created in 1999 by Leipzig architect Ingo Andreas Wolf using container modules, is something of an exception, possessing more spatial qualities than many of the other neglected and dilapidated commercial buildings around Leipzig.

A certain degree of scepticism about Leipzig's rosy development future is nevertheless warranted. Unemployment here is running at more than twenty per cent and there is a similar percentage of empty housing. But Leipzig's new transport situation is beginning to sway the situation. The new airport by Stuttgart architects Brunnert & Partner may not yet be regarded as central Germany's international hub, but it is certainly a fascinating technoid landmark with a highly efficiently organised traffic structure. By the time its final phase reaches completion, it will fully span the motorway and railway routes that currently separate the two airfields.

Proximity to the airport and to the two major north-south and east-west motorways was very probably an important consideration for the relocation of BMW, Porsche and DHL. But in spite of the enormous international acclaim, the new BMW building by Zaha Hadid (2005) is not entirely convincing. It currently stands on open land, far from the city and completely isolated. The grand gesture of her highly lauded entrance building is simply lost in the wide-open landscape it faces. Its barely visible back, almost completely overshadowed by the sheer mass of the factory complex designed by BMW's own engineers, is turned to the city, the motorway and the access route. However, her simulation of a

Olympia-Kandidatur in der Schublade verschwanden. Allein zwei Projekte wurden erfolgreich realisiert: Die multifunktionale Arena Leipzig (2002) der Architekten Arat Siegel Schust am alten Sportforum, dessen »Stadion der 100.000« von einer Projektgemeinschaft unter dem Schweizer Architekturbüro Wirth + Wirth 2003 radikal verkleinert und modernisiert wurde. Der Baukörper ihres neuen Fußballstadions spannt sich in zwei sehr gelungenen, dynamischen Halbschalen über die Zuschauer, die hier jenseits der Fußballweltmeisterschaft nur die Spiele eines Oberligisten erleben können.

David Chipperfield gab auf Grund von drastischen Budgetkürzungen den Umbau des Grassi-Museums entnervt ab. Mit etwa der Hälfte des Etats realisierten die Leipziger Ilg Friebe Nauber die Modernisierung des Zwanziger-Jahre-Komplexes so sensibel wie effektiv und machen dessen expressionistisch-monumentale Architekturmischung wieder erlebbar. In der Trabantensiedlung Leipzig-Grünau haben die Architekten mit dem Maria-Montessori-Schulzentrum (2002) eine der räumlich interessantesten Plattenbau-Transformationen in Ostdeutschland geschaffen, nahe einer Schwimmhalle von Behnisch + Partner.

In Bezug auf bürgerliche Toleranz und Engagement stand der Olympia-Slogan der Leipziger Freiheit für eine Stadt unterschiedlicher Lebenskulturen. Während in Grünau radikal abgerissen wird, die meisten Turm-Wohnhochhäuser bereits verschwunden sind, die der Trabantensiedlung ihre unverwechselbare Silhouette gaben, leben einzelne Viertel des 19. und frühen 20. Jahrhunderts wieder auf. Hier kommt Leipzig seine alte Doppelstruktur zugute, seine kleinteilige Mischung aus bürgerlichen Villenvierteln und sehr dichten Industriearbeitervierteln, die Arbeiten und Wohnen bereits früher sehr eng miteinander verwoben.

Der große Leerstand und die geringen Preise haben neue Raumpioniere hervorgebracht, die die vielfältigen Raumangebote für sich zu nutzen verstehen. Für jeden Lebensstil findet sich ein Angebot, wenn auch etwa der Wandel vieler alter Etagenfabriken zumeist noch dem Auge entzogen bleibt, viele Fabriken auch weiterhin verfallen. Zumindest in Leipzig-Plagwitz gibt es einige sichtbare Zeichen des Wandels. Prächtig strahlen wieder die bunten Ziegel der ausgedehnten Buntgarnfabrik, deren Lofts jedoch weniger überzeugen. Große kulturelle Ausstrahlung hat hingegen die Baumwollspinnerei entwickelt – als Sitz verschiedener Künstler und Kunstgalerien, Kulturinitiativen und Freizeitangebote in einem leicht morbiden Fabrikkomplex.

Der kleine Fluss Pleiße, der nur als Industriekanal genutzt worden war, wurde in Plagwitz wie zuvor schon in der Innenstadt von der Leipziger Architektin Angela Wandelt wieder freigelegt. Das Berliner Landschaftsarchitekturbüro »Lützow 7« schuf ihm zur Seite einen modernen Stadtteilpark. Landschaftsarchitektonische Transformationen haben sich hier wie an vielen Orten der Stadt vollzogen, wo Brachen, Industrie- und Abrissflächen nach prägnanten, aber pflegeleichten Gestaltungen verlangen. Ein Pionier ohne Nachfolge war leider das Jahrtausendfeld der »Schaubühne Lindenfels«, ein dezentrales Projekt der Expo 2000, das einen Sommer lang eine Stadtbrache mit einem weiten Sonnenblumenfeld füllte.

Unweit davon bauten die Leipziger Architekten Weis & Volkmann eine industriell stark kontaminierte Fabrik aus den dreißiger Jahren zum Dienstleistungs- und Gastronomie-Ensemble »Stelzenhaus« um. Das Neue wurde partiell und sehr sensibel in die freigeräumten Baustrukturen implantiert. Vis-à-vis befindet sich das

Behnisch, Hermus, Schinko und Schumann, Sozialpädiatrisches Zentrum, Frühförderstelle, 1999–2005
Behnisch, Hermus, Schinko und Schumann, Social and educational centre, early learning facility, 1999–2005

post-industrial teamwork situation in the dynamic interior is carried off with aplomb. This piece of international avant-garde architecture has undoubtedly benefited Leipzig, if only in terms of the publicity it has brought. The gleaming silver mushroom-like pavilion of the Porsche factory by von Gerkan, Marg & Partner can be seen from the motorway and immediately arouses the viewer's curiosity, yet it has been virtually ignored.

Some of the other projects by internationally renowned architects such as Kees Christiaanse, Peter Kulka, Peter Eisenman or Barkow-Leibinger have not fared so well, getting no further than the drawing board once it became clear that the Olympic bid had failed. Only two of the projects planned at that time have been built: The multi-purpose Arena Leipzig (2002) by architects Arat Siegel Schust on the site of the old Sportforum, originally intended as a stadium with a capacity of 100,000, was radically reduced in size and modernised by Swiss architects Wirth + Wirth in 2003. Their new football stadium comprises two dynamic half-shells spanning the terraces, but apart from hosting some World Cup games, it will now only see the occasional premier league match.

David Chipperfield threw in the towel in exasperation at the drastically reduced budget for the Grassi Museum redevelopment and was replaced by Leipzig architects Ilg Friebe Nauber who subsequently refurbished this 1920s complex on a shoestring of half the funds and did so with great sensitivity, effectively reviving its architectural blend of expressionism and monumentality. In the dormitory town of Leipzig-Grünau, the same architects have achieved one of eastern Germany's most interesting conversions of prefab architecture in creating the Maria Montessori School (2002), near a swimming pool designed by Behnisch + Partner.

The Olympic motto of "Leipzig Freedom" was coined to reflect the tolerance and civic pride of the city's diversity. While radical demolition work in Grünau has rid the district of most of the high-rise apartment blocks that were once its hallmark, other districts dating from the nineteenth and early twentieth centuries have undergone a renaissance. Leipzig's age-old dual structure has served the city well, with a small-scale mix of bourgeois villas and densely populated working-class areas creating a situation in which working and living have always been closely interwoven.

A large number of empty buildings and low property prices have attracted a new kind of pioneer who knows exactly how to

Behnisch, Hermus, Schinko und Schumann, Neugestaltung Thomaskirchhof, 2000–2006

Behnisch, Hermus, Schinko and Schumann, Redesign of Thomaskirchhof, 2000–2006

»Technologiezentrum GaraGe«, eine neue Form von privatem Industriemuseum und Berufsfindungsinstitution im alten Fabrikgehäuse, die Jugendlichen einen aktiven Einblick in die spätere Berufspraxis ermöglicht. Nach der architektonischen Konzeption des Kölner ArchitekturBüro Felder wurde 2001 die alte Textilfabrik wiederum von Weis & Volkmann sehr sachlich und materiell höchst taktil transformiert.

Geburtsort des Begriffs der »perforierten Stadt« ist Leipzig. Die Stadtplanerin Martha Doehler vom Büro für Urbane Projekte bezeichnete damit die größte Herausforderung für die ostdeutschen Städte im 21. Jahrhundert, nämlich die unumgängliche Diskussion, wie Urbanität bei geringerer Bevölkerung und Baudichten möglich ist. Im Rahmen des bundesweiten Programms »Stadt 2030« entstand mit Beteiligung der Bevölkerung ein Masterplan für den Rückbau des Leipziger Ostens, der teilweise realisiert wurde.

Eine andere Folge der Diskussionen war die kommunale Initiative »Stadthäuser«, Wohneigentum mit geringeren Dichten in der Stadt auf Brachen zu ermöglichen. Nur 19 der 50 Standorte fanden aber Interessenten. Von den größeren Projekten konnten bislang nur die Hausanlagen in der Biedermannstraße von Gerd Heise des Leipziger Büros HPP sowie an der Pleiße von Weis & Volkmann architektonisch überzeugen, die Schweizer und britischen Vorbildern folgen. Im kleineren Maßstab gelangen ebenfalls I. A. Wolf mit seinem Wohnhaus am Schillerweg, Henchion + Reuter mit ihrem »Haus hinter der Schlossmauer« sowie hobusch + kuppardt

make the best of the available space. There is something here for every taste, though the potential conversion of defunct factory buildings still seems to escape notice, with many of them continuing to fall into a dilapidated state. In Leipzig-Plagwitz, at least, there are some signs of change. The bright bricks of the old yarn factory have been restored to their former glory, but the lofts inside leave something to be desired. The old cotton mill, on the other hand, has real cultural charisma now, with artists' studios and galleries, events and leisure facilities all housed in a shabby-chic factory complex. There, among the art, literature and architecture, is the Federkiel foundation, whose exhibitions and panel discussions are highly regarded nationwide.

The little River Pleiße, formerly used only as an industrial canal, has now been opened up in Plagwitz, as it has been in the city centre, by Leipzig architect Angela Wandelt, while Berlin landscape architects Lützow 7 have created a modern urban park on its banks. Here, as elsewhere in the city, landscaping has been used to transform wastelands, industrial areas and gap sites. One pioneering project that has unfortunately found no emulators is the Schaubühne Lindenfels – a project on the fringes of Expo 2000 that involved creating a huge field of sunflowers on an urban gap site.

Not far from here, Leipzig architects Weis & Volkmann converted an industrially polluted 1930s factory into the Stelzenhaus service and catering ensemble by sensitively implanting the new structure partially into the cleared-out building shell. Just opposite this is the GaraGe Technology Centre – a new form of privately run industrial museum and career advice centre housed in an old factory that offers young people hands-on work experience. In 2001, the old textile factory was given a very functional and highly tactile transformation by Weis & Volkmann on the basis of a concept drawn up by Cologne architects Felder.

Leipzig is the birthplace of the "perforated city". This was the phrase coined by urban planner Martha Doehler of the Office for Urban Projects to describe the greatest challenge facing eastern Germany's cities in the twenty-first century: the unavoidable issue of reconciling urbanity with a dwindling population and low-density housing. As part of a nationwide programme entitled "City 2030", in intense consultation with the local population, a master plan was drawn up for the eastern districts of Leipzig, which has already been partially completed.

This particular debate also resulted in a community initiative by the name of "Townhouses" which involved allowing low-density owner-occupied housing to be built on inner-city gap sites. But only 19 of the 50 earmarked sites met with any interest. To date, the only large-scale projects of any architectural merit to emerge from this initiative have been the complexes on Biedermannstrasse by Gerd Heise of the Leipzig architectural firm HPP and on the banks of the Pleiße by Weis & Volkmann, based on Swiss and British examples. On a smaller scale, noteworthy projects include I. A. Wolf's house on Schillerweg, Henchion + Reuter's "House by the Palace Wall" and hobusch + kuppardt's three houses in Connewitz, all of which are architecturally interesting examples of leafy urban living.

Leipzig has come to regard itself as a kind of "plus-minus city", meaning that it is a city of growth and decline, leaning more towards the block-type architectural density of the European city – which can only be achieved within the relatively small confines of the city centre. On the square formerly known as Sachsenplatz, the new Museum of Art by Berlin architects Hufnagel Pütz

Schulz & Schulz Architekten, Erweiterung Neue Nikolaischule, 2000–2003
Schulz & Schulz Architekten, Extension of Neue Nikolaischule, 2000–2003

mit ihren drei Häusern in Connewitz interessante Wohngebäude eines Wohnens im Grünen in der Stadt.

Mittlerweile versteht sich Leipzig als eine ›PlusMinusStadt‹ zwischen Wachstum und Schrumpfung, die mehr auf die Vorstellung der europäischen Stadt mit einer dichten Blockrandbebauung setzt, welche aber fast nur im überschaubaren Leipziger Stadtzentrum ihre Umsetzung finden kann. Auf dem früheren Sachsenplatz steht so das 2003 eröffnete neue Museum der bildenden Künste der Berliner Architekten Hufnagel Pütz Rafaelian, das einmal aus dem Hof einer Blockrandbebauung leuchten soll. Gute, leicht erneuerbare DDR-Bauten wie die nahen Scheiben-Wohnhochhäuser am Brühl sollen dann ebenfalls verschwunden sein. Ein seltsamer Zwitter zwischen Minimalismus und einer sehr pathetischen Monumentalität ist dieses Museum, das mit seinen überdimensionalen Lufträumen eher einschüchtert. Wie komplex Architektur sein und sich im Dialog mit der Kunst räumlich verändern kann, beweist die zeitgleiche Erweiterung der Galerie für Zeitgenössische Kunst durch die jungen Architekten von AS-IF am Volkspark. Sie bietet neue Perspektiven und veränderbare Räume an, die stets eng mit ihrem Stadtraum verknüpft sind.

Man geht in Leipzig nicht besonders verständnisvoll mit dem baulichen Erbe der DDR um. Vielen Denkmalpflegern fehlt noch das Verständnis für die historisch belastete Architektur, währenddessen sich vor allem die Jungen um deren Erhalt und Modernisierung bemühen. Am Alten Markt verschwanden schon alle Bauten des 20. Jahrhunderts. Die unterirdische Messehalle wurde für den Bau einer von vier Stationen des ehrgeizigen

Rafaelian opened its doors in 2003, and is intended to be enclosed by block developments in the future so that it will eventually occupy a courtyard situation. Good quality and easily renewable GDR buildings such as the nearby apartment blocks at Brühl will also have disappeared by then. This museum is a strange cross between minimalism and pathos-laden monumentality with a spatial presence that is quite forbidding. Just how complex architecture can be and how it can change spatially in dialogue with art is demonstrated by the extension of the Gallery of Contemporary Art on Volkspark by the young team of AS-IF architects, which offers new views and flexible spaces that are always closely linked with their urban setting.

In Leipzig, there is little respect for the architectural heritage of the communist era. Many conservationists still lack any understanding of this historically freighted architecture, and it is primarily the younger generation that is endeavouring to retain it and modernise it. All the twentieth-century buildings on Alter Markt have already disappeared. The underground trade fair hall has been demolished to make way for one of four stations on the ambitious new underground regional railway network. The former trade fair office has been replaced by a commercial and office building designed by Christoph Mäckler, which overwhelms the Old Town Hall with its brazen urbanity that flaunts the notion of diversity where the real driving force is merely maximum floor space. By contrast, the unspectacular new Messehof by Weis & Volkmann is well conceived, but for the fact that it was built at the cost of demolishing one of the finest GDR buildings by the Frieder

Hobusch + Kuppardt Architekten, Stadthäuser, 2006
Hobusch + Kuppardt Architekten, Townhouses, 2006

Regionalbahntunnel-Projektes zwischen Hauptbahnhof und Bayrischem Bahnhof abgerissen. Das Messeamt wich den Fassaden eines Geschäfts- und Bürohauses von Christoph Mäckler, das dem kleinteiligen Alten Rathaus nun allzu großstädtisch Konkurrenz macht und Vielfalt vorgaukelt, wo allein auf Nutzfläche gesetzt wurde. Gelungener wirkt der unaufgeregte neue Messehof von Weis & Volkmann, wäre für ihn nicht einer der besten DDR-Bauten vom Kollektiv um Frieder Gebhardt im Stile der Neuen Sachlichkeit abgerissen worden. Zwischen Alt und Neu vermittelt überzeugender die neue Gestaltung des nahen Thomaskirchhofs von Behnsch, Hermus, Schinko und Schumann, die am Rande Leipzigs Gebäude prägnanter Gestalt und räumlicher Vielfalt bauten.

Fast widerspruchslos wurde der Messehof angenommen, während um den Augustusplatz ein leidenschaftlicher Bürgerstreit entbrannte. Vom Dresdner Vorbild initiiert, einigte man sich hier aber erst auf einen Kompromiss, wie die zu Zeiten der DDR gesprengte, gotische Paulinerkirche innerhalb der Modernisierung des Universitätskomplexes wieder erstehen könnte. Letztlich entsteht jedoch nun das neue Universitätsquartier von Behet Bondzio Lin bis auf ein Gebäudeteil völlig neu, da der Umbau der DDR-Gebäude zu hohe Kosten bedeutet hätte. In zeitgenössischer Nachempfindung und mit neuen Materialien ist darin die Kirche als multifunktionale Universitäts-Aula umgesetzt, wofür Erick van Egeraat ein kristallines Gebäude mit dem alten Hallenraum verknüpft.

Eine Rekonstruktion blieb Leipzig somit erspart, und der neue Universitätskomplex mit seinem Hybriden verspricht den Platz aufzuwerten, wenn auch einmal mehr die Schicht der DDR verschwindet. Denn der sonst so überzeugende Sachse Peter Kulka sah für den früheren Universitätsturm des DDR-Stararchitekten Henselmann nur eine Natursteinverkleidung vor, die den ehemals leichten Turm nun überaus schwer erscheinen lässt. Im Gegensatz zu seinem dunklen »MDR-Klangkörper«-Monolithen am Fuße des Hochhauses ist der neue Konzertsaal der Dortmunder Gerber Architekten im Innenhof der Musikhochschule »Felix-Mendelssohn-Bartholdy« sensibel wie markant eingefügt, mit einer materiell überraschenden Winkelkonstellation und Verklammerung seiner Räume.

Ungleich vielen anderen ostdeutschen Städten besitzt Leipzig eine sehr lebendige Architekturszene mit vielen jungen Architekten. In der Initiative »L21« haben sich 2000 15 junge Architekten der Leipziger Büros KARO-Architekten, m.f.s.-architekten, S.E.P., kombinat 4 und hobusch + kuppardt zusammengeschlossen, die mit Artikeln im Stadtmagazin »Kreuzer«, mit öffentlichen Aktionen und städtebaulichen Gegenprojekten die eher traditionellen Sicht- und Planungsweisen der Kommune offensiv hinterfragen. Dem schmerzhaften Prozess der Stadtschrumpfung in vielen Vierteln

Gebhardt collective in the style of Neue Sachlichkeit. A more persuasive example of the dialogue between old and new can be found in the nearby Thomaskirchhof designed by Behnisch, Hermus, Schinko and Schumann, who have created buildings of distinction and diversity on the edge of the city.

While the Messehof was accepted with virtually no dissent, the development on Augustusplatz became the subject of heated debate. Inspired by the example of Dresden, a compromise was eventually met as to how the gothic Paulinerkirche, demolished under the communist regime, could be reconstructed within the modernisation of the university complex. In the end, however, the new university district designed by Behet Bondzio Lin is being built completely from scratch, apart from one small section, since the cost of converting the GDR buildings would have been prohibitive. The church has now been turned into a multi-purpose university hall in a contemporary interpretation and using new materials, linking Erick van Egeraat's crystalline building with the old interior space.

With that, Leipzig has been spared a reconstruction project and the new university complex with its hybrid buildings promises to enhance the site, even though this means erasing the traces of the GDR once again. The otherwise locally patriotic Saxon Peter Kulka came up with nothing better than adding a natural stone cladding to the former university tower built by the GDR's star architect Henselmann, which now makes the previously light tower appear rather unwieldy. Unlike his dark "MDR Resonator" monoliths at the foot of the high-rise, the new concert hall by Dortmund-based architects Gerber in the inner courtyard of the Felix Mendelssohn Bartholdy music school is both sensitive and distinctive, featuring a surprising angular constellation and handling of space.

In contrast to many other eastern German cities, Leipzig has a vibrant architectural scene with many young architects. In the year 2000, fifteen young architects from the Leipzig firms of KARO-Architekten, m.f.s.-architekten, S.E.P., kombinat 4 and hobusch + kuppardt got together to form "L21", publishing critical and analytical articles in *Kreuzer* magazine, staging public events and urban development counter-initiatives that openly challenge the somewhat traditional views and planning approaches of the local authorities. They endeavour to gain something positive from the otherwise painful process of urban decline that afflicts so many parts of Leipzig. With an urban mix of Land Art, existing structures and implants, they develop strategies and projects for the city's increasingly abandoned eastern districts and Lützner Strasse.

Henchion, Reuter und Partner, Haus hinter der Schlossmauer, 2005
Henchion, Reuter and Partner, House by the Palace Wall, 2005

Gerber Architekten, Konzertsaal, 1995–2001
Gerber Architekten, Concert hall, 1995–2001

Leipzigs versuchen sie positive Möglichkeiten abzugewinnen. Mit Stadtraum-Amalgamen aus Land Art, Vorhandenem und Implantaten entwickeln sie Strategien und Projekte für den entleerten Leipziger Osten oder die »Lützner Straße«.

Aus dem Büro für Urbane Projekte sind die sehr jungen Architekten von »urbikon« hervorgegangen, die Architektur und Städtebau als eine Frage von Kommunikation und neuen Medien behandeln. Arbeitet das Büro für Urbane Projekte sehr intensiv mit den Mitteln von Film und Foto, historischen Ausstellungen sowie moderativen Planungsprozessen, so setzt urbikon aufs Internet, auf mobile Events oder temporäre Provisorien, was sie mit »archileagu« verbindet, einem weiteren Zusammenschluss junger Architekten, die Gebäude temporär besetzen und noch stärker an der Transformation von Vorhandenem arbeiten.

Die klassischen Berufsbilder lösen sich im Osten noch stärker auf als im Westen, wo private Auftraggeber bislang eher selten sind und die Architekten ihre Programme häufig selbst initiieren müssen. Nur wenige junge Büros wie Schulz & Schulz verstehen es, auch überregional mit Wettbewerben erfolgreich zu sein. Mit der konstruktiven Architektur ihrer Leipziger Stadtwerke (2001) oder der Experimentalanlage »Wolkenlabor« (2005) verfolgen sie sachliche, klare Objektlösungen mit großer räumlicher Offenheit, die bis ins Detail überzeugend sind. Mit dem Vorhandenen arbeiten, Transformationen mit geringen Mitteln durchführen, ist die Herausforderung, die sich vor allem in Leipzig stellt. Seine Stadtkultur und Architekturszene sind dazu bereits weiter entwickelt als die Stadtpolitik, die zwischen Wachstumseuphorie und Schielen aufs Vergangene eher schlingert denn steuert.

The Office for Urban Projects has spawned a group of young architects by the name of "urbikon", who address architecture and urban development from the point of view of communication and new media. Whereas the Office for Urban Projects relies heavily on film and photography, historic exhibitions and moderative planning processes, "urbikon" uses the internet, mobile events and temporary installations along the lines of "archileagu" – another group of young architects who temporarily occupy buildings and work even more strongly on transforming existing architecture.

Conventional divisions between the professions are dissolving even faster in the east than they are in the west, where private clients are the exception and architects often have to launch their own programmes. Only a handful of architectural firms such as Schulz + Schulz have managed to make their mark at national level in design competitions. With the constructive architecture of their Leipziger Stadtwerke (2001) and their experimental Cloud Laboratory (2005) they pursue sober, clear-cut designs of great openness and attention to detail. Working with what already exists and undertaking conversions on a shoestring is the challenge to be tackled – especially in Leipzig. In that respect, the city's urban culture and its architectural scene are already far ahead of its official policies, which are still wavering between the euphoria of a prospective boom and nostalgia for the past.

TRUGBILD ›EUROPÄISCHE STADT‹
WIE SOLL SIE AUSSEHEN, DIE VIEL BESCHWORENE ›NEUE URBANITÄT‹?
THE ILLUSION OF THE "EUROPEAN CITY"
IN SEARCH OF THE "NEW URBANITY"

Falk Jaeger

»Zurück in die Stadt« titelt die FAZ Anfang Februar 2006 und berichtet über eine Umkehrung der Stadt-Umland-Wanderung in Berlin und die Bevölkerungszunahme von bis zu zehn Prozent in manchen Innenstadtbezirken. ›Inneres Wachstum‹ der Städte liegt im Trend, der sich keineswegs auf Berlin beschränkt.

Die verstärkte Arbeitsorientierung der Frauen, differenziertere Lebensstile abseits der Kleinfamilie und die Kombinutzung von Wohnraum führen zu einem Raumbedarf, der mit standardisierten Familienwohnungen nicht zu decken ist. Die neuen Lebens- und Wohnformen lassen sich besser in den Innenstädten realisieren, vorzugsweise in räumlich wenig determinierten Altbauwohnungen. »Das individuelle Wohnen wird gleichsam Standard« (Hartmut Häußermann).

Spricht man von der Renaissance der Innenstädte als Lebensraum, als Ort der Arbeit und des Wohnens, wird von Interesse sein, wann und weshalb die City in Verruf gekommen ist. Der Drang nach dem Häuschen im Grünen hatte und hat nur zum Teil soziologische Gründe wie das Streben nach Unabhängigkeit von Vermietern und Nachbarn. Primärer Segregationsfaktor waren die Minderung der Lebensqualität in den Innenstädten einerseits und die sinkende Toleranz demgegenüber sowie die wirtschaftliche Potenz breiter Bevölkerungskreise, diesen unliebsamen Verhältnissen ausweichen zu können. Konnte man Mitte der fünfziger Jahre in der Innenstadt noch ein Kind ohne Begleitung zum Kindergarten schicken, hatte der Verkehr bereits 1960 einen Umfang angenommen, der dies unmöglich machte. Als dann in den sechziger und siebziger Jahren die Warenhäuser mit Elefantenfüßen in die Stadtzentren einbrachen und man versuchte, durch die Innenstädte autogerechte Schneisen zu schlagen, wurde dies als endgültige Zerstörung der Innenstadt als Lebensort empfunden.

Heute wird die Randwanderung der Einkaufszentren Richtung Autobahnanschluss und die damit einhergehende Austrocknung der Cityfunktionen beklagt. Doch der Rückzug umweltbelastender Industriebetriebe und der Wegfall flächenintensiver Bahn- und Militärnutzungen in der Stadt werden als Chance für die notwendige Wiederbelebung der Innenstadt als Wohn- und Lebensort verstanden und propagiert.

Neu ist die Erkenntnis allerdings nicht. Sie ist vor allem ein Medienereignis, das freilich Aktionismus fördert und die in den Planungsämtern ohnehin angestrebte Entwicklung zu beschleunigen vermag. Der exorbitante Siedlungsflächenverbrauch seit den sechziger Jahren war den Fachleuten spätestens in den Siebzigern als fatale Tendenz aufgefallen. Schon damals sprachen Stadtplaner von der Unumgänglichkeit der Verdichtung. Damals ging es um die Eindämmung des Flächenwachstums, die Schonung stadtnaher Natur und die bessere Nutzung der Infrastruktur, alles Ziele, die auch heute noch angestrebt werden. Einzig der ökologische

In February 2006 the *Frankfurter Allgemeine Zeitung* ran an article headed "Back to the City" reporting on a reversal of the trend that, for years, had seen an exodus from Berlin to the surrounding areas, and pointing out that the urban population had risen by as much as ten percent in some inner city areas. Berlin is by no means the only city currently undergoing this "inner growth".

Conventional, standard family accommodation can no longer meet the needs of a society in which women are increasingly career oriented, lifestyles have diversified beyond the nuclear family and many homes double as offices. The inner city with its stock of historic buildings offering flexible accommodation is far better suited to the new modes of living. "Individuality in housing is becoming standard" (Hartmut Häußermann).

If we are to speak of a renaissance of the inner city as a place to live and work, we might do well to consider how and when the city fell into disrepute in the first place. The lure of the green belt was only partly a question of sociological factors such as the wish to be free of landlords and neighbours. The main factor was the declining quality of life in the inner cities, which people were no longer willing to accept, combined with the fact that an increasingly affluent society meant that many now had the financial means to vote with their feet against the conditions they found intolerable. While it may still have been possible, in the mid-1950s, for a child to walk to kindergarten alone, by 1960 the volume of traffic had already increased to such a degree that this was no longer an option. The traffic-friendly policies of the 60s and 70s finally rang the death knell for inner city living, with urban motorways being carved through the centre of town and department stores being built on elephantine stilts.

Today, out-of-town retail parks are blamed for draining the city of its urban functions. But the closure of environmentally pollutant industrial premises and of extensive railway and military sites within the city are seen as an opportunity to be seized for the necessary revival of the inner city as place to live and work.

Not that this insight is new. It is above all a media event – though admittedly one that encourages action and may even speed up the development that the planning departments are already aiming for. By the 1970s at the latest, experts realised that the vast urban sprawl that had been continuing apace since the 60s was unsustainable. Even back then, urban planners were talking of the inevitability of more high-density developments. At the time, the aim was to stem the tide of urban sprawl, conserve the

Grüntuch Ernst, Wohn- und Geschäftshaus Monbijouplatz 3, Berlin, 1997–2001
Grüntuch Ernst, Residential and office building at Monbijouplatz 3, Berlin, 1997–2001

Peter Kulka, Wohnbebauung Hollerborn/Kleinfeldchen, Wiesbaden, 1994–1998
Peter Kulka, Residential development Hollerborn/Kleinfeldchen, Wiesbaden, 1994–1998

Aspekt ist neu. Wenn ein Planer 1975 durch stadtplanerische Maß-
nahmen, Verdichtung und Nutzungsmischung versuchte, die Ent-
stehung von Verkehr zu minimieren, dann mit der Absicht, den
allerorten drohenden Verkehrsinfarkt zu vermeiden. Verdichtung
heute hat noch ein anderes Ziel, nämlich in Immobilien und Mobi-
lien den Einsatz von Primärenergie zu minimieren.

Das ›Wohnen in der Stadt‹ wurde damals propagiert, ohne
gleich von einer Renaissance der Stadt zu reden. Das ›Stadthaus‹
wurde kreiert, das individuelle, mehrgeschossige Familienwohn-
haus in der Reihe oder im Cluster, für das man etwa in Bremen
historische Vorbilder fand. Insbesondere Gerhard Laage propa-
gierte die urbanen Wohnformen und wies nach, dass mit Wohn-
hochhäusern bei Anwendung hiesiger Vorschriften kein Landge-
winn verbucht werden kann. Stattdessen machte das Schlagwort
vom ›verdichteten Wohnen‹ die Runde. Darunter verstand man
puebloartige Wohnlandschaften, mit denen Wohnblockdichte
erreicht werden konnte, ohne in Wohnblockschematismus zu verfallen. Durch vielfältigste Wohnungszuschnitte, individuelle
Zugänge, halbprivate Bereiche als informelle Treffpunkte und viel
Grün sollten die Nachteile des in Verruf geratenen Massenwoh-
nungsbaus vermieden werden. Als innenstadtnahe Grundstücke
boten sich aufgegebene Standorte der ersten Industrialisierungs-
phase an sowie die ersten nutzlos gewordenen Bahngelände.

Eine Reihe von Projekten ist schon Ende der siebziger Jahre
ausgiebig diskutiert und publiziert worden, etwa die Konversion
des Stollwerck-Geländes in Köln in ein innerstädtisches, dicht

green belts and optimise the infrastructure – aims that are still
pursued today. All that is new is the ecological aspect. In 1975,
planners implementing measures to increase density and intro-
duce a mix of functions in order to minimise traffic did so with the
aim of averting traffic chaos. Today, high-density development has
a different aim: to minimise energy and fuel consumption.

In the 70s, living in the city was propagated without any talk of
an urban renaissance. A new kind of townhouse was created in
the form of an individual family home over several storeys, either
terraced or in clusters, based on examples of traditional architecture in cities such as Bremen. Gerhard Laage, a particularly fervent
advocate of urban living, proved that, under prevailing planning
legislation, high-rise apartment blocks did not actually bring land-
saving benefits. Instead, there was much talk of creating pueblo-
style developments that could achieve the density of apartment
blocks without their sterile anonymity. Varied layouts, individual
access, semi-private areas as informal meeting places and lots of
green spaces were meant to avoid the negative aspects of the
kind of mass housing that had by now become so maligned. Former industrial premises and defunct railway grounds, now abandoned, offered suitable inner-city sites for such developments.

Several projects were widely discussed and published in the
late 70s, including the conversion of the Stollwerck factory
grounds in Cologne to create a high-density residential district in
the heart of the city (dt8 group of architects) and the Darmstädter
Hof Quarter in Heidelberg with its wide range of facilities from

bebautes Wohnquartier durch die Architektengruppe dt8, oder das Quartier Darmstädter Hof in Heidelberg mit einer beachtlichen Nutzungsvielfalt vom Appartement bis zu Kaufhalle und Schwimmbad (Architekten Hauss Walla Partner). Wenn sich derlei Projekte nicht in großem Stil durchgesetzt haben, dann auf Grund der problematischen Komplexität der rechtlichen, planerischen und bautechnischen Umsetzung sowie der Organisation und Unterhaltung. Profitable Investorenprojekte sehen anders aus.

›Die Innenstadt als Wohnort‹ war Thema und Schlagwort der IBA 1984/87 in Berlin. Wenngleich sie primär angetreten war, die spezifischen Westberliner Probleme der vergleichsweise späten Behebung der Kriegsfolgen zu lösen, brachte sie doch Aspekte ins Gespräch, die in der Folge auch in westdeutschen Städten durch den Paradigmenwechsel der Industrie neuerlich akut wurden.

Neu ist also der ökologische Ansatz, der vor allem dem Planer am Herzen liegt, den Stadtrandbewohner jedoch nur sekundär tangiert, etwa beim Bezahlen an der Tankstelle. Zusätzlichen Sog erzeugt jedoch die wachsende Bedeutung der Stadt als Lebens- und Entfaltungsort für Jugendliche und Erwachsene. Die Verlagerung vieler Kommunikationsvorgänge in den medialen, virtuellen Raum hat nicht die noch vor 15 Jahren befürchtete Stadtflucht mit sich gebracht. Offenkundig lassen sich zwischenmenschliche Kontakte, informelle im Szenelokal, sportliche im Fitnesscenter oder konspirative beim Geschäftsessen, gruppendynamische im Fußballstadion oder gesellschaftliche bei einer Vernissage nicht durch Agieren im virtuellen Raum ersetzen.

Hinzu kommt das Bemühen der Städte, durch Eventkultur Anziehungskräfte sowohl auf Besucher als auch auf potenzielle Neubürger zu entwickeln. Aus gelegentlichen Stadtjubiläen, Bundesgartenschauen und Turnfesten ist längst eine Festivalisierung der Stadtkultur geworden. Oft genügt schon die Bewerbung als Kulturhauptstadt Europas, als Austragungsort für eine WM oder Olympische Spiele, um eine ganze Region zu elektrisieren und einen Entwicklungsschub zu evozieren. Ob runde Jahrestage bei Einstein, Mozart oder Preußen anstehen, gefeiert wird immer, zuweilen ein ganzes Jahr lang.

Staunend beobachtet der Bürger, was simple fünf Fußballspiele in seiner Stadt bewirken können. Dass eine Fußballweltmeisterschaft zum Anlass genommen wird, neue Stadien zu errichten oder alte zu erneuern, mag noch verständlich sein. Dass neue Verkehrswege entstehen, dass alle Baustellen einschließlich der des Hauptbahnhofs im Dreischichtbetrieb hastig fertig gestellt werden, dass allerlei Kulturereignisse auf die vier WM-Wochen konzentriert werden (Fußballfans als Ausstellungsbesucher?) und schließlich der Ladenschluss ausgesetzt wird (für bundesweit 3,2 Millionen Spielbesucher?), hat dann doch nicht mehr so viel mit 450 Minuten Kampf ums runde Leder zu tun, sondern ist Folge der Festivalhochstimmung, auf der die Stadtväter so geschickt wie möglich surfen, solange die Welle der Euphorie trägt.

Empfänglich für die Eventkultur sind vor allem Singles, die als Wohnungsinhaber auf dem Vormarsch sind. Sie nutzen das Freizeitangebot intensiver als Familien, sie profitieren von der anregenden, unterhaltsamen, dichten Urbanität am meisten. Die Entwicklung kindgerechter Infrastruktur in den Innenstädten kommt dagegen nur langsam voran.

So sind es denn keineswegs preiswerte Familienwohnungen, die als Beleg für die Renaissance der Innenstadt angeführt werden. Das ›Townhouse‹, von dem jüngst auf dem Friedrichswerder in Berlin 65 Exemplare durch unterschiedliche Architekten gebaut wurden, ist allerdings trotz des albernen englischen

Schaller Theodor, Wohnbebauung auf dem ehemaligen Stollwerck-Gelände, Köln, 1987

Schaller Theodor, Residential development on the former Stollwerk grounds, Cologne, 1987

apartments to shops and swimming pool (architects Hauss Walla Partner). If projects like these failed to take hold on a grand scale, it was mainly because of the sheer complexity of actually implementing all the legislative, architectural and technical aspects involved, as well as the organisation and maintenance. Profitable investment projects look rather different.

"The City Centre as a Place to Live" was the theme and slogan of the 1984–87 IBA in Berlin. Although it was aimed primarily, and comparatively late in the day, at resolving problems specific to West Berlin arising from the legacy of war, the IBA actually fuelled a wider discussion of aspects affecting other West German cities in the wake of industrial change.

What was new was the ecological approach. Crucial as this may have seemed to the planner, it affected suburbanites only indirectly – for instance when it came to paying for petrol. What really added to the appeal of the city was its growing importance as a place where young people and adults can enjoy life to the full. The communications revolution that brought a shift towards the realms of virtual media did not trigger the urban exodus that was feared 15 years ago. Evidently, the kind of direct social contact we find in the local pub, the gym, at a business lunch, a football stadium or a gallery opening simply cannot be replaced by virtual communication. What is more, cities are now endeavouring to attract visitors and potential residents by launching a whole raft of events. Where there was once the occasional city jubilee, horticultural show or athletics meet, there is now a veritable festival of urban culture. Simply being a candidate for European City of Culture or bidding to host a World Cup or an Olympic games can be enough to electrify an entire region and unleash a mini boom. Whatever the anniversary – Einstein, Mozart or Prussia – there is always a reason to celebrate, and sometimes even all year long.

People are watching in amazement at the effect that just five football matches are already having on their hometown. The fact that hosting a World Cup might be taken as an opportunity to build a new stadium or refurbish some old ones may come as no surprise. But constructing new roads, rushing to complete every building site, including the main railway station, in double and treble time, scheduling all manner of cultural events for the four

Fink und Jocher, Wohnbauten am Olympiaberg, Am Ackermannbogen, München, 2004
Fink and Jocher, Residential buildings at Olympiaberg, Am Ackermannbogen, Munich, 2004

Marketingtitels nichts anderes als der von Laage definierte Typus ›Stadthaus‹, ein drei- bis fünfgeschossiges Reihenhaus-Eigenheim. Schon 1978 sind Stadthäuser auf der »Hamburg Bau« oder 1984 von der IBA Berlin im südlichen Tiergartenviertel gebaut worden. Die neue Berliner Version ist – dem Preis und der Lage Nähe Schlossplatz und Unter den Linden geschuldet – einem privilegierteren Klientel vorbehalten. Luxuswohnungen mit Ateliers oder Kanzleien werden darin Platz finden, Familien mit Kindern die Ausnahme bilden. Wenn auch das Vorbild der Frankfurter Saalgasse aus den achtziger Jahren an postmoderner Formenvielfalt nicht erreicht wird, kommt doch eine Kleinteiligkeit wieder in die Stadt, die Überschaubarkeit und Sicherheit suggeriert. Auch das neue, sich dynamisch und weltoffen gebende Kulturbürgertum sucht und findet hier sein (teuer bezahltes) Refugium.

Kein allgemeingültiges Beispiel also, aber ein Fanal, das Nachahmung auf Normalniveau evoziert. Vom Einzug des Einfamilienhauses in die Stadt auf breiter Front kann jedoch noch nicht gesprochen werden, wenngleich gerade dessen typische Bewohnerschaft die Vielfalt des städtischen Lebens um einen entscheidenden Sektor bereichern würde.

weeks of the World Cup and even extending shop opening hours (to cater to an anticipated 3.2 million visitors) has less to do with 450 minutes of kicking a ball around than it has with generating a festive mood that the city authorities will use to their best advantage for as long as the euphoria allows.

The people most likely to embrace this "event culture" are the singletons who are now climbing the property ladder. They make more use of the leisure and cultural facilities than families do and are the ones who benefit most from the exciting, entertaining concentration of city life. The development of inner city facilities for children, on the other hand, is moving much more slowly.

Accordingly, it is not affordable family homes that are cited as proof of the inner city's renaissance. The 65 houses recently completed at Friedrichswerder in Berlin by various architects and marketed under the pseudo-English title of "Townhouse Quartier" are in fact nothing other than the same type of traditional three- to five-storey townhouse defined by Laage. As early as 1978, such townhouses were built at the "Hamburg Bau" and in 1984 in the southern Tiergarten district as part of the IBA Berlin. The new Berlin version, thanks to the close proximity of Schlossplatz and

Es sind dann eher großflächige Konversionen, die Platz für städtische Familienwohnungen bieten. Etwa in München die Theresienhöhe, wo die Chance bestand, das ehemalige Messegelände neu zu strukturieren, in Riem das Gelände des ehemaligen Flughafens (eine Aufgabe, die beim Flughafen Berlin-Tempelhof noch ansteht) oder im Ackermannbogen, einem früheren Kasernenareal. Während in Riem zwischen den schematisch aufgereihten Wohnblocks räumliche Großzügigkeit herrscht, die nicht dazu angetan ist, innerstädtische Gefühle aufkommen zu lassen, ist im Ackermannbogen nahe dem Olympiagelände als Reaktion auf die höheren Grundstückspreise die Dichte auf eine GFZ von 1,2 gesteigert worden. Die mehrheitlich vier-, im Einzelfall siebengeschossigen Wohnhäuser sind je nach Situierung in langen, lärmabschirmenden Riegeln und kürzeren Blocks orthogonal arrangiert. Trotz der Kompaktheit wird auch hier keine überaus städtische Befindlichkeit aufkommen. Es handelt sich bei diesen Wohnquartieren eher um parasitäre vorstädtische Wohnformen, die sich der vorhandenen Infrastruktur an ihren Rändern – Verkehrsanbindung, wohnungsnahe Grundversorgung – bedienen.

Das gilt auch für die Neubebauung der Theresienhöhe, wo großformatige Bürogebäude entlang der Verkehrsachse mit acht- bis fünfzehngeschossigen Wohntürmen hinterfüttert sind. Otto Steidles bunte Fassaden, neckische Befensterungsmuster sowie wahrnehmungs- und verhaltenspsychologisch indiskutable Schubladenbalkons (›Präsentiertellereffekt‹) gaukeln eine mediterrane Nonchalance vor, die über die Monostruktur und den harten Schematismus der Anlage hinwegtäuschen soll.

Wie man mit großen Gesten doch keine Großstadt erzeugt, zeigte Peter Kulka auf der ehemaligen Industriebrache Hollerborn am Rand der Wiesbadener Innenstadt. »Kompromisslos modern« seien die lang gestreckten, fünf- bis siebengeschossigen Wohnblocks, beteuert Kulka und nimmt als Vorbilder Bruno Taut und Ernst May in Anspruch. Indes kommen Ludwig Hilberseimers rigide Utopien endloser stereometrischer Blocks den Vorstellungen Kulkas weitaus näher: das 19. Jahrhundert als Feindbild, nicht nur was die Semantik betrifft, sondern auch die Struktur. Von der Nutzung vorgegebene Differenzierungsmöglichkeiten wurden bewusst ignoriert. Die immergleichen Fensterreihen geben keinen Hinweis auf die Wohnungen im Inneren. Großer Maßstab, weite Grünräume, Absenz von Urbanität, in dieser Konsequenz wird die Charta von Athen heute nur noch selten befolgt.

Die Chance, in größeren Chargen innere City neu zu planen, hat es in Deutschland in den letzten Jahren nur in Berlin gegeben. Bereits vor dem Bau viel gescholten, wurde die Bebauung des Potsdamer Platzes trotzdem zur Erfolgsgeschichte. Schon vor dem Fall der Mauer als autonomes Zentrum geplant, galt es nach der Wende, durch Bebauung des Leipziger Platzes die Anbindung an Berlin-Mitte zu leisten. Nachdem es gelungen war, die Baustelle an sich zur Touristenattraktion zu machen, hielt sich das Interesse auch nach der Fertigstellung. Besucher wie Einheimische bevölkern Passage und Kinoszene, und man muss schon miserables Wetter aussuchen, um im Debis-Quartier allein auf der Straße zu sein. Der Mut zur Dichte und zur urbanen Mischung wurde belohnt. Den Wohnungen im Quartier mangelt es an Großstadtfeeling bestimmt nicht.

Freilich gibt es signifikante Leerstände bereits nebenan, in den Wohnungsbauten entlang des Tilla-Durieux-Parks und in den oberen Geschossen des Leipziger Platzes, Folge der wenig attraktiven Architektur einerseits und der Renditevorstellungen der Vermieter oder Verkäufer andererseits. Die langfristig unumgängliche

Unter den Linden, as well as to the high price, is within grasp of only a privileged clientele. They will house luxury flats with studios or offices. Families with children will be the exception. Even though these new houses do not match the postmodern diversity of the Saalgasse development that was built in Frankfurt in the 1980s, they do bring a certain intimacy of scale back into the fabric of the city. This is where the new middle class of dynamic, cosmopolitan, cultural sophisticates will seek and find their des res – and pay dearly for the privilege.

So, while this may not be universally applicable, it does set an example to be emulated on a more modest level. Not that there is any sign as yet of the one-family home becoming a widespread phenomenon in the city, even though the typical residents it would attract constitute a crucial sector that would enrich the diversity of urban life.

Instead, it is the large-scale conversion projects that offer space for urban families. Take for instance the city of Munich, where an opportunity arose to redevelop the former trade-fair grounds at Theresienhöhe, and the former airport at Riem (a challenge still to be tackled at Berlin's Tempelhof airport) as well as the former barracks at Ackermannbogen. Whereas the rows of housing blocks at Riem are spaced so generously that they hardly create a sense of urban density, real estate prices at Ackermannbogen near the Olympic stadium prompted a floor-space index of as much as 1.2. The predominantly four-storey buildings, interspersed with some seven-storey buildings, are orthogonally arranged in long, sound-insulating blocks and shorter blocks,

Hilmer, Sattler und Albrecht, Drei Wohnhäuser Theresienhöhe München, Haus Ganghoferstraße 35, 2001–2002
Hilmer, Sattler and Albrecht, Three residential buildings at Theresienhöhe Munich, Ganghoferstrasse 35, 2001–2002

Anpassung des Preisniveaus wird jedoch auch diese Wohnlagen mit Standortvorteil beleben. Das gilt womöglich auch für die Wohnungen im oberen Luxus-Segment im Beisheim-Center nördlich des Potsdamer Platzes. Ob hier, am Pariser Platz oder in der Friedrichstraße, die Renaissance der Innenstädte in den 1a-Gebieten wird ein stagnierendes Projekt bleiben, solange die Investoren den ihnen mühsam abgerungenen Wohnungsanteil lieber leer stehen lassen, als ihn zu günstigeren, marktgängigen Preisen zu belegen.

Große Chancen sehen die Städte in der attraktiven Kombination Innenstadt und Wasser, das heißt die Erweiterung der City um angrenzende ehemalige Hafengebiete. Sind es in Köln an der Rheinau und in Berlin am Osthafen schmale Uferbezirke, so haben Frankfurt am Main mit dem Osthafen, Düsseldorf, Duisburg oder gar Hamburg größere Hafenareale, die derzeit konvertiert werden. Ziel ist in allen Fällen ein Maximum an Urbanität, die Erweiterung der City um intensiv genutzte Wohn- und Bürostandorte mit möglichst hohem Prestigewert. Nur durch die dadurch erwartete Wertschöpfung sind die notwendigen Investitionen zu akquirieren.

Die Planer stecken freilich in einem Dilemma. Cityfunktionen lassen sich nicht beliebig vermehren. Ihr Umfang ist vom Gesamtareal und Potenzial der Stadt abhängig – und von der wirtschaftlichen Prosperität. Urbanität hat Dichte, Körnung und Nutzungsmischung zur Voraussetzung, Verhältnisse also, wie sie in historischen Innenstädten ›gewachsen‹ sind. Diese Verhältnisse aber sind mit den vorherrschenden Bodenverwertungsmechanismen nicht zu haben. Dichte bedeutet weitgehender Verzicht auf Stadtgrün, was beim Bürger auf reflexartige Ablehnung stößt. Körnung bedeutet Kleinteiligkeit der Grundstücks- und Eigentumsverhältnisse, wobei viele Investoren von vornherein abwinken. Und Nutzungsmischung bedeutet Akzeptanz auch weniger profitabler Nutzungen im Interesse des Ganzen, wie etwa Sozialeinrichtungen, Cafés oder Wohnungen normalen Standards, auch dies keine Lieblingsvorstellung der Einzelinvestoren. Seitens der Stadtplanung steuernd eingreifen zu wollen, ist bei der gegenwärtigen wirtschaftlichen Großwetterlage illusorisch. Allenfalls kann man das enorme Überangebot an Büroflächen als Druckmittel ein-

Hilmer und Sattler, Wohnhaus Kurfürstenstraße Berlin, 1982–1987, IBA-Projekt
Hilmer and Sattler, Residential building on Kurfürstenstrasse, Berlin, 1982–1987, IBA-Project

depending on the site position. In spite of this compact layout, the atmosphere here is not overtly urban either. These housing developments have more in common with the kind of parasitic suburban housing that feeds on the existing infrastructure of transport and utilities around it.

This is also true of the new development at Theresienhöhe, where large-scale office buildings flank the main traffic route, with housing blocks of eight to fifteen storeys set behind them. Otto Steidle's colourful facades, whimsical window patterns and frankly unspeakable drawer-like balconies (offering all the privacy of a goldfish bowl) try to create an illusion of Mediterranean nonchalance that is meant to distract from the structural monotony and harsh schematism of the development.

Grand gestures do not make a city, as Peter Kulka has demonstrated on the former industrial wasteland of Hollerborn in Wiesbaden. Kulka claims that his elongated five- to seven-storey housing blocks are "uncompromisingly modern" and cites Bruno Taut and Ernst May as sources of inspiration. But Kulka's design demonises the structure and semantics of nineteenth-century architecture in a way that is more akin to Ludwig Hilberseimer's inflexible utopian vision of endless stereometric blocks. No attempt whatsoever has been made to exploit the potential for diversity that the function and use of this development actually offers. The repetitive rows of windows give no indication of the homes inside. Huge in scale, with large expanses of green space and a complete absence of urban atmosphere, it follows the Athens Charter to the letter in way that is rarely seen today.

Berlin is the only city in Germany that has offered an opportunity for major inner-city redevelopment in recent years. Much maligned before construction had even started, the development of Potsdamer Platz has proved an unexpected success story. Potsdamer Platz had already been earmarked as an independent and distinctive urban centre before the fall of the Berlin Wall. Afterwards, the development of Leipziger Platz created a link with Berlin-Mitte. The building site itself became a veritable tourist attraction and interest in the project did not wan after completion either. Visitors and locals alike now flock to its shops and cinemas, and the weather has to be truly grim for the Debis complex to be anything like deserted. The courage to create urban density and diversity has been richly rewarded. The apartments in this district certainly have no shortage of urban atmosphere.

There are, however, some significant empty buildings close by: the apartments along Tilla-Durieux Park and on the upper floors of Leipziger Platz have failed to find favour, partly because they lack architectural appeal and partly because landlords and investors have set their profit margins a little too high. Once prices have come into line here, as indeed they must in the long term, these centrally located apartments too will be occupied. That may also be true of the top-end luxury apartments in the Beisheim Center to the north of Potsdamer Platz. Here, at Pariser Platz and in Friedrichstrasse, the inner-city renaissance will continue to stagnate in prime areas as long as investors choose to let their property stand empty rather than renting or selling at more reasonable prices.

Cities have set their sights on the attractive combination of water and urban living, taking the opportunity of expanding into former dockland areas near the centre. While Cologne has its Rheinau and Berlin its Osthafen, both with relatively narrow shorelines, Frankfurt, Düsseldorf, Duisburg and even Hamburg all have considerably larger docklands that are currently undergoing conversion. In all these cases, the aim is to achieve a maximum of

Rob Krier, Francy Valentiny/Hubert Hermann, Aldo Rossi, Henry Nielebock, Klaus-Theo Brenner/Benedict Tonon, Giorgio Grassi, Hans Hollein, Stadtvillen an der Rauchstraße, Berlin, 1980–1984, IBA-Projekt

Rob Krier, Francy Valentiny/Hubert Hermann, Aldo Rossi, Henry Nielebock, Klaus-Theo Brenner/Benedict Tonon, Giorgio Grassi, Hans Hollein, Townhouses on Rauchstrasse, Berlin, 1980–1984, IBA-Project

setzen, um Investitionswillige zum Wohnungsbau zu bewegen.

Die Folgen sind in Hamburg zu erleben. 110 Hektar Hafengebiet stehen südlich der City und der historischen Speicherstadt zur Verfügung und haben die Phantasie der Planer und Stadtherren beflügelt. Die Ausfüllung des Masterplans mit konkreten Gebäudeplanungen kommt zwar nur mühsam in Gang, da die Nachfrage nach Büroraum auf einem Tiefpunkt ist, doch haben diese Verhältnisse auch ihre positive Seite. Der Wohnungsbau ist als Alternative attraktiv. So entstehen neben Arbeitsplätzen im tertiären Sektor auch genügend Wohnungen (allerdings der höheren Preisgruppe), die zu der erstrebten Mischnutzung führen.

Es ist jedoch augenscheinlich, dass der Citycharakter, die urbane Atmosphäre, die noch in der Speicherstadt anzutreffen ist, schon nebenan bei den ersten Neubauten auf Grund mangelnder Dichte jäh abbricht. So sind am Sandtorkai erste Wohngebäude entstanden, respektable Architektur von Peter Schweger, von Böge Lindner-Böge, von ASTOC, BRT und anderen. Es sind wunderbare Wohnungen in siebengeschossigen, mäßig großen Hauseinheiten, nach Süden orientiert, mit Blick übers Wasser, aber es sind die am nächsten zur Innenstadt gelegenen und es werden die letzten sein, deren Bewohner auf den PKW werden verzichten können. Schon

urbanity and to expand the city centre by the creation of intensely used housing and office districts with a high prestige value. Only if this is achieved will the areas attract the necessary investment.

The planners, however, are faced with a dilemma. Urban functions cannot simply be replicated at will. They depend on the overall size and potential of the city itself – and on its economic prosperity. The urban fabric requires the same density, graining and diversity that have grown organically in historic inner cities. But such a situation cannot be achieved under the present development legislation. Density means less green space, and that tends to be automatically unpopular. Graining means smaller sites and smaller properties, and that tends to put off investors. Diversity means having to accept less profitable facilities in the interests of the community, such as welfare centres, cafés and housing of a normal standard, none of which are favoured by individual investors. In the current economic climate, it is illusory for urban planners to intervene. At best, they can point out the huge oversupply of office space and use that argument as leverage to persuade potential investors to build housing.

The consequences can be seen in Hamburg. To the south of the city and the historic Speicherstadt, 110 hectares of docklands

Potsdamer Platz, Berlin, Zustand 2004
Potsdamer Platz, Berlin, Status 2004

wer jenseits des Sandtorhafens, am Dalmannkai wohnen wird, ist auf das Auto angewiesen – wenn er nicht gerade in Herzog & de Meurons zukünftiger Philharmonie am Endes des Kais zu arbeiten hat.

Letztlich lebt und arbeitet es sich doch nur in den traditionellen Kerngebieten mit dem ultimativen Metropolengefühl, in schicken Lofts in den ehemaligen Brauereien, Mietfabriken und Spinnereien, in umgewidmeten Kirchen, in ausgebauten Dachgeschossen und in baulückenfüllenden Appartementhäusern. Den Charme der Stadt des 19. Jahrhunderts durch gänzlich neue Quartiere zu synthetisieren, will nirgends so recht gelingen. Die Europäische Stadt ist ein Trugbild, man sieht sie deutlich, doch man erreicht sie nicht mehr.

Die Renaissance der Stadt bedeutet somit, dass Firmen die ›weichen Standortfaktoren‹, wie Kulturangebot und Unterhaltungsmöglichkeiten, für qualifizierte Mitarbeiter schätzen lernen und deshalb wieder in die Stadt ziehen, dass veränderte Lebens- und Beziehungsformen Platz greifen, die sich nur im innerstädtischen Umfeld verwirklichen lassen, und dass die Attraktivierung des Stadtlebens durch eine offensive Event- und Festivalkultur Wirkung zeigt. Sie bedeutet nicht, dass die ganze Stadt zur City mit einem Maximum an Urbanität gemacht werden kann. Dichte,

have fired the imagination of the planners and city authorities. But fleshing out the master plan with actual designs for specific buildings is taking a long time to get off the ground, as demand for office space has slumped. Yet this situation also has its benefits. Housing development has become an attractive alternative. And so, alongside tertiary sector workplaces, enough apartments (albeit in the upper price bracket) are also being built to ensure the desired diversity.

It is, however, evident that the urban atmosphere to be found in the Speicherstadt is not replicated in the adjacent new-build development, which lacks density. At Sandtorkai the first housing has already been built. This is respectable architecture by the likes of Peter Schweger, Böge Lindner-Böge, ASTOC, BRT and others. These are wonderful south-facing apartments with sea views, in modestly scaled seven-storey building units, but even those closest to the city centre will require cars. Anyone living beyond Sandtorhafen, on Dalmannkai, will depend on a car for transport – unless they just happen to have a job in Herzog & de Meuron's future Philharmonic Hall at the end of the quay.

Ultimately, it is only the traditional core areas that really do offer that city buzz, where people can live and work in chic loft conversions of former breweries, factories, spinning mills and

David Chipperfield, Parkside Apartments, Potsdamer Platz, Berlin, 2005
David Chipperfield, Parkside Apartments, Potsdamer Platz, Berlin, 2005

Mischung und menschlicher Maßstab sind die Zutaten für Urbanität, die in den bestehenden Innenstadtgebieten durch Lückenschließungen und Nachverdichtung erschlossen werden kann. Die neuen, großformatigen, noch als innenstadtnah geltenden Entwicklungsgebiete jedoch werden Zwitter bleiben, keine pulsierende, Tag und Nacht lebendige City, aber auch keine verschlafene Trabantenstadt. Die viel beschworene Europäische Stadt sieht anders aus.

churches, in attic conversion and in gap-site apartment buildings. Nowhere does it seem possible to create the charm of the nineteenth-century city. The European city is an illusion. We can see it clearly, but we cannot reach it.

In this respect, the renaissance of the city is about companies beginning to appreciate the importance of "soft location factors", such as culture and entertainment, for their skilled workforce. It is about the changing lifestyles and relationship structures that can only thrive in an inner-city environment. It is about the burgeoning event and festival culture that makes urban life more attractive. It is not about turning an entire town into a city centre with a maximum of urbanity. Density, mix and a human scale are the ingredients for the urban atmosphere that can be fostered in existing inner cities by developing gap sites and increasing density. The new, large-scale developments near the centre will remain hybrids: neither vibrant urban centres full of life day and night, nor sleepy dormitory towns. The much-vaunted European city is something else.

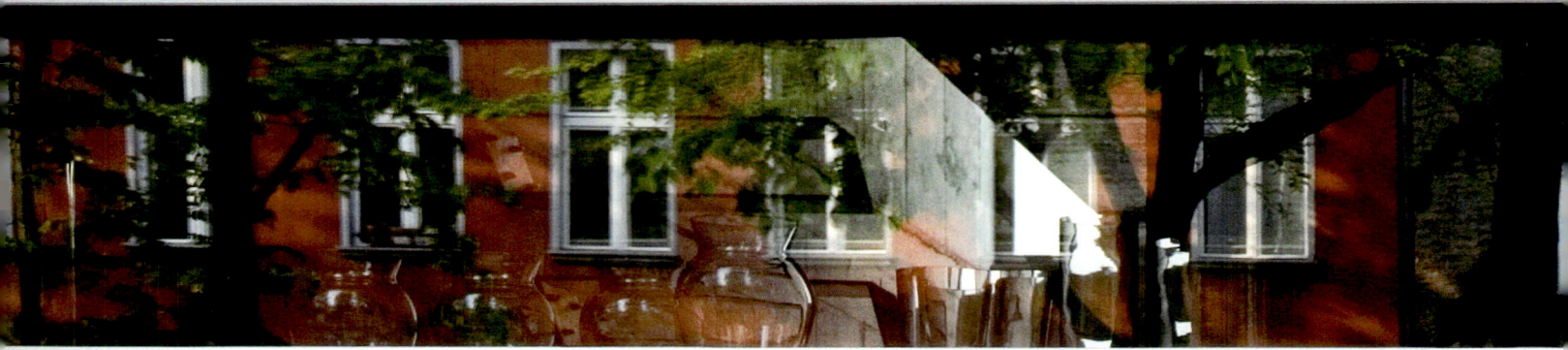

WOHNEN IN DER STADT
LIVING IN THE CITY

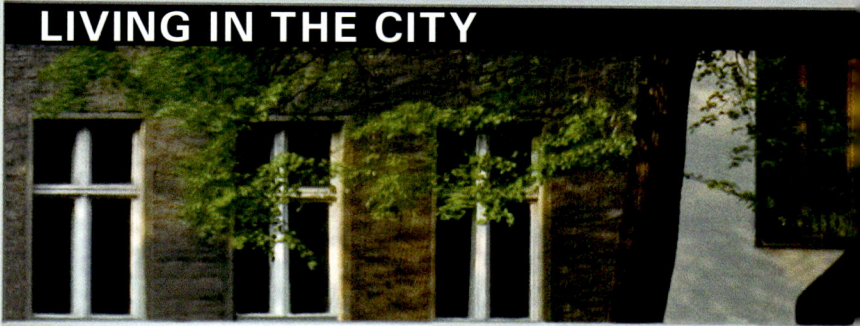

WOHN- UND GESCHÄFTSHAUS, MÜNCHEN
COMMERCIAL AND RESIDENTIAL BUILDING, MUNICH

Allmann Sattler Wappner

Es gibt viel zu sehen hier: Detailverliebte historische Gebäude schmiegen sich an funktionalistisch strenge Bauten der Nachkriegszeit – die Narben der Bombardements während des Zweiten Weltkriegs gehören zum kontrastreichen Bild der Nymphenburger Straße. Deren große Dimensionen und die vorgestellten Baumreihen, die hier den Straßenraum säumen, verraten noch etwas von der einstigen Bedeutung als wichtige Verbindung zum prachtvollen Schloss Nymphenburg.

Heute wird der erste sinnliche Eindruck, den man von diesem Straßenzug gewinnt, vor allem durch den Verkehrslärm der vorbeifahrenden Autos hervorgerufen. Just an diesem Ort, nur zwei U-Bahn-Stationen vom Hauptbahnhof entfernt, errichteten die Münchener Architekten Allmann Sattler Wappner ein neues Wohn- und Geschäftshaus. Durch den Abriss eines maroden, seit Jahren leer stehenden Wohnhauses ergab sich für sie die Chance, eine passende Antwort auf diesen diffizilen Kontext zu finden. Während der Altbau noch räumliche Nähe zu seinen Nachbarn besaß, entschieden sich die Architekten nun für einen deutlich freigestellten Solitär, der als monolithischer Körper nachhaltig in Erscheinung tritt. Links und rechts des Neubaus betonen große Fugen seine Distanz zu einem tristen Flachdachbau aus den 1960er-Jahren und einem pastellgelben Gründerzeithaus. Aber nicht nur räumlich, auch gestalterisch sucht das neue Haus die Abgrenzung zu seinen Nachbarn. In die bunte Melange des Straßenzugs fügten die Architekten ein zeitloses Stadthaus, das seiner heterogenen Nachbarschaft auf subversive Weise antwortet. An Stelle der vertrauten, klassischen Dreiteilung aus Sockel, Wand und Dach erscheint dieses Haus in einem äußerst homogenen Kleid aus cremefarbenem Putz: Lediglich die Körnung der Oberflächen changiert noch ein wenig – doch selbst die Dachflächen sind mit einem Kunstharzputz in identischem Farbton gedeckt. Weit vorspringende Balkone oder Erker gehören nicht zu diesem Konzept – nur im Erdgeschoss schieben sich zwei kleine Kuben aus der Fassade. Ansonsten wurde hier alles möglichst flächenbündig gestaltet, um den Eindruck des soliden, kompakten Körpers zu bestärken. Bedruckte Glasscheiben vor den eloxierten Aluminiumfenstern unterstreichen nicht nur den Eindruck der Flächenbündigkeit, sie erhöhen auch den Barriereeffekt gegenüber dem Straßenlärm, von dem die Hausbewohner profitieren.

Und das subversive Spiel geht weiter: Während aus der Nachbarschaft die rigiden Fassaden von Symmetrie und funktionaler Dominanz künden, überrascht der Neubau mit seinen »tanzenden Fenstern«. An drei Seiten des Hauses sind die Fensteröffnungen stets gegeneinander versetzt – und kokettieren mit den Konventionen der Nachbarn. Nur nach Süden, zur lärmgeschützten Hofseite, öffnet sich das Haus betont großzügig mit raumhohen Fensterbändern und lenkt den Blick auf ein saniertes Fabrikgebäude aus

There is plenty to see here: flamboyantly ornamented historic buildings rub shoulders with the sober functionality of the postwar era. The scars of wartime bombing are part and parcel of the architectural diversity along the broad, tree-lined boulevard of Nymphenburger Strasse that was once a major approach road to the magnificent palace of Schloss Nymphenburg.

Today, the first impression of this street is mainly that of a busy thoroughfare with heavy traffic. Here, just two metro stops away from the main railway station, Munich-based architects Allmann Sattler Wappner have created a new commercial and residential building. The demolition of a house that had stood empty for several years offered an opportunity for addressing a rather difficult urban situation. Whereas the old building huddled close to its neighbours, the architects chose to make the new design more clearly separate by creating a strikingly monolithic edifice standing well apart from the bleak flat-roofed 1960s building and the pastel-coloured nineteenth-century building on either side of it. But it is not just physical distance that sets this new building apart from its surroundings. The design itself stands out. The timeless townhouse that the architects have created seems almost subversive amid the motley architectural jumble of this street. Instead of the familiar classical division into plinth, wall and roof, it has an extremely homogeneous look in cream-coloured render, broken only by the grainy texture of the finish. Even the roof areas are finished in synthetic resin plaster of exactly the same colour. With no broadly jutting balconies or bays – just two small cubes protruding from the facade at ground-floor level – the overall effect is one of smoothness and flatness, underlining the solid, compact look of the building. Panes of printed glass in front of the anodised aluminium windows add to this impression while at the same time increasing the sound insulation that screens the occupants from the noise of heavy traffic.

The subversiveness does not end there, either. Whereas the surrounding facades have a rigidity of design that speaks of symmetry and functionality, this new building surprises us with its "dancing windows". On three sides, the window apertures are staggered, as though to mock the conventions of the surrounding architecture. Only on the quiet, south-facing courtyard facade does the building open up with large floor-to-ceiling windows, drawing the eye towards the refurbished brick-built factory that is the architects' own studio. Narrow loggias across the entire back of the building provide sheltered and secluded outdoor spaces. One might assume that the varied wall apertures reflect the varied layouts of the apartments within. But that is not the case. In fact, from the first floor to the fourth, the layout is the same throughout. The 115-square-metre north-south apartments provide flexible accommodation with daylight from three sides. Since none of

Architekten Architects Allmann Sattler Wappner Architekten, München, www.allmannsattlerwappner.de; Team: Karin Hengher, Michael Frank, Christine Himmler **Bauherr** Client Privat **Private Tragwerk** Structure Seeberger Friedl und Partner, München **Bauzeit** Construction Period 2001–2005 **Standort** Location Nymphenburger Straße 127, 80636 München **Abbildungen** Photo Credits Florian Holzherr

Straßenansicht, Wohnhaus
Street elevation, residential building

Hofansicht, Geschäftshaus
Courtyard elevation, commercial building

Ziegeln, das Büro der Architekten. Schmale Loggien, die sich über die gesamte Rückseite ausdehnen, bieten hier die geschützten privaten Außenräume. Die Wohnungen, so könnte man vermuten, haben unterschiedliche Grundrisse, und diese Differenzen führten dann zu den variierten Wandöffnungen. Doch dem ist nicht so: Vom ersten bis zum vierten Geschoss gibt es denselben Grundriss. Die rund 115 Quadratmeter großen Nord-Süd-Typen verfügen über drei Tageslichtseiten und können flexibel eingeteilt werden. Auf die großzügige Öffnung des Wohnraums nach Süden wollte bislang keiner der Mieter verzichten, deshalb sind keine 4-, sondern ausnahmslos 3-Zimmer-Wohnungen entstanden.

Seine Prägnanz im Stadtraum erfährt das Haus jedoch nicht nur durch die Fassaden dieser neun Wohnungen. Der Möbelladen, dessen zurückgesetzter Eingang in den Sockel des Monolithen tief einschneidet, und die Penthousewohnung im Dachgeschoss kontrastieren mit ihren großzügigen horizontalen Fensterflächen die bewegten Lochfassaden. Während der Sockelbereich jedoch noch als solide wahrzunehmen ist, wirken die gläsernen Einschnitte in die Dachflächen – besonders an der rückwärtigen Hofseite – etwas zu groß. Was hier innenräumlich sinnvoll erscheint, konterkariert den äußeren Eindruck des Monolithischen und das sublime Spiel mit den vertrauten Dachflächen.

Betritt man das Haus, spürt man unvermittelt den Habitus der Reduktion. Eine Treppe, deren Unterseiten von Neonlichtstreifen beleuchtet werden, windet sich skulptural nach oben. Jegliches Ornament, jeglicher Zierrat würde diesen konsequent reduzierten Aufgang in Frage stellen. Man läuft über Platten aus hellem kroatischem Kalksandstein im Treppenhaus und Eichenparkett in den Wohnungen – eine asketisch-reine, aber keineswegs strenge Sprache erfüllt die Räume. Das neue Haus ist ein ebenso klares wie überzeugendes Plädoyer für die öffentliche Dimension privaten Bauens. Es ist vor allem ein privates Wohnhaus; doch nicht nur dessen Mieter, auch die Nymphenburger Straße darf sich über Stadthäuser dieser hohen Qualität freuen.

Hans-Jürgen Breuning

the tenants wanted to forgo the open southerly aspect, there are no four-room apartments here, but only three-room apartments.

It is not just the facades that lend this building such a distinctive presence in the urban fabric. The furniture store with its set-back entrance cutting deep into the base of this monolithic block and the rooftop penthouse with its huge horizontal swathes of glass contrast starkly with the sense of motion created by the window alignment of the facades. Whereas the ground floor has an appearance of solidity, the glass inserts in the roof area – especially on the courtyard side – seem almost too big. Appropriate as this may be in terms of the interior design, it actually counters the monolithic impression of the building and the fascinating play on conventional rooftops.

Inside the building, there is a distinct sense of reduction. A staircase lit by neon strips from below sweeps upwards like a sculpture. Any form of ornament here would undermine its rigorous simplicity. Pale Croatian lime-sand brick flooring in the stairwell and oak parquet flooring in the apartments create an air of ascetic purity that is far from sterile. Here is a new building that makes a clear and compelling case for the public aspect of privately commissioned architecture. This may be first and foremost a private house, but the occupants are not the only ones who benefit from it. A townhouse of such quality enhances the entire Nymphenburger Strasse.

Hans-Jürgen Breuning

Hofansicht, Wohnhaus
Courtyard elevation, residential building

Lageplan
Site plan

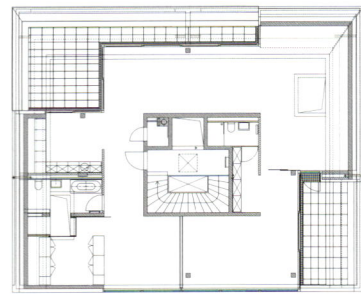

Wohnzimmer im Obergeschoss mit Balkon
Living room on upper floor with balcony

Grundriss Dachgeschoss
Top-floor plan

Grundriss Obergeschoss
Upper-floor plan

Grundriss Erdgeschoss
Ground-floor plan

Penthousewohnung im Dachgeschoss
Penthouse apartment on top floor

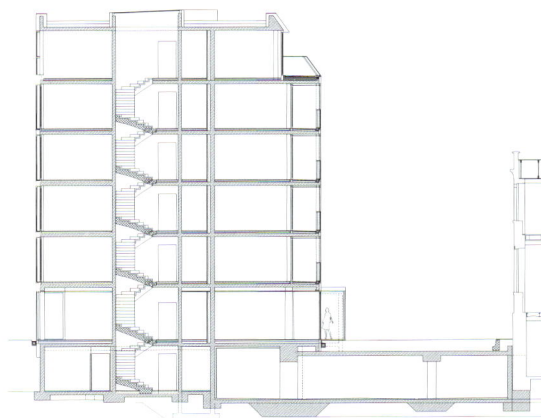

Querschnitt, Wohnhaus
Cross section, Residential building

Treppenhaus von oben
Staircase from top

Treppenhaus von unten mit Neonlichtstreifen
Staircase from below with neon light strips

WOHNHAUS, HAMBURG
APARTMENT BUILDING, HAMBURG

Blauraum Architekten

Versteckt in einer eher unattraktiven und ehemals rein gewerblich geprägten Stichstraße im ansonsten noblen Hamburger Stadtteil Harvestehude, in der Nähe der bekannten Grindelhochhäuser, hat das junge Büro blauraum architekten sein erstes Gebäude mit allen Leistungsphasen in einem Direktauftrag fertig gestellt. Das heute holzverkleidete ›Schmuckkästchen‹ war einst ein einfaches Bürogebäude und Parkhaus aus den 70er-Jahren. Während eines Streifzugs durch Hamburg auf der Suche nach einem geeigneten Grundstück für ein innerstädtisches Wohnungsbauprojekt, fanden die Architekten Anfang 2003 das schmucklose und leer stehende Bürohaus – nur die Parkebenen im Erd- und Untergeschoss wurden auf Grund der immerwährenden innerstädtischen Parkplatznot noch intensiv genutzt. Da die Substanz des Betonskelettbaus gut erschien, die Lage in der Stadt hervorragend war und die bestehende Tiefgarage im Untergeschoss den geforderten Stellplatznachweis vereinfachte, wagten sich die Architekten gemeinsam mit einem Projektentwickler und einem Makler an das Unterfangen: statt des geplanten Neubaus wollten sie nun das bestehende Gebäude auf einem verhältnismäßig teuren Grundstück zu einem hochwertigen, neuartigen Wohnhaus umbauen. Nachdem die Bauvoranfrage mit großer Interessensbekundung von Seiten der Stadt erwidert wurde, machten sich blauraum architekten auf einen Parforceritt durch die Bauleistungsphasen. In anderthalb Jahren wurde das alte Gebäude bis auf die Grundstruktur entkernt und durch einen erlesenen Bau mit gänzlich neuer Erscheinung ersetzt.

In dem schicken Altbauviertel fällt heute jedem Passanten das neue Haus sofort ins Auge – teilweise zum Leidwesen der Bewohner, die sich auf ihren Balkonen und hinter den großen Fensterflächen manchmal zu stark beobachtet fühlen. Die monotone ›Kiste‹ wurde besonders zur Straßenseite hin aufgebrochen. Aus der Lochfassade zur Bogenallee schieben sich geschosshohe, erkerartige Boxen über zwei Meter hinaus. Die Fenster befinden sich bei diesen Boxen in den Seitenwänden, so dass die Wohneinheiten miteinander zu kommunizieren scheinen. Der Blick von innen kann nur auf das eigene Haus, auf die eigene Wohnung stattfinden, während die direkt gegenüberliegende, unattraktive Umgebung nicht Teil des Blickfelds ist. Auch der Pkw-Aufzug ins Untergeschoss versteckt sich unauffällig in einer der ebenerdigen Kisten. Zur Hofseite gen Westen zeigt sich der Bau großzügig verglast: mit Terrassen zum ruppig gestalteten Garten im Erdgeschoss und mit durchgehenden, vorgestellten Balkonen in den Obergeschossen. Der gesamte Baukörper wurde ringsum mit horizontal ausgerichteten und hinterlüfteten HPL-Platten (künstliches Hochdrucklaminat) und darauf einer Dekoschicht aus dunklem Echtholzfurnier bekleidet und erhält dadurch ein edles Erscheinungsbild. Es scheint, als sei die hölzerne Innenverkleidung nach außen gestülpt worden. Gleichzeitig werden durch die ungewohnte Materialität

Tucked away in a rather unattractive and formerly entirely industrial side street in Hamburg's otherwise upmarket neighbourhood of Harvestehude, near the famous Grindelhochhäuser [Germany's first high-rise buildings, now listed monuments], the young blauraum team of architects have created their first complete and directly commissioned work. This wood-clad gem was once a simple 1970s office building with underground car park. It was in 2003, on a stroll through Hamburg in search of a suitable inner-city development project that the architects spotted this plain, empty office building (only the basement and ground-floor parking areas were still in use, due to the lack of alternative spaces in the city). The overall structure of the concrete skeleton building appeared to be sound, the location was outstanding and the existing underground car park level provided a built-in solution to the statutory requirement to provide parking facilities for new buildings. So the architects joined forces with a project developer and an estate agent to take up the challenge. Instead of the planned new building, they decided to convert the existing building on its prime site into a high quality new-style apartment building. The local authorities welcomed their outline planning application with open arms and blauraum architects promptly embarked on the Herculean task of gutting the building and transforming it into an exquisite residential property within the space of just eighteen months.

Today, the new building is a striking feature in this chic district of traditional architecture. A little too striking for some residents, who feel exposed to the gaze of curious passers-by on the balconies and behind their huge windows. The monotony of the structure has been broken, especially on the street facade. The perforated facade on Bogenallee now has floor-to-ceiling oriel-like boxes protruding more than two metres outwards. The windows are set into the side walls of these boxes so that the residential units appear to communicate with one another. The view from inside focuses onto the residents' own home and apartment, thereby screening out the unattractive immediate surroundings. The car lift to the basement is discreetly hidden in one of the ground-level boxes. At the western side, towards the courtyard, the building is extensively glazed: with terraces leading to the rambling garden on the ground floor and protruding balconies on the upper floors. The entire structure has been clad all round in rear-ventilated horizontal HPL panels with a dark real-oak veneer that lends it a sophisticated appearance. It almost looks as though the wooden inner cladding has been turned out to the exterior. At the same time, the unusual material and form break with

Ansicht Straßenseite
Elevation, street side

Architekten Architects blauraum architekten, Hamburg, www.blauraum.de; Team: Carsten Venus, Claudia Große-Hartlage, Hanna Haerdter, Michael Maurer, Dirk Fischer-Appelt **Bauherr** Client Cogiton Projekt Harvestehude GmbH **Tragwerk** Structure WTM Windels Timm Morgen, Hamburg **Ausführung** Construction April 2004 – Januar 2005 **Standort** Location Bogenallee 10–12, 20144 Hamburg **Abbildungen** Photo Credits Dominik Reipka, Christian Schaulin

Ansicht Hofseite
Elevation, courtyard side

und Form bisher bestehende Bilder des Wohnungsbaus aufgebrochen. Leider wurden auf Erdgeschossebene hohe, undurchsichtige Gartentrennwände errichtet, die das ansonsten homogene Bild des Gesamtkörpers stören.

Im Inneren verbergen sich hinter zwei Hauseingängen fünfzehn unterschiedlich große und verschieden ausgestattete Wohneinheiten (mit zwei bis drei Zimmern, eine Maisonettewohnung) auf vier Geschossen. Eine Klientel vom Yuppie-Single bis zur Familie mit Kind findet hier helle Neubauwohnungen in der jeweils passenden Größe von 80 bis 110 m². Allen gleich ist jedoch die durch den Altbau vorgegebene geringe Deckenhöhe (gut zweieinhalb Meter), die durch eine offene Grundrissgestaltung mit raumhohen Fenstern und Türen und durch die Freilegung der Unterzüge in der Decke geschickt überspielt wird. Nur die in allen Geschossen übereinander liegenden Versorgungskerne für Küche und Bad stehen als unverrückbare Bestandteile fest. Je nach Bedarf können die großen Pendeltüren einzelne Bereiche zimmerartig abteilen oder einen offenen Raum zum Kochen, Essen, Wohnen oder Spielen erlebbar machen. Ein einheitlicher dunkler Parkettboden unterstreicht das Großraumgefühl von der Garderobe bis zur Fassade.

Die eigentlich durch geringe Quadratmeteranzahl und einen vorerst simplen Grundrisszuschnitt gekennzeichneten Wohnungen werden durch die nach außen gestülpten so genannten ›flexboxen‹ ganz wesentlich belebt. So werden die einzelnen Einheiten erweitert und individualisiert und schaffen einen höheren Identifikationsfaktor in dem ansonsten gleichförmigen Gesamtensemble. Im Inneren dieser Boxen finden Raumerweiterungen von Küche, Schlafraum oder Badezimmer Platz – ein Essplatz, eine Leseecke oder auch eine Sauna sind damit möglich. Je nach Bedarf des Eigentümers sollten diese ursprünglich ›maßgeschneidert‹ im Grundriss platziert werden, mussten dann aber doch im Vorhinein festgelegt werden. Die potenziellen Käufer können also die schon vorbereitete und von den Architekten entwickelte Vorauswahl ›von der Stange‹ erwerben.

Den jungen Architekten ist es hervorragend gelungen, ein leer stehendes und unattraktives Bürogebäude in ein neuartiges und ästhetisch hochwertiges Wohngebäude umzuwandeln. Nun müssen nur noch die zahlungswilligen Nutzer einziehen, damit es auch belebt wird.

Anna Hesse

conventional images of housing construction. The otherwise homogeneous appearance of the building as a whole is marred only by the non-transparent garden partition walls.

Two separate main entrances lead into the building, in which there are fifteen apartments of differing sizes and design (two- to three-room flats and a maisonette) on four floors. They offer bright, modern apartments of 80 to 110 square metres for a clientele ranging from single young professionals to families. Though the original building dictated a relatively low ceiling height of about two-and-a-half metres, this is cleverly offset by the open plan layouts and the floor-to-ceiling windows and doors. The only feature that cannot be varied is the location of kitchen and bath, determined by the core structure for utilities that runs vertically through the building. Large swing doors allow the separate areas of each apartment to be opened up or closed off as required to create a large open space for cooking, dining, living and play. Dark parquet flooring throughout further underlines the sense of space, from wardrobe to facade.

In spite of their relatively modest dimensions and simple layouts, these apartments have been given a real wow factor by the so-called flex-boxes protruding outwards to add extra space and individuality, making each one highly distinctive within an otherwise uniform overall ensemble. The flex boxes can extend the kitchen, bedroom or bathroom to accommodate a dining area, a reading zone or even a sauna. Originally, the flex boxes were meant to be tailor-made to cater to the needs of the respective owner, but in the end they had to be pre-determined. Now potential buyers can select an off-the-peg flex box from the architect's short list.

These young architects have succeeded magnificently in transforming a faceless, empty office building into an innovative and aesthetically pleasing apartment building. All it needs now is a few willing buyers to move in and breathe life into the place.

Anna Hesse

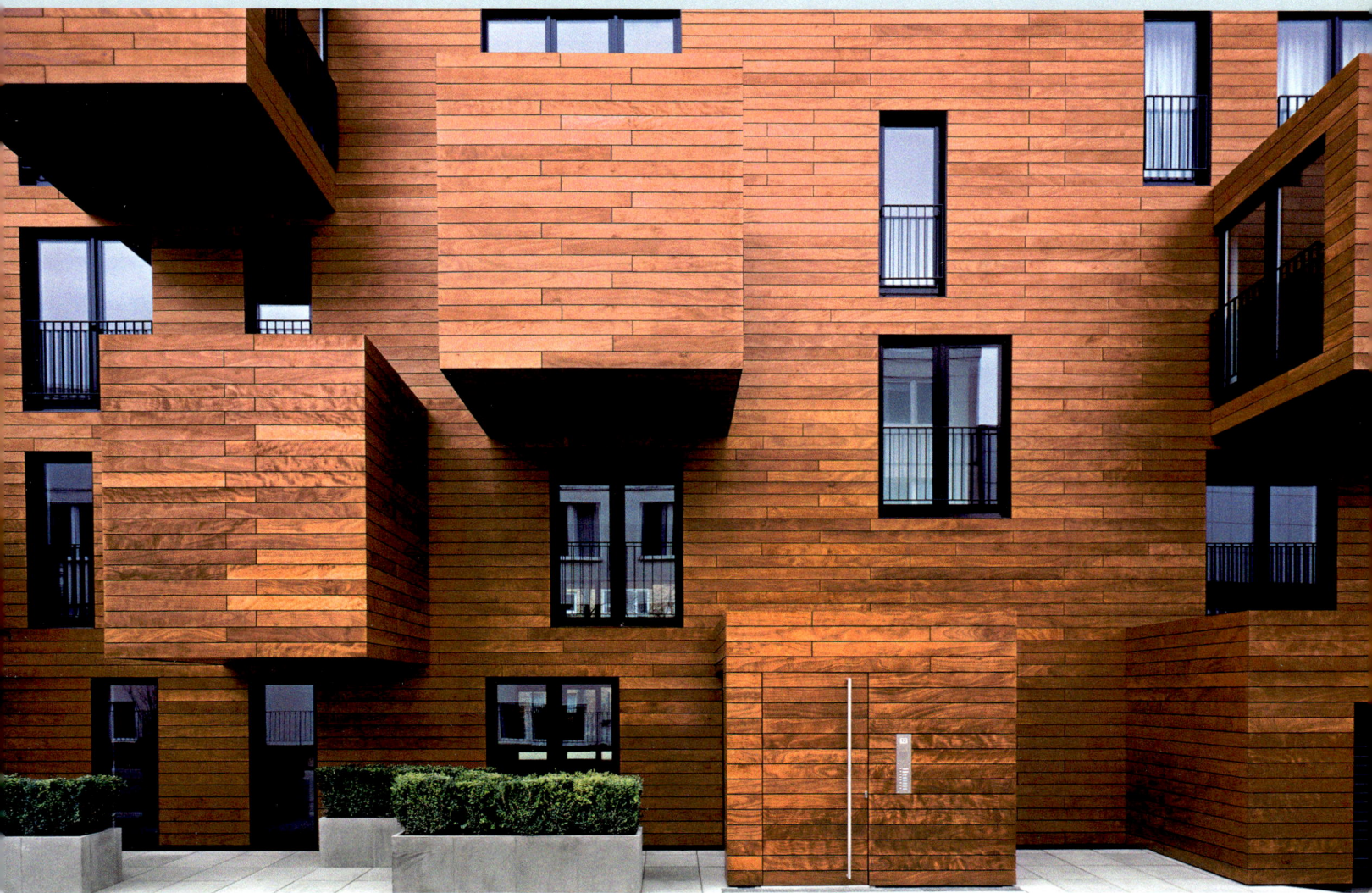

Hauseingang
House entrance

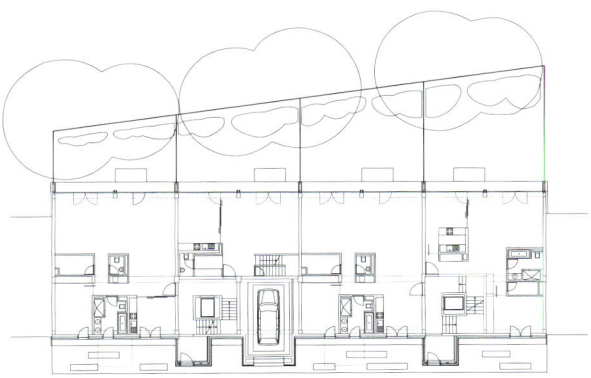

Grundriss Erdgeschoss
Ground-floor plan

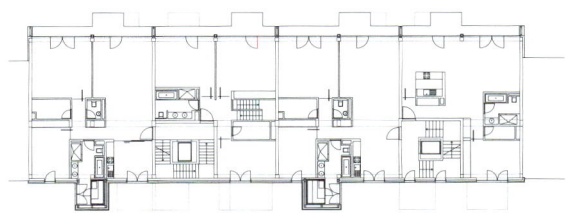

Grundriss 1. Obergeschoss
First-floor plan

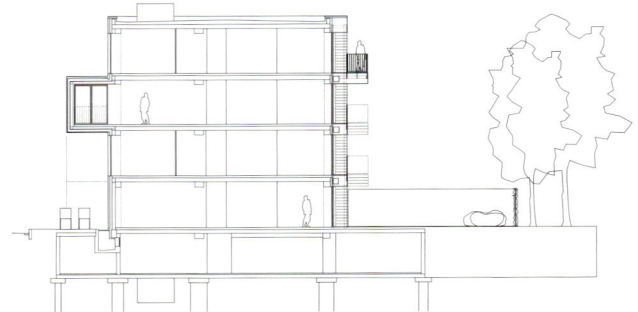

Querschnitt
Cross section

›Flex-box‹ mit Badewanne
"Flex-box" with bathtub

Schlafzimmer mit raumhoher Tür
Bedroom with room-high door

Wohnraum mit Blick Richtung Balkon
Living room with view towards balcony

Garderobe
Wardrobe

WOHN- UND GESCHÄFTSHAUS, BERLIN
RESIDENTIAL AND COMMERCIAL BUILDING, BERLIN

Jörg Ebers

Wo in der alten neuen Mitte Berlins die Kleine Hamburger Straße diagonal auf die Auguststraße trifft, steht seit einem Jahr klein und grün ein Haus, das dort eigentlich nicht stehen dürfte. Seine Existenz hat es der Fantasie seines Architekten Jörg Ebers zu verdanken.

Er hat die bekanntermaßen enge Berliner Bauordnung, die für Mehrfamilienhäuser ein vom Erdgeschoss bis zum Dach durchgängiges Treppenhaus verlangt, kreativ ausgelegt, indem er für das nur 7,80 Meter breite Grundstück einen Bauantrag für offiziell zwei Gebäude einreichte. Im Erdgeschoss befindet sich ein durch Brandwände und -decken abgeschotteter Laden. Darüber stapeln sich ein Einzimmerappartement und eine Maisonettewohnung, so dass ein vertikales Doppelhaus entsteht. Der Trick dabei: Doppelhäuser benötigen kein durchgängiges platzraubendes Treppenhaus. Ob die Wohnungen nebeneinander oder übereinander liegen, schreibt die Bauordnung nicht vor.

Das Gebäude steht selbstbewusst neben seinen gründerzeitlichen Nachbarn, ohne sie zu dominieren. »Ein fremder Freund«, so nennt es der Architekt. Er unterstreicht diese Haltung in der Straßenfassade dadurch, dass sich zwei der vier großen Fenster direkt an das Nachbargebäude anlehnen, ohne aber dessen Höhenlinien aufzunehmen.

Die Fassade weist noch andere Besonderheiten auf: Sie ist vollständig mit grünen, schimmernden Mosaikfliesen verkleidet. Die Eingangstür zu den Wohnungen fällt durch bullaugenartige Öffnungen auf. Durch diese Bullaugentür gelangt man in ein schmales Treppenhaus. Wieder begegnet man der Farbe Grün, diesmal als Brüstung, die sich an einer Betontreppe mit eingesetzten Eichenholzstufen nach oben windet. Auf den Treppenpodesten sind ganzflächig borstige Teppiche bündig in den Boden eingelassen, Riesenfußmatten als praktisches Detail.

Das Appartement im ersten Stock besteht aus einem Raum mit unterschiedlichen Deckenhöhen, die die verspringenden Ebenen der Wohnung darüber erahnen lassen. Dort nämlich hat sich der Architekt seine eigene Wohnung auf insgesamt fünf unterschiedlichen Niveaus nach sehr individuellen Wünschen zugeschnitten. Auf einem Rundgang gelangt man von einem quadratischen, über zwei Geschosse hohen Raum in eine höhlenartige, etwa 3 Meter hohe Nische, durchquert ein Bad, ganz mit rot-orangefarbenen Mosaikfliesen ausgelegt. Dahinter verbirgt sich ein Gästezimmer einige Stufen tiefer, in das man schon gleich nach Betreten der Wohnung einen Blick geworfen hat.

Eine Ebene höher kommt man in die halb offene Küche, das Herz der Wohnungslandschaft, die den Blick nach oben in einen blau gestrichenen Schacht und durch Fenster in den Himmel lenkt. Nach unten sieht man über eine Galerie zurück in den überhohen Wohnraum. Durch dessen große Fensteröffnung blickt man hinein

Right in the centre of Berlin, where Kleine Hamburger Straße converges diagonally with Auguststrasse, there is little green house that shouldn't really be there at all. Built a year ago, it owes its existence to the imaginative approach of architect Jörg Ebers.

His creative interpretation of Berlin's notoriously strict planning regulations for apartment buildings, which require a stairwell running from the ground floor to the roof, meant that when he submitted his planning application for developing the narrow 7.80-metre-wide site, he officially sought permission for two buildings. The commercial premises on the ground floor are completely self-contained, with firewalls and fire-ceilings. Above that he has stacked a one-room apartment and a maisonette above one another. The loophole in the legislation is this: a duplex house [*Doppelhaus*] does not require a space-guzzling ground-to-attic stairwell. But the planning legislation does not actually specify that the units of a duplex house have to be side by side. So he built them one on top of the other.

The building stands confidently alongside its turn-of-the-century neighbours without dominating them. "Like a stranger who's also a friend", is how the architect describes it. He underscores this in the street facade by placing two of the four large windows so that they directly abut the neighbouring building without reiterating the line of the window heights on the older building. And that's not all that is different about this facade. It is completely covered in shimmering green mosaic tiles. The entrance door leading to the apartments has round apertures like portholes. This porthole-door leads into a narrow stairwell. Again, we find the colour green here – this time in the handrail that sweeps up along the concrete stairway into which oak treads have been set. On the landings, brush-type doormat inserts, flush with the floor, add a practical touch.

The first-floor apartment consists of a single room with different ceiling heights, reflecting the various levels of the apartment above where the architect himself lives. His apartment on five different levels, is tailored to his highly individual requirements. A tour of this apartment takes you from a square room with a high ceiling open over two floors into a den-like niche with a ceiling height of three metres, through a bathroom completely tiled in orange mosaic, and down a few steps into the guest room you saw the moment you entered the flat. On the upper level is the semi-open-plan kitchen that is the heart of the apartment. Here, a blue shaft catches the eye and draws the gaze upwards to the skylights. A galleried area looks down into the high-ceilinged living area with its large window giving a view of the diagonal street axis. It is a

Straßenansicht, Nachtaufnahme
Street elevation, night exposure

Architekten Architects Ebers Architekten, Berlin, www.ebers-architekten.de; Team: Jörg Ebers, Daniel Buchheit **Bauherr** Client Jörg Ebers **Tragwerk** Structure ifb Frohloff Staffa Kühl Ecker, Berlin **Entwurf** Design 2002 **Ausführung** Construction 2003–2005 **Standort** Location Auguststraße 26a, 10117 Berlin **Abbildungen** Photo Credits Linus Lintner

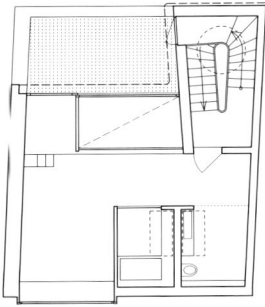

Grundriss 1. Obergeschoss
First-floor plan

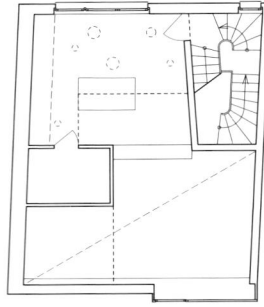

Grundriss 2. Obergeschoss
Second-floor plan

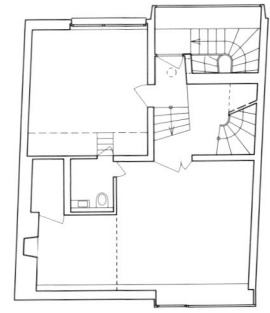

Grundriss 3. Obergeschoss
Third-floor plan

in die diagonal verlaufende Straßenachse. Der Blick bleibt nicht an der gegenüberliegenden Hauswand hängen, sondern holt die Stadt ins Haus.

Die Küche wird durch einen drehbaren Block, der Herd und Spüle in einem ist, dominiert – eine Spielerei des Architekten. Ungewöhnlich sind die Betonwände und die Holztüren der Einbauschränke ausgearbeitet: Wand- und Schrankflächen weisen dieselbe Riffelung auf. Die Türgriffe bestehen aus doppelt gelegten Lederriemen, die exakt die Breite und Tiefe des Rillenprofils – 20 auf 6 Millimeter – aufweisen.

Wie man aus der Wohnebene bereits einen optischen Bezug zur Küchenebene gewinnt, erahnt man auch von dort hinter dem blauen Schacht weitere Räume: Über die Fortsetzung der gewendelten Treppe gelangt man in die Schlafebene. Wie in einem Eisenbahnwaggon zweigen von einem schmalen Gang Nischen ab, zwei Sanitärnischen in Weiß beziehungsweise Grün und eine Schlafnische. Gegenüber steigt man über einige Stufen auf eine Dachterrasse. Sie schwebt wie ein Nest über einem engen Hinterhof. Eine weitere Tür führt zurück ins Treppenhaus; wieder ist ein interner Rundgang geschlossen. Spätestens hier fällt das stets wiederkehrende Kreismotiv auf, das schon an der Eingangstür durch die Bullaugen eingeführt wurde: In kreisförmigen Deckenvertiefungen sind schlichte Glühbirnen eingelassen.

Auf insgesamt 120 Quadratmetern hat Jörg Ebers eine Abfolge von Räumen unterschiedlichster Qualität ineinander geschoben. Der Wohnraum mit 4,20 auf 4,20 auf 4,20 Meter garantiert das ›Altbauerleben‹, auf das moderne Architekten so ungern verzichten. Angegliedert sind immer wieder teils farbig gehaltene niedrigere Rückzugsräume (zwei Abstellkammern sind so geschickt integriert, dass sie erst beim Studieren des Grundrisses auffallen). Raffiniert geführte Blickachsen durch die unterschiedlichen Niveaus der Wohnung erzeugen eine Weite, die man bei diesen Abmessungen nicht erwart. Die optische Durchlässigkeit kündigt die einzelnen Ebenen an – jede für sich überrascht mit eigenen Details.

Gerne bezeichnet der Architekt sein Haus im Haus als bewohnbares Möbel. Gefragt nach Vorbildern, fällt erwartungsgemäß als Stichwort der Loos'sche Raumplan, aber auch der Vergleich mit dem mexikanischen Architekten Luis Barragán liegt nahe.

Folgt man dem Trend, sich die Innenstadt als Wohnraum zurückzuerobern, ist ein solches Haus eine wirkliche Entscheidungshilfe.

Christina Gräwe

view that seems to bring the city right into the building.

The dominant feature of the kitchen is an island, which can be rotated, housing the cooker and sink – a personal detail by the architect. The concrete walls and the wooden doors of the built-in wardrobes are unusual in that the walls and the cupboard have the same grooved surface. The doorhandles are made of double strips of leather in exactly the same width and depth as the grooves – 20 x 6 millimetres.

Just as the kitchen is partly visible from the living area, so too do we realise in the kitchen that there must be more rooms behind the blue shaft. The continuation of the winding staircase leads to the bedroom level. There is a narrow corridor with niches, like the compartments of a train: two bathrooms in white and green, respectively, and a small sleeping area. This open space has just enough room for a double bed and a pair of slippers. A few steps lead from here to the roof terrace that hovers like a nest over a small courtyard. Another door leads back to the stairs – and we find we have come full circle again. It is at this point, at the latest, that we become aware of the circular motif that was already indicated by the portholes of the entrance door. Simple light-bulbs are set into circular indentations in the ceiling.

On a total floor space of 120 square metres, Jörg Ebers has created a sequence of highly distinctive rooms and spaces that dovetail with one another. The living area, measuring 4.20 x 4.20 x 4.20 gives a sense of the kind of generous traditional architecture that modern architects seem to hanker after. Off this area there are more intimate spaces with lower ceilings (and two large storage cupboards are so cleverly integrated that they might only be noticed when looking at the actual plan). Vistas open up through the various levels of the apartment, creating a spaciousness that is hardly to be expected in a home of this size. This handling of space provides a visual openness that constantly leads the eye towards the next level – each one harbouring some unexpected detail.

The architect likes to describe his house as a piece of furniture for living in. When asked who his role models are, it comes as no surprise when he mentions Loos. But there is also something of the Mexican architect Luis Barragán here.

For anyone thinking of following the trend towards regaining the inner city as a place to live, this house really does make the decision easier.

Christina Gräwe

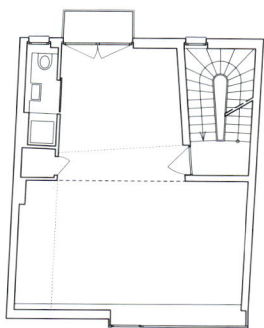

Grundriss Dachgeschoss
Top-floor plan

Straßenansicht
Street elevation

Blick von der Terrasse, Dachgeschoss
View from terrace, top floor

Wohnzimmer, 2. Obergeschoss
Living room, second floor

Küche, 3. Obergeschoss
Kitchen, third floor

Gästebad, 2. Obergeschoss
Guest bathroom, second floor

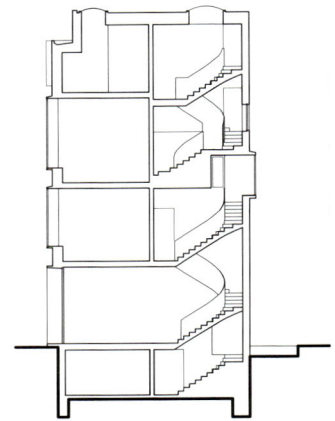

Längsschnitt
Longitudinal section

Treppenhaus
Staircase

PENTHOUSE, Frankfurt am Main
PENTHOUSE, Frankfurt/Main

Meixner Schlüter Wendt

Der Bauherr hatte sich entschieden, nicht in einem der Außenbezirke von Frankfurt zu leben, sondern in der Innenstadt wohnen zu bleiben. Als überzeugter Stadtbewohner kaufte er für sich und seine Frau die beiden oberen Stockwerke des damals gerade in Planung befindlichen, mehrgeschossigen Wohngebäudes am Rothschildpark. Im Äußeren war die Architektur dieses Bauwerkes durch die Fensteröffnungen, Erker und Balkone bereits festgelegt. Hinzu kam die unveränderbare Lage des Treppenhauses, des Aufzugsschachtes und der statischen Anschlusspunkte. Da der Bauherr jedoch im vierten und fünften Geschoss eine individuelle Lösung anstrebte, die sich zudem im abschließenden Geschoss als Penthouse auch nach außen gestalterisch zeigen sollte, beauftragte er das Frankfurter Architektenteam Meixner Schlüter Wendt, ein Wohnkonzept zu erarbeiten.

Die Architekten fanden somit einen zweigeschossigen ›leeren‹ Raum von 150 Quadratmetern Grundfläche vor, den es – unter Berücksichtigung der besonderen Position innerhalb des Gebäudes, der Situation inmitten der Stadt sowie der Bedürfnisse des Bauherrn – zu strukturieren galt. Dabei sollte das zur Verfügung stehende räumliche Volumen als Ganzes erlebbar und nachvollziehbar sein, was eine große Offenheit und Transparenz bedingte. Die Entwürfe der Architekten sind dadurch charakterisiert, jenseits konventioneller Raumstrukturen neue räumliche Gebilde zu entwickeln und damit innovative Raumerfahrungen zu offerieren. Hier gingen sie von einer Stapelung alltäglicher Dinge aus, die sie in ihrer Gegenständlichkeit abstrahierten und deren Raumgefüge sie in eine additive Zuordnung verschiedener Raumelemente transformierten. Solch eine plastisch-konzeptionelle Denkweise bildet stets die Grundlage ihrer räumlichen Kompositionen. Durch dieses Prinzip, das der bildenden Kunst verwandt ist, geht es ihnen um ein Öffnen von Räumen und Hohlräumen, um experimentelle Raumerfahrungen und das Sichtbarmachen variabler, räumlicher Schichten. So bestimmte bei diesem Projekt das Schaffen beziehungsweise die Vergegenständlichung von Räumen mithilfe unterschiedlicher Einzelelemente das Entwurfskonzept. Durch die ›Subtraktion‹ von Wänden fungieren sie als Raumandeutungen und markieren im Gesamtraum einzelne Bereiche. In der Imagination ergeben sich durch diese Formen, die aus der Funktion entwickelt wurden und somit eine flexible Methode darstellen, geschlossene Räume, die in der Realität jedoch ineinander übergehen oder zueinander gefügt wurden.

Das Penthouse am Rothschildpark umfasst zwei übereinander liegende, räumliche Ebenen, auf deren unterer sich der Eingangsbereich mit der Garderobe und der nach oben führenden Treppe befindet. Dieser trennt zugleich den westlichen, privatesten Wohnbereich – mit dem Schlaf- und Ankleidezimmer, dem Fitnessraum, der Sauna und den Badräumen –, der eine unerwartete

The client had decided not to move to the suburbs of Frankfurt, preferring instead to stay in the city centre. So, in order to enjoy an urban lifestyle, he bought the two upper floors of a still unfinished apartment complex at Rothschildpark for himself and his wife. The outer appearance of the building was already clearly defined by the window apertures, oriels and balconies. The stairwell, lift shaft and structural connecting points were other fixed features that could not be changed. However, as the client wanted the fourth and fifth floors that he intended to occupy to have an individually tailored solution that would also be outwardly legible as a penthouse, he commissioned Frankfurt architects Meixner Schlüter Wendt to draw up a concept.

The architects had the brief of structuring a two-storey "empty" space with a floor area of 150 square metres while taking into account the particular position of the penthouse within the building, the location of the building within the urban fabric and also the specific needs of the client. In order to give a clear overall sense of the available space, there had to be maximum openness and transparency. The architects came up with a design that would create new and innovative spatial impressions beyond the bounds of conventional room layouts. They took as their basis the material properties of everyday objects, which they abstracted and collated into a sequence of spatial elements. Such a sculptural and conceptual approach has always underpinned their compositional handling of space. It is a principle closely related to the world of fine art, involving opening up spaces and hollows, experimenting with volume and revealing variable spaces and layers. In this project, the design concept is driven by the creation, or rather reification, of spaces by means of different individual elements. By "subtracting" walls, they indicate spatial divisions and mark out individual areas within the overall space. These forms, developed on the basis of their respective functions, provide a flexible and versatile way of creating enclosed spaces that, in reality, dovetail or flow into one another.

The penthouse at Rothschildpark comprises two levels. The lower one contains the entrance area, cloakroom and stairs up to the next level. The stairway also separates the western and most private area of the apartment – bedroom, dressing room, gym, sauna and bathrooms, which are surprisingly small-scale – from the eastern area of the apartment with its spacious study, library, guest bedroom and guest bathroom, without actually interrupting the spatial fluidity on this side of the building. This is achieved by using only a few cubic elements to indicate the different rooms, furnish them and create upward continuity. The cubes are used as cupboard and storage areas. One of them is the vertical block of the chimney that also doubles as a zoning element in the study and in the living room above with its fireplace. On the upper level,

Architekten Architects Meixner Schlüter Wendt Architekten, Frankfurt am Main, www.meixner-schlueter-wendt.de; Team: Claudia Meixner, Florian Schlüter, Martin Wendt, Georg Hefter **Bauherr** Client Familie Morgen **Tragwerk** Structure Ingenieurbüro Lenz Weber, Frankfurt am Main **Entwurf** Design 2004 **Ausführung** Construction 2005–2006 **Standort** Location Am Rothschildpark, 60389 Frankfurt am Main **Abbildungen** Photo Credits Christoph Kraneburg

Blick aus dem Wohnzimmer
View from living room

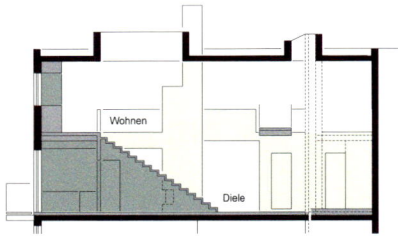

Schnitt B-B
Section B-B

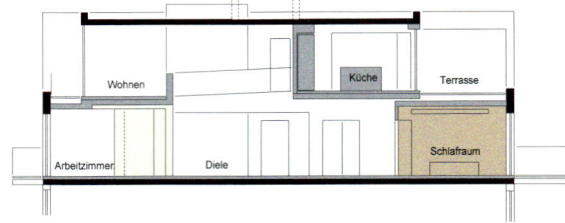

Schnitt A-A
Section A-A

Kleinteiligkeit aufweist, von dem östlichen Wohnbereich – mit großzügigem Arbeitszimmer, Bibliothek, Gästezimmer und Gäste-bad –, ohne dass der Raumfluss auf dieser Seite unterbrochen wird. Denn bereits hier sind es nur wenige kubische Elemente, welche die unterschiedlichen Räume andeuten, möblieren und nach oben eine Fortsetzung bilden. Sie werden als Schränke oder Stauräume genutzt, und einmal ist es der vertikale Kaminblock, der über die Funktion als raumzonierendes Element hinaus sowohl im Arbeitszimmer als auch in dem darüber liegenden Wohnraum eine Feuerstelle erhielt. Auf der oberen Ebene, die – von außen betrachtet – das eigentliche Penthouse bildet, befinden sich west-lich die offene Küche mit dem Essbereich und gegenüber davon, auf der östlichen Seite, der großzügig bemessene Wohnraum. Während auf der unteren Ebene die Räume aufgrund ihrer Einbin-dung in den Baukörper des Wohnhauses durch die vorgegebenen Fensteröffnungen, Balkone und einen Wintergarten eine Kommuni-kation mit dem Außenraum eingehen, sind es auf der oberen Ebene die gänzlich verglasten Fronten, welche eine uneinge-schränkte, faszinierende Sicht auf die Stadt gewährleisten. Durch die vor dem Wohn- und dem Essbereich liegenden Terrassen besteht mit dem Luftraum der Stadt eine direkte Verbindung. Sowohl die Besonnungsverhältnisse als auch die Blickbeziehungen spielten bei der Disposition der Räume eine bedeutende Rolle.

Zu den funktionalen Elementen auf der oberen Raumebene zäh-len auch die vor der Treppe geführte kurze Brücke und die gegen-über davon sich erstreckende, leicht ansteigende Rampe, die neben den vielgestaltigen, rechtwinkligen Formen eine diagonale Verlebendigung des Raumes bewirkt. Im Sinne einer ›promenade architecturale‹ erlaubt sie nicht nur Ein- und Durchblicke in die Struktur des gesamten zweigeschossigen Raumvolumens, son-dern macht auch die Gruppierung aller Räume um das offene, zentrale Treppenhaus wahrnehmbar. Dessen imaginärer Kubus wird durch den Lichteinfall des orthogonalen Glasdaches unterstri-chen. Im Ganzen werden die spezifischen Raumelemente mit ihren ›fließenden‹ Zwischenräumen plastisch als Fragmente begriffen, die durch unterschiedliche Materialien und Farbnuancen erkennbar sind, und ein ungewöhnliches, ganzheitliches Raumgefüge erge-ben haben.

Sabine Brinitzer

which, seen from the outside, forms the penthouse proper, there is an open-plan kitchen and dining area to the west and a spacious living area to the east. Whereas the rooms on the lower level com-municate with the outside through their integration into the struc-tural volume of the building with predetermined window aper-tures, balconies and a winter garden, the upper-level achieves this dialogue through the fully glazed frontage that affords fantastic views of the city. The patios opening out from the living and din-ing areas create a direct link with the urban air space. The layout of the rooms was largely determined by the direction of sunlight and the views.

Among the functional elements of the upper level, there is a small bridge in front of the stairway and a gently sloping ramp providing a dynamic diagonal contrast to the right-angled forms, which adds vitality to the space. This forms a "promenade archi-tecturale" providing views and vistas through both levels of the two-storey apartment while at the same time emphasising the alignment and grouping of the rooms around the open, central stairwell. The imaginary cube of the stairwell is further underlined by the light flooding in through the orthogonal glass roof. Overall, the specific room elements with their "fluid" interim spaces thus appear as sculptural fragments defined by different materials and nuanced colours, creating a highly unusual yet cohesive sense of space.

Sabine Brinitzer

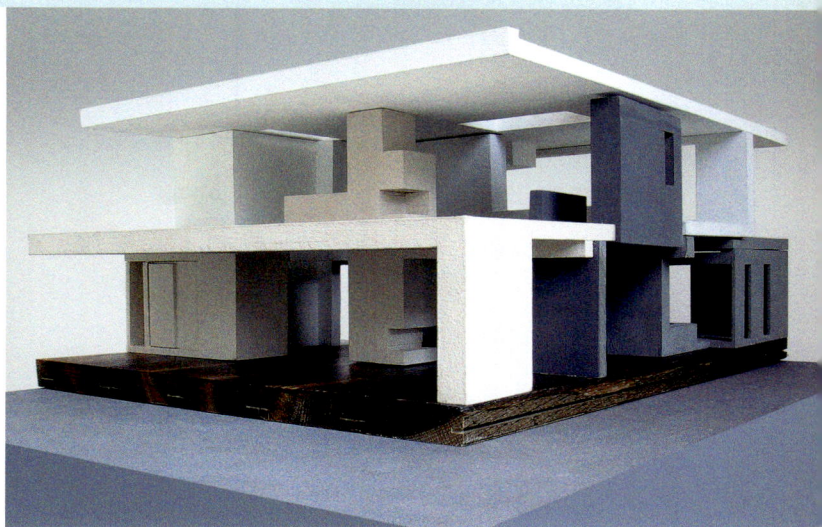

Modell
Model

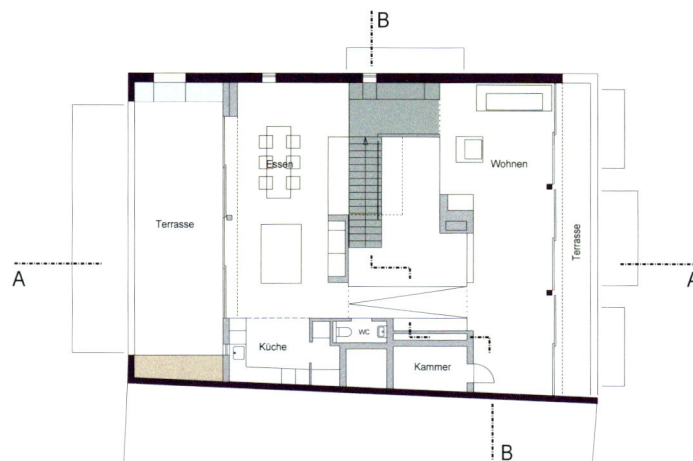

Grundriss Dachgeschoss
Top-floor plan

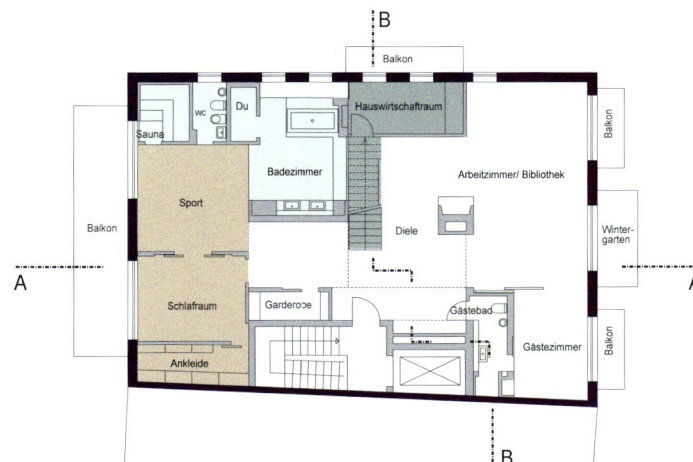

Grundriss 4. Obergeschoss
Fourth-floor plan

Ansicht Penthouse Elevation, penthouse

Eingang Entrance

Badezimmer
Bathroom

Blick Richtung Esszimmer
View towards dining room

Treppenraum
Staircase

Wohnzimmer
Living room

WOHNHAUS, BERLIN
APARTMENT BUILDING, BERLIN

Roedig Schop Architekten

Würde beispielsweise Alain Delon in einem Film dieses Haus betreten, so dächten die Zuschauer vermutlich an eine Szene aus dem Paris der siebziger Jahre. Aber das Haus steht in Berlin Mitte und ist von heute. Selten sah man bei einem Neubau an der Randzone eines Stadtteils zwischen Leerstand und Gentrifizierung eine lapidarere Fassade: mausgrau, ein kleiner Eingang, das Erdgeschoss hinter einer quer geriffelten Betonrustika mit hoch angesetzten, breiten Fenstern wie für die Wohnung der Concierge, in den Geschossen darüber dann raumhohe Fenstertüren, und das alles europäisch modern in der Erscheinung und zeitlich nicht recht zu fassen.

Es ist das Haus mit Eigentumswohnungen einer Baugruppe von zehn Menschen, zu denen auch die beiden Architekten gehören. Sie haben bezahl- und gestaltbaren Wohnraum mitten in der Stadt gesucht, diese Baulücke in einer baumbestandenen Straße mit typischen Gründerzeithäusern und einfachen, ordentlichen Nachbarn aus der Vor-Plattenzeit der DDR gefunden und ihr Haus für gut 1600 Euro pro Quadratmeter einschließlich Grundstückskosten in kurzer Zeit geplant und gebaut. Sie verstehen ihre Wohnungen als gestapelte Eigenheime, deren Individualität sich in zehn verschiedenen Grundrissen ausdrückt: von der schmalen Maisonette im Erd- und 1. Obergeschoss bis hin zum loftartigen Großraum im 5. Obergeschoss. Dort bieten zwei zusammengelegte Wohnungen eine Fläche von 135 Quadratmetern. Die Fenstereinteilung der nach Südwesten ausgerichteten Straßenfassade aus grau durchgefärbten Faserzementplatten zeichnet ebenso wie jene zum Hof und Garten im Nordosten diese Variationen innerhalb eines typologischen Rahmens nach, und zwar mit einer konventionell verputzten weißen Lochfassade. Die besonders schmal profilierten Holzfenster sind unterschiedlich angeschlagen und sorgen so auch in der Tiefe der Öffnungen für Abwechslung. Der innenbündige Anschlag der Fenstertüren zu den stählernen Kleinstbalkons an der Straße erlaubt es, die Flügel um 180 Grad und damit vor die Wand zu drehen, so dass sich der gesamte Innenraum weit zum Außenraum öffnet und außerdem die Möglichkeit besteht, vor die Fassade zu treten.

Bindend für die Grundrissorganisation sind allein der Kern des Betontreppenhauses mit Fahrstuhl und groß dimensioniertem Podest vor den Wohnungstüren sowie die Versorgungsschächte, um die herum Bäder und Küchen frei im Raum oder an einer Außenwand angeordnet wurden. Es gibt keine Stützen oder Unterzüge in den 2,80 Meter hohen Wohnungen, und die Innentüren nehmen dieses Maß auf.

Die innere Ordnung des Hauses folgt dem Prinzip des Durchwohnens bei größtmöglicher Variabilität. Grundsätzlich können die Wohnungen auf einer Ebene zu einer Einheit zusammengeschlossen werden. Freigehaltene Sichtachsen bieten auch aus

If we were watching a film in which Alain Delon stepped into this building, we would probably think it was set in Paris in the 1970s. But this is Berlin-Mitte and the house is new. For a new building on the edge of an urban neighbourhood that is a mix of the empty and the gentrified, it is remarkably laconic in style: mouse-grey, with a small entrance, a rusticated plinth of horizontally corrugated concrete, broad, high-level ground-floor windows redolent of a concierge's apartment and floor-to-ceiling French windows on the upper floors – all of which smack of continental modernism and yet seem somehow timeless.

The building houses the owner-occupied apartments of ten members of a construction group that also includes the two architects. They had been looking for affordable, versatile accommodation in the city centre when they found this gap site in a tree-lined street of typical, late-nineteenth-century architecture and simple, clean-cut buildings from East Germany's communist era that pre-date the state's later ubiquitous prefabricated blocks. They designed and built the house within a short time span at a cost of some 1,600 Euros per square metre, including the cost of the actual site. They regard their apartments as stacked homes, with ten different individually tailored layouts ranging from the narrow maisonette on the ground and first floors to the loft-like space on the fifth floor where two apartments merge to create a floor area of 135 square metres. On the street side, the interior variations are echoed within a typological framework by the window alignment in the grey-tinted, fibre cement south-west facade and on the courtyard and garden side by the conventional, white-rendered, punctuated north-east facade. The extremely narrow profiles of the wood-framed windows are fitted in different ways, creating variations in the aperture depths. The French windows opening onto the tiny steel balconies overlooking the street are set flush to the inner wall, allowing them to be opened to 180 degrees and folded right back against the wall so that there is a fluid continuity between the interior and outside world, offering the possibility of stepping out in front of the facade.

The only fixed elements of the layout are the core of the concrete stairwell with its elevator and spacious landings in front of the apartment doors and the service tracts around which the bathrooms and kitchens can be arranged either as freestanding internal spaces or set against an external wall. The ceiling height of 2.80 metres with neither pillars nor joists is reiterated by the dimensions of the internal doors.

The interior layout of the building is based on the principle of maximum versatility. In principle, all the apartments on any given

Ansicht Anklamer Straße
Elevation, Anklamer Strasse

Architekten Architects roedig schop architekten, Berlin, www.roedig-schop.de; Team: Christoph Roedig, Ulrich Schop, Beate Marvan, Lukasz Sadura, Christine Rokstein, Alexander Hülsey **Bauherr Client** Baugruppe A52 GbR, Berlin **Tragwerk Structure** Jockwer und Partner, Berlin **Planung und Ausführung Planning and Construction** 2003–2005 **Standort Location** Anklamer Straße 52, 10115 Berlin **Abbildungen Photo Credits** Peter Gruchot, Andrea Kroth, Stefan Müller

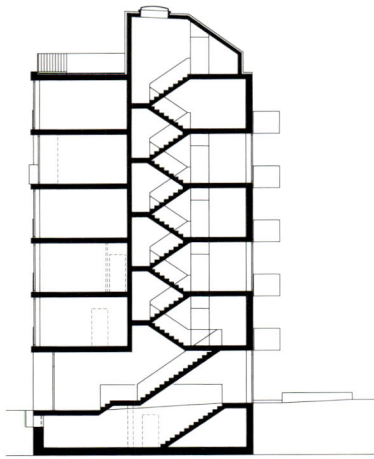

Schnitt
Section

nebenrangigen Perspektiven Ausblicke auf das Grün der Straße und die spitzwinklig an der Rückseite anschließende Freifläche eines Friedhofs. Trotz ihrer Tiefe wirken die Wohnungen luftig und großzügig inmitten der Dichte der umgebenden Blockstruktur. Die mächtige Brandwand des Nachbarhauses, die sich über die gesamte Grundstückstiefe erstreckt und auch den Garten begrenzt, scheint durch das Haus weiterzuführen, da die Betonaußenwand der anliegenden Maisonettewohnung dieses Motiv aufnimmt. Über zwei Geschosse sichtbar, verdeutlicht sie eindrucksvoll, dass der Neubau Teil einer geschlossenen Straßenbebauung ist und zwischen zwei alten Mauern steht.

Das Haus ist das Muster eines Pfadfinderprojekts für kleine Architekturbüros, die sich gut in ihrer Stadt auskennen, diverse Aufgaben kumulieren und daraus einen handhabbaren Auftrag entwickeln. So etwas ist keine singuläre Erscheinung und funktioniert im Augenblick gut in Städten, deren Wohnungsmarkt nicht von Hektik gekennzeichnet ist – wie gerade in Berlin. Anspruchsvolle Eigenbauvorhaben mit einer überschaubaren Teilnehmerzahl sind nicht nur kostengünstig realisierbar, sie können auch in hohem Maße individuelle Wünsche berücksichtigen und als Ganzes elegant aussehen. Durch die gemeinsame Planung lässt sich ein Maximum an Flexibilität der Grundrisse erreichen, was den Wert der Wohnungen langfristig sichert oder steigert. Eine auch in ihrer Zurücknahme selbstbewusste Architektur wie diese entsteht aus mehr als nur der dreidimensionalen Reflexion von Bewohnerwünschen, gepaart mit den gestalterischen Vorlieben der Entwerfer. Weil ihre Struktur und ihr Erscheinungsbild den Kontext der Nachbarschaft aufgreifen und weiterentwickeln, fügt sie sich gut in die Stadt ein.

Filmtauglich wie die Fassade sind auch der allen Bewohnern offen stehende, holzbeplankte Dachgarten und eine kleine Gästewohnung. Beide bieten einen Panoramablick auf das Zentrum der Stadt, und von hier oben wird deutlich, dass es Berlin ist.

Ulrich Höhns

level can be merged into one. Open vistas afford views of the leafy street and the nearby cemetery from almost any angle. In spite of their depth, the apartments are light, airy and spacious within the density of the surrounding block structure. The massive firewall of the adjacent building that stretches the entire depth of the site and forms the boundary of the garden appears to continue through the new building because of the way the concrete exterior wall of the maisonette apartment echoes it. Visible over two levels, it impressively demonstrates that this new building stands between two old walls as part of a cohesive street development.

This building is exemplary as a project for small architectural firms who know their local city well and are able to use their experience of small-scale contracts to develop something more robust. Such projects are few and far between, and they work well in cities where the property market is not quite as frenetic as it is in Berlin. High-quality home ownership projects involving a limited number of participants are not only an economically viable option, but also offer a high degree of flexibility in catering to individual needs within an elegant overall structure. By drawing up the plans together, it is possible to achieve a maximum of versatility in the layout, which ensures that the apartments retain and even increase their value in the long term. Architecture as subtle and quietly confident as this is about more than just the three-dimensional realisation of the occupants' wishes and their aesthetic preferences. Because its structure and appearance respect and add to the surrounding neighbourhood, it fits well into the urban context.

The facade is not the only thing about this building that makes it fit for a film location: there are also the shared roof garden with wooden decking and a small guest apartment offering panoramic views of the city centre. From up here, there can be no mistaking the fact that we are in Berlin.

Ulrich Höhns

Betonrustika
Concrete bossage

Seite 69 oben Page 69 top
Dachgarten mit Gästewohnung
Roof garden with guest apartment

Seite 69 unten Page 69 bottom
Ansicht vom Friedhof
View from cemetery

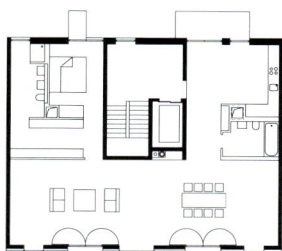

Grundriss 5. Obergeschoss
Fifth-floor plan

Grundriss 4. Obergeschoss
Fourth-floor plan

Grundriss 3. Obergeschoss
Third-floor plan

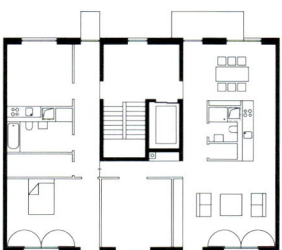

Grundriss 2. Obergeschoss
Second-floor plan

Grundriss Erdgeschoss
Ground-floor plan

Treppe und
Küchenzeile in
Wohnung 3,
Erdgeschoss
Stair and kitchen
unit in apartment
3, first floor

Küchenzeile in Wohnung 4, 2. Obergeschoss
Kitchen unit in apartment 4, second floor

Badezimmer in Wohnung 2, 1. Obergeschoss
Bathroom in apartment 2, first floor

NEUES BAUEN AM HORN, WEIMAR
NEW DEVELOPMENT AM HORN, WEIMAR

Diener & Diener, Krischanitz, Snozzi

Eine Mustersiedlung für das 21. Jahrhundert?
A Model Development for the Twenty-first Century?

Wohnen im Stadtzentrum oder in dessen fußläufiger Nähe ist wieder gefragt. Die Absenkung der Entfernungspauschale und die Abschaffung der Eigenheimzulage werden diesen Trend in den kommenden Jahren noch verstärken. Wie aber gelingt es, individuellen Wohnraum, gar den Traum vom Einfamilienhäuschen im Grünen auch in der Stadt zu realisieren? Wie vor allem kann dieser Wohnungsbau ästhetisch, ökologisch, aber auch wirtschaftlich anspruchsvoll gestaltet werden?

In Weimar wagte man vor gut zehn Jahren ein Experiment und ersann eine Mustersiedlung. Die Initiative ging von der dortigen Bauhaus-Universität aus. Geplant wurde für einen legendären Ort: Am Horn. Dort hatte das Bauhaus unter der Leitung von Walter Gropius bereits um 1920 eine Mustersiedlung erwogen. Realisiert wurde aber lediglich ein Haus nach dem Entwurf von Georg Muche.

Das Areal ist – wie der Name schon sagt – ein rechts der Ilm bis an das Flussufer heranreichender Bergrücken in Form eines Horns. Dort liegt auch Goethes berühmtes Gartenhaus. Im Norden wird das Gelände von der heutigen Leibnizallee, der einstigen Schlossallee, begrenzt, die schnurgerade über die Sternbrücke auf das Schloss zuführt. Ab der Mitte des 19. Jahrhunderts entwickelte sich an der Leibnizallee eine Militäranlage, die nach dem Zweiten Weltkrieg auch von den Sowjets genutzt wurde.

Mit dem Abzug der sowjetischen Streitkräfte stellt sich die Frage nach einer neuen Nutzung dieses rund 10 Hektar großen Gebietes. Die Bauhäusler finden schnell Gehör mit ihrer Idee einer zeitgenössischen Mustersiedlung unter dem Titel »Neues Bauen am Horn«. Dabei ist ihr Ansatz wesentlich pragmatischer als einst unter der Ägide von Gropius. Es sollte ein Wohnquartier entstehen, »das in städtischer Vielfalt modellhaft Sparsamkeit im Umgang mit natürlichen Ressourcen, die Offenheit der Bauwerke für soziale Veränderungen und den Respekt vor der bestehenden Stadt in hoher ästhetischer Qualität demonstriert«.

Die Planungshoheit liegt bei der Stadt Weimar, die LEG (die Landesentwicklungsgesellschaft Thüringen ist die treuhänderische Verwalterin der von den Sowjettruppen genutzten Liegenschaften) sorgt für eine gewinnbringende Vermarktung, während die Architekturfakultät der Bauhaus-Universität das Planungsverfahren betreut und vor allem in einem Baubeirat die architektonische Gestaltung überwacht.

1996 wurde nach einem Planungsworkshop mit Teilnehmern aus mehreren europäischen Ländern ein städtebauliches Gutachten in Form eines begrenzten Wettbewerbes durchgeführt. Die drei erstplatzierten Vorschläge von Diener & Diener, Adolf Krischanitz und Luigi Snozzi wurden in einem Masterplan zusammengefasst. Das war ohne großen Reibungsverlust möglich, da alle drei Preisträger ihre Stärken in einzelnen Teilbereichen hatten.

Blick von der Streichhan-Kaserne auf das Wohnquartier nach Süden
Looking south towards the residential district from the Streichhan Barracks

Inner-city living, or at least living within easy walking distance of the city centre, is in again. With cutbacks in tax deductible allowances for commuting and fewer incentives for homebuyers, it is a trend that looks set to increase in the coming years. But how is it going to be possible to achieve individually tailored housing, let alone the dream of a family home in leafy surroundings, within the city? More importantly still, how can such housing be created in an aesthetically pleasing, ecologically sound and still financially viable way?

Weimar grasped that particular nettle some ten years ago and took the risk of experimenting with a new kind of housing development. The initial idea came from the city's own Bauhaus University. The site that was earmarked was the legendary Am Horn, where the Bauhaus, under the direction of Walter Gropius, had already planned an experimental housing estate around 1920. In the end, only one house, designed by Georg Muche, was actually built.

The site is a slope on the right bank of the Ilm that runs down to the river in the form of a horn – as the name suggests. This is

Planungshoheit Planning Authority Stadt Weimar **Baubeirat** Advisory Board Adolf Krischanitz, Roger Diener, Vertreter der LEG, der Bauhaus-Universität Weimar, des Stadtentwicklungsamtes Weimar, des Thüringer Ministeriums für Bau und Verkehr (Abteilung Städte- und Wohnungsbau) **Planungswerkstatt** Planning Workshop 1996–1997 **Masterplan** Masterplan 1997 Diener & Diener, Basel, Luigi Snozzi, Locarno, Adolf Krischanitz, Wien **Erschließungsplanung** Developmental Planning seit since 1998 **Vermarktung** Marketing seit since 1999 LEG Landesentwicklungsgesellschaft Thüringen **Ausführung** Construction seit since 2000; Häuser 1–4 **Architekt** Architect ARGE Prof. Walter Stamm-Teske, Weimar **Ausführung** Construction 2002–2003; Häuser 5–6 **Architekten** Architects Bernd Rudolf, Weimar und AFF Architekten, Magdeburg/Berlin **Ausführung** Construction 2001–2002; Häuser 7–8 **Architekten** Architects AFF Architekten, Magdeburg/Berlin **Ausführung** Construction 2001; Haus Hopp **Architekt** Architect Max Dudler, Berlin **Ausführung** Construction 2002–2003; Haus Schmitz **Architekt** Architect Karl-Heinz Schmitz, Weimar **Ausführung** Construction 2000–2001; Haus Bauer **Architekten** Architects Bauer Architekten, Weimar **Ausführung** Construction 2001–2002 **Abbildungen** Photo Credits Christoph Eckelt, Frank Müller

where Goethe had his famous garden house. To the north, the site is bounded by Leibnizallee (formerly known as Schlossallee) – a boulevard running straight across Sternbrücke to the palace. From the mid-nineteenth century onwards, a military complex grew up along Leibnizallee, which was also used by the Soviet forces after the Second World War.

With the departure of the Soviet forces, a new function was sought for this 10-hectare site. The Bauhaus quickly came up with the welcome suggestion of a contemporary experimental housing development under the title "Neues Bauen am Horn". However, they have taken a considerably more pragmatic approach than Gropius did. The idea was to create a neighbourhood "of urban diversity, exemplary in its economic use of natural resources, versatile in coping with social and demographic change, and demonstrating both respect for the existing urban fabric and a high aesthetic quality".[1]

The planning authority in charge is the city of Weimar. The Thuringian LEG (Landesentwicklungsgesellschaft – a venture that

Das circa fünf Hektar große Gebiet für die Mustersiedlung südlich der Kasernenbauten wurde nach dem Vorschlag von Adolf Krischanitz entwickelt. Leitbild der Planung war es, durch eine dichte, aber nicht geschlossene Bebauung und einen ›durchfließenden‹ Grünraum unterschiedliche Bereiche zu definieren. Das Areal wurde zunächst in zehn große Baufelder geteilt, die durch die Erschließungswege begrenzt sind. Das Zentrum bildet ein lang gestreckter Anger, dessen Schmalseiten von den Fahrstraßen gesäumt werden und so eine Durchquerung in west-östlicher Richtung ermöglichen. Von der Leibnizallee aus erfolgt die nördliche Erschließung. Hier stört allerdings die breite Zufahrt in eine zentrale Tiefgarage unter dem Anger den ersten Eindruck. Neben diesen wenigen Verkehrsstraßen gibt es ein dichtes Netz aus Fußwegen.

Die Baufelder wurden nach einem sehr durchdachten System in einzelne Parzellen unterteilt. Die Basis bildet ein Grundmodul: eine Parzelle von 7,5 Metern Breite und mit einer Länge zwischen 37 und 74 Metern. Maximal drei solcher Grundmodule können nebeneinander geschaltet werden. Um dieses gleichförmige Raster zu durchbrechen, wurde eine kleine Parzelle von 7,5 Metern Breite bei nur 30 bis 35 Metern Länge eingestreut. So ergibt sich ein abwechslungsreicher ›Parzellenteppich‹, der das Rückgrat für die gelungene Gesamtstruktur des Areals bildet.

Für die Bebauung hat Krischanitz ein komplexes Reglement – eine »Grammatik des Bauens« – festgelegt. Die schmalen Grundstücke können bis an die seitlichen Grenzen bebaut werden. Bei den 15 Meter breiten Doppelparzellen kann das Haus an einer der seitlichen Grenzen stehen. Die großen Grundstücke sind in offener Weise zu bebauen. Für die Häuser am Anger gab es die Verpflichtung, direkt an die Parzellengrenze zu bauen, um so eine deutliche Raumkante zu schaffen. An den Verkehrsstraßen sind die Häuser durch schmale Vorgärten vom Fahrweg getrennt. Auch für

manages sites and properties formerly used by the Soviet troops) is in charge of financially viable marketing. The architecture faculty of the Bauhaus University is undertaking the planning process and supervising the architectural design through an advisory committee.

In 1996, following a planning workshop involving participants from several European countries, an urban development proposal was drawn up by way of a restricted competition. The three winning proposals submitted by Diener & Diener, Adolf Krischanitz and Luigi Snozzi were then combined to create a master plan. This process went relatively smoothly, as all three winners had focused on individual areas that did not necessarily overlap.

The five-hectare site for the housing to the south of the barracks was developed according to the proposal by Adolf Krischanitz. The main aim of this plan was to delineate various areas by means of dense, but not closed, building development with a green space flowing through it. First of all, the area was divided into ten large sites bounded by access roads. At the centre is an elongated green space bounded at its narrow end by roads providing a west-east link. The northern access is from Leibnizallee, though it has to be said that the broad sliproad leading into the central underground car park below the green space does detract somewhat from the otherwise favourable first impression. Apart from these few roads, there is a well-connected network of footpaths.

The sites have been further subdivided into individual plots according to a carefully considered system based on the following module: each plot is 7.5 metres wide and 37 to 74 metres long. No more than three of these basic modules can be juxtaposed. In order to break through the uniformity of the grid, smaller plots measuring 7.5 metres by just 30 to 35 metres are scattered among the larger plots. The result is a varied tapestry of building plots that forms the basis for the successful overall structure of the area.

Krischanitz has created a complex development system –

1 ARGE Prof. Walter Stamm-Teske
2 AFF Architekten | Bernd Rudolf
3 Max Dudler
4 Karl-Heinz Schmitz
5 Bauer Architekten
6 Schloss Palace
7 Haus am Horn House am Horn

Lageplan Site plan

Blick auf den zentralen Anger gegen Süden. Die Häuser stehen direkt auf der Grenzlinie, um so eine deutliche Platzbegrenzung zu schaffen.
Looking south over the central green. The houses are built right on the edge to create a distinct boundary.

die Aufrissgestaltung der Häuser gibt es eine Grammatik. Sie dürfen maximal drei Geschosse haben und müssen mit einem Flachdach abschließen. Der Baukörper muss ein kompaktes kubisches Erscheinungsbild aufweisen, ein Rücksprung ist nur an einer Seite möglich.

Mit diesen strengen Vorgaben sollte bei aller Unterschiedlichkeit der einzelnen Bauten eine strukturelle Ähnlichkeit erzeugt werden. Das ist ohne Zweifel gelungen und führt zu einem harmonischen Gesamteindruck, wie er in Wohnquartieren nur selten erreicht wird. Auf den ersten Blick hat man den Eindruck einer gewissen Uniformität, der sich aber schnell abschwächt, da die Bauten in den Details sehr unterschiedlich sind. Es erfüllt sich Krischanitz' Anspruch von der »Vielfalt in der Einheit«. Im Detail zeigen sich jedoch auch deutlich die Stärken und Schwächen der einzelnen Bauten. Die durchdachte Gesamtplanung verkraftet aber selbst die weniger gelungenen Häuser. Die von manchen als rigide empfundene Grammatik des Bauens hat nur eine bestimmte Bauherrenschaft angezogen, so dass man in Weimar auch vom »Architektenhügel« spricht. Dieses Reglement aber ist ein wichtiger Bestandteil für das gelungene Experiment, ebenso wie der Baubeirat, der die Einhaltung überwacht hat und den sehr hohen Beratungsaufwand der Bauherren steuerte. Hierin könnte vor allem ein zukunftsträchtiges Modell liegen.

Ursula Kleefisch-Jobst

1 *neues bauen am horn. Eine Mustersiedlung in Weimar*, hrsg. v. Lars-Christian Uhlig, Walter Stamm-Teske, Weimar 2005, S. 26.

a "grammar of building". The narrow plots can be developed right up to the side boundaries. In the case of the 15-metre-wide double plots, the building can be constructed at one of the side boundaries. There is a stipulation that the houses directly by the green space have to be built right up against the plot boundary in order to create a clear spatial delineation. The houses along the roads have small front gardens separating them from the actual roadway. There is even a "grammar" for the facades. The houses can be no more than three stories high and must have a flat roof. The building must be of compact, cuboid appearance with recesses, if any, only on one side.

These strict regulations were intended to ensure a structural similarity between the individual buildings in spite of their diversity. This has undoubtedly been achieved, resulting in a harmonious overall impression that is rarely found in residential areas. At first glance, there appears to be a certain uniformity, but this is soon countered by the wide variety of details. This meets entirely with Krischanitz's demand for "diversity in unity". Although the details also clearly show up the strengths and weaknesses of the individual buildings, the overall plan is so well thought out that it can easily absorb and offset even the less successful designs. This "grammar of building", dismissed by some as too inflexible, has attracted a certain clientele, with the result that some people in Weimar have dubbed the place Architektenhügel [Architects' hill]. Yet it is the stringency of the rules that has proved the key to the success of this experiment – together with the strong involvement of the advisory committee that has ensured the rules are observed. That in itself could be a model for the future.

Ursula Kleefisch-Jobst

1 *neues bauen am horn. Eine Mustersiedlung in Weimar,* edited by Lars-Christian Uhlig, Walter Stamm-Teske, Weimar 2005, p. 26.

Häuser 1–4 (Entwurf ARGE Prof. Walter Stamm-Teske/Weimar)
Houses 1–4 (designed by ARGE Prof. Walter Stamm-Teske/Weimar)

Die beiden Häuser 5–6 am Anger (Entwurf Bernd Rudolf/Weimar und AFF Architekten/Magdeburg, Berlin)
mit den beiden dahinter liegenden Häusern 7–8 (AFF Architekten)
The two houses 5–6 on the green (designed by Bernd Rudolf/Weimar and AFF Architekten/Magdeburg, Berlin)
and the two houses 7–8 behind them (AFF Architekten)

Haus Schmitz (Entwurf Karl-Heinz Schmitz/Weimar)
Schmitz House (designed by Karl-Heinz Schmitz/Weimar)

Haus Bauer (Entwurf Bauer Architekten/Weimar)
Bauer House (designed by Bauer Architekten/Weimar)

Haus Hopp (Entwurf Max Dudler/Berlin) bestehend aus zwei schwarzen Kuben, dem Atelierhaus am Anger und dem dahinter liegenden Wohnhaus
Hopp House (designed by Max Dudler/Berlin) consisting of two black cubes, the studio on the green and the actual house behind it

ARCHITEKTUR IN DEUTSCHLAND
ARCHITECTURE IN GERMANY

HAUS K., GMUND AM TEGERNSEE
HOUSE K., GMUND/TEGERNSEE

Titus Bernhard

Von München kommend, ist Gmund das Tor zum Tegernsee. Entlang dem Ostufer des Sees gelangt man über den Ort Tegernsee nach Rottach-Egern an der Südspitze, eine andere Straße führt am Westufer entlang nach Bad Wiessee. Das Blau des Sees, die sattgrünen Weiden sowie die Wälder des Vorgebirges und schließlich die darüber aufragenden Spitzen der Alpengipfel haben dem bäuerlich geprägten Tegernseer Tal seit Beginn des 19. Jahrhunderts einen stetigen Zustrom von Besuchern beschert. Wie in anderen Alpenregionen wandelte sich der Fremdenverkehr in den Jahrzehnten nach dem Zweiten Weltkrieg zur Tourismusindustrie, die Ortsbilder vor allem von Rottach-Egern und Bad Wiessee haben sich grundlegend verändert. Hotelkomplexe und Boutiquen muten an wie ›Outposts‹ des Münchner Zentrums, und Tankstellen, Appartementensembles und Feriensiedlungen tarnen sich mit Imitaten der für die Region typischen, flach geneigten Satteldächer.

Gmund, weniger stark zum See hin orientiert als die Nachbarorte, ist von derlei Versehrungen am ehesten verschont geblieben. Hügelaufwärts gehend, trifft man auf verstreut zwischen Feldern und Weiden gelegene alte Bauernhöfe: lang gestreckte, breit gelagerte Gebäude – vorne der Wohnteil mit umlaufenden hölzernen Balkonen, dahinter der Stalltrakt mit Heuboden.

St. Quirin ist ein Ortsteil von Gmund, der sich auf halbem Weg nach Tegernsee am Hang zwischen Ufer und Waldrand erstreckt. Ferienhäuser sind auch hier schon seit längerem entstanden, wie nicht zuletzt ein – heute veränderter – Bau von Sep Ruf am Kramerweg beweist. Ruf errichtete überdies das Wohnhaus von Ludwig Erhardt oberhalb des Bahnhofs von Gmund sowie das Gulbransson-Museum im Kurpark von Tegernsee. Er ist neben Olaf Andreas Gulbransson, dem Kirchenarchitekten und Sohn des Karikaturisten, ein Architekt, dem es überzeugend gelang, Elemente der Moderne in die bayerische Kulturlandschaft einzubeziehen.

Heute ist derlei nicht mehr so einfach, selbst wenn im fernen Berlin das Schlagwort Baukultur als Dauerthema gilt. Das mussten – und müssen – der Architekt Titus Bernhard und sein Bauherr erfahren. Das Gebäude, das der Augsburger Architekt für einen Münchner Anwalt in St. Quirin errichtete, steht unmittelbar oberhalb des Gebäudes von Ruf am Kramerweg – auf einem der wenigen noch bebaubaren Grundstücke mit Seeblick oberhalb des Tegernsees.

Beruflich hatten Architekt und Anwalt – jetzt Bauherr – schon einmal Kontakt: Die Kanzlei, in welcher der Jurist arbeitet, ist spezialisiert auf Architekten als Klientel. Titus Bernhard musste ihre Hilfe in Anspruch nehmen, nachdem um das mit Altmühltaler Dolomit in Gabionen verkleidete und mit einem Zeltdach gedeckte Haus 9 x 9 in Stadtbergen bei Augsburg ein Streit mit der Gemeinde entbrannt war. Einen positiven Nebeneffekt hatte die Auseinandersetzung, erklärt Bernhard im Gespräch: Haus 9 x 9

Arriving from the direction of Munich, Gmund is the gateway to the Tegernsee lake district. Along the shores of the lake, you pass through the town of Tegernsee to Rottach-Egern on the southern tip while another road leads along the western shore to Bad Wiessee. The blue of the lake, the verdant green of the meadow and the forests fringing the foothills of the Alps that tower in the distance have attracted increasing numbers of tourists to this largely rural area since the early nineteenth century. As in other Alpine regions, the tourism of the post-war years has become a veritable tourist industry, radically changing the face of towns such as Rottach-Egern and Bad Wiessee whose hotel complexes and boutiques now look like outposts of Munich city centre, with petrol stations, apartment blocks and holiday homes camouflaged in the style of the region's vernacular architecture with its typical gently-pitched saddle roofs.

Gmund, less strongly oriented towards the lake than some of the neighbouring towns, has been left relatively unscathed by such developments. Walking uphill, we find old farmsteads scattered among the fields and meadows. They are long, squat buildings with the wooden-balconied living quarters at the front and the byres and haylofts at the back.

St Quirin is a district of Gmund located on the slope halfway between the shore of the lake and the edge of the forest. Here, too, the construction of holiday homes has been going on for some time, as a (now altered) building by Sep Ruf on Kramerweg demonstrates. Ruf also built the home of Ludwig Erhardt above the railway station in Gmund and the Gulbransson Museum in Tegernsee Park. Along with the church architect Olaf Andreas Gulbransson, son of the legendary satirical caricaturist, Sep Ruf was an architect who succeeded with aplomb in combining elements of modernism with the Bavarian cultural landscape.

Today, even in an era in which "architectural culture" is something of a buzzword in faraway Berlin, that is no longer such an easy task, as architect Titus Bernhard and his client were to discover. The house that the Augsburg-based architect designed for a Munich lawyer in St Quirin stands directly above Ruf's building on Kramerweg, on one of the very few still available plots with lake views over Tegernsee.

The architect and his lawyer client had already met before. The client's legal firm specialises in architectural issues and had represented Titus Bernhard when his House 9 x 9 in Stadtbergen – a pyramid-roofed building clad in gabions of Altmühltaler dolomite stone – had met with howls of protest in the community. As Bernhard relates, the lawsuit had a very positive effect, making House 9 x 9 one of the most internationally publicised family homes.

Titus Bernhard is no agent provocateur. He had no plans to unleash a scandal when he started designing the house in

Architekten Architects Titus Bernhard Architekten, Augsburg, www.titusbernhardarchitekten.com; Team: Daniela Spuhler, Helmut Schmid, Stefan Krippl **Bauherr** Client Familie Kaltenegger, Gmund **Tragwerk** Structure Kurt Winter, Friedberg **Fertigstellung** Completion 2005 **Standort** Location Kramerweg 13, 83703 Gmund am Tegernsee/St. Quirin **Abbildungen** Photo Credits Christian Richters

Lage im Tegernseer Tal Site in the Tegernsee Valley

Blick vom Schlafzimmer auf die Terrasse
View from the bedroom towards the terrace

Grundriss Erdgeschoss Ground-floor plan
Grundriss Sockelgeschoss Basement plan

avancierte zum meistpublizierten Einfamilienhaus in der in- und ausländischen Presse.

Titus Bernhard ist kein Provokateur, und so hatte er auch keinen Skandal im Sinn, als er mit der Planung für St. Quirin begann. Im Gegenteil: Die Bauherrschaft wünschte über Gebäudeform und Materialien eine harmonische Eingliederung in die ortstypische Bebauung. Weitere Vorgaben waren eine offene Raumfolge und der Bezug nach außen, also die Ausrichtung auf den See.

Sensibel wurde das neue Volumen so auf dem Hanggrundstück platziert, dass möglichst wenige Eingriffe in die Geländemodulation vorgenommen werden mussten. Von der Erschließungsstraße aus gelangt man zum Eingang im Sockelgeschoss an der südöstlichen Stirnseite. Tritt man über die Schwelle, steht man in der schmalen, aber die gesamte Höhe des Hauses beanspruchenden Treppenhalle. Schon hier werden die Charakteristika des Hauses offenbar. Zum einen die reduzierte Materialpalette: Lebendige, kraftvolle Travertinplatten am Boden, weißer Putz an den Wänden, Meranti-Holz für Fenster und Einbauten. Zum anderen die Präzision in der Behandlung der Details – diese erweist sich zum Beispiel an der skulptural wirkenden Treppe, deren Läufe durch Lichtfugen von der Wand abgesetzt sind, oder am Zuschnitt der Bodenplatten, deren Raster perfekt auf den Innenausbau abgestimmt wurde.

Neben dem Eingang birgt das Sockelgeschoss die Garderoben, Technikräume sowie eine Einliegerwohnung, die als Betonbox talwärts aus der Kubatur des Gebäudes hervortritt.

Das Wohngeschoss – doppelt so lang wie der Sockel – wird durch eine Wegachse erschlossen, welche die gesamte Länge des Gebäudes durchmisst. Links, also talseitig, öffnet sich zunächst

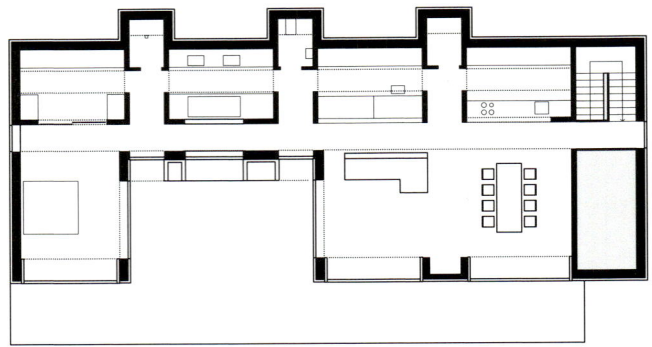

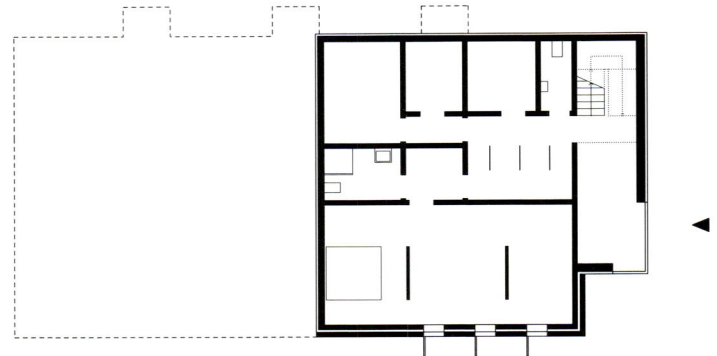

St Quirin. One the contrary: the client wanted the form and materials of the building to blend harmoniously with the local architecture. He also wanted an open sequence of rooms and a dialogue with the outside, looking towards the lake.

The new building was sensitively positioned on the sloping site in a way that intervened as little as possible in the topography. From the access road, we arrive at the entrance set in the southeastern narrow end of the plinth. On crossing the threshold, we find ourselves standing in a narrow stairwell that opens upwards to the full height of the building. Even here, the main characteristics of the house are already clearly evident. One of these is the minimal use of materials: strong and vibrant travertine flooring, white plastered walls, meranti wood for the windows and fittings. Another is the painstaking attention to detail – as in the sculptural stairway with its treads separated from the walls by lighting gaps, or the way the flooring slabs are cut to echo the exact dimensions of the interior fittings.

The basement houses not only the entrance area, but also the cloakrooms, technical utilities and a small guest apartment in the form of a concrete box protruding from the cuboid main building towards the valley.

The level above is double the length of the plinth and is accessed by an axial passage that runs the entire length of the building. On the left, towards the valley, is the spacious living and dining area with two large panorama windows, between which there is a fireplace, offering expansive views of the surroundings, the lake and Bad Wiessee on the opposite shore. A third window looks onto the patio area cut into the building and also onto the bedroom at the end of the central axis. On the side facing the

Ansicht, Eingang im Sockelgeschoss
Elevation, entrance in the basement

der großzügige Wohn- und Essbereich; zwei große Panoramafenster, zwischen denen sich der Kamin befindet, bieten einen weiten Ausblick über die Umgebung, den See und auf Bad Wiessee am anderen Ufer. Durch ein drittes Fenster blickt man auf die in das Gebäude eingeschnittene Terrasse – und auf das Schlafzimmer am Ende der zentralen Erschließungsachse. Bergseitig reihen sich entlang der zentralen Achse vier identisch dimensionierte Nebenräume, welche funktional auf ihr Gegenüber bezogen sind: Küche, Bibliothek, Bad und Ankleide. Getrennt sind diese Räume durch Miniaturkorridore, die zu kleinen, die nordöstliche Längswand gliedernden Zellen (Speisekammer, WC) führen. Über die Miniaturkorridore hinweg sind die Nebenräume durch eine sekundäre Wegachse verbunden, die sich partiell durch Schiebetüren (Bad) unterbrechen lässt. Da das Gebäude auf dieser Seite in den Berghang eingeschnitten ist, dienen Oberlichte als indirekte Lichtquellen.

Titus Bernhard ist mit dem Haus K. eine überaus intelligente und wohl kalkulierte Grundrisslösung gelungen. Von den kleinen Raumzellen über die mit Oberlichten erhellten Nebenräume schiebt sich das Haus gleichsam aus dem Berghang heraus und kulminiert in der räumlichen Opulenz der Wohn- und Schlafbereiche mit der vorgelagerten Terrasse. Durch die zwei parallelen Erschließungsachsen ergeben sich variierende Durchblicke. Gemeinsam mit den kreuzenden Korridoren entsteht ein räumlicher Raster, der vielfältige Modulationen zwischen Intimität und Offenheit erlaubt und in Zusammenwirkung mit der lichten Höhe die einzelnen Raumbereiche größer erscheinen lässt, als sie in Wirklichkeit sind. Bernhard konnte auch die Innenausstattung übernehmen: Bibliothek, Küche und Esstisch entstanden nach

mountain, there are four identically sized rooms off the central axis, all of which relate to the function of the rooms opposite them: kitchen, library, bathroom and dressing room. These rooms are separated by mini corridors that lead to small cells (larder, WC) which structure the north-east wall. Beyond the mini corridors the auxiliary rooms are linked by a secondary axis that can be partially blocked by sliding doors (bathroom). As the building is cut into the slope on this side, there are skylights to provide indirect lighting.

Titus Bernhard has succeeded here in creating a thoroughly intelligent and carefully calculated layout. From the small cells to the skylit auxiliary rooms, the house seems to push out of the slope, culminating in the opulently spacious living and sleeping areas with a terrace beyond. The two parallel axes create a variety of vistas and views, while the intersecting corridors form a spatial grid that allows a wide variety of modulations between privacy and openness which, in combination with the high ceilings, makes the individual areas appear larger than they really are. Bernhard was also commissioned as interior architect: the library, kitchen and dining table are all designed by him. The painstaking care with which the entire design has been executed is evident in the smallest details. For instance, two narrow windows above the corridor allow a view over the Tegernsee from the bathtub.

The house with its saddleback-roof (pitched at 20 degrees in accordance with local planning regulations) is clad in larch wood shingle – not only the walls, but also the roof, giving the entire volume a homogeneous appearance. Even though House K. is in a relatively secluded setting on the edge of the town, cannot be seen easily and has a wood shingle cladding that fits in with the

Wohn- und Essbereich
Living and dining area

Schlafzimmer
Bedroom

seinen Entwürfen. Wie durchdacht das Konzept ist, zeigt sich nicht zuletzt an kleinen Details: Liegt man in der Badewanne, ermöglichen zwei schmale Fenster über die Erschließungsachse hinweg die Aussicht auf den Tegernsee.

Umhüllt ist das mit einem Satteldach gedeckte Haus (mit einer Neigung von 20 Grad entspricht das Dach der örtlichen Gestaltungssatzung) von Lärchenholzschindeln. Diese finden sich nicht nur an den Wänden, sondern auch auf dem Dach, so dass das Volumen homogen erscheint. Auch wenn das Gebäude relativ abgelegen am Ortsrand liegt, nur teilweise einsehbar ist und sich überdies nicht zuletzt mit seinem Schindelkleid in die Umgebung einfügt: Auch Haus K. hat einen Rechtsstreit provoziert, der noch nicht ausgestanden ist. Durch den Verzicht auf einen Dachüberstand und die Fenstersprossung habe man gegen die am 1. Februar 1996 erlassene Gestaltungssatzung verstoßen, so der Vorwurf. Wer aufmerksam durch Gmund geht, bemerkt, dass man mit Hilfe einer Gestaltungssatzung architektonische Qualität nicht erzeugen kann. Wohl aber, sollte die Gemeinde sich durchsetzen, verhindern.

Über Gestaltung wird beiläufig auf der untersten Ebene entschieden, und das vielfach von Personen, denen es an geschmacklichem Verständnis mangelt. Wenn ein Architekt und sein Bauherr bereit sind, diese Mechanismen offen zu legen, so ist das praktizierte Baukultur.

Hubertus Adam

surroundings, it has already provoked a legal battle that is still to be resolved. The reason? With its lack of overhanging eaves and window mullions it has fallen foul of the planning regulation of 1 February 1996. A stroll through Gmund with open eyes is proof enough that a planning regulation cannot ensure architectural quality – but it can certainly damage it if the authorities win their case.

Planning regulations on design details such as these tend to be passed arbitrarily at the lowest level of government, often by people with little or no aesthetic awareness. When an architect and his client are willing to show up the flaws in this mechanism, that is "architectural culture" in practice.

Hubertus Adam

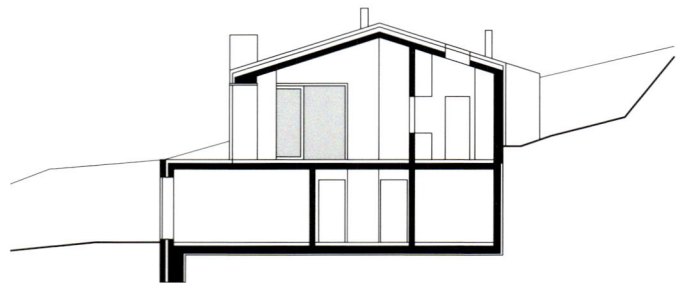

Querschnitt Cross section

Treppenhalle
Stair-hall

LITERATURMUSEUM DER MODERNE, MARBACH AM NECKAR
MODERN LITERATURE MUSEUM, MARBACH/NECKAR

David Chipperfield

Nimmermüde Schiller-Verehrer richteten 1859 das etwas ärmliche, mitten in Marbach gelegene Geburtshaus des Dichters als kleine Gedenkstätte ein. Um den Ruhm des Dichters jedoch effizient zu mehren, bedurfte es eines repräsentativen Hauses, das 1903 am Ortsrand hoch über dem Neckar gebaut wurde. Eisenlohr & Weigle verbanden die Bautypen Pantheon und Schloss im ›Baustil von Schillers Heimatjahren‹ miteinander – das Haus erlitt dann eine Beeinträchtigung seiner Proportionen, als 1934 beidseitig je drei Fensterachsen hinzukamen. Heute ist Marbach mit seiner imposanten Doppelinstitution aus Literaturarchiv und Schiller-Museum, an der über einhundertsiebzig Mitarbeiter wirken, international bekannt. Das Haupthaus, das Archiv sowie ein Gästehaus aus den siebziger und achtziger Jahren wuchsen zu einem uneinheitlichen Architekturensemble stattlicher Größe. Doch gerade das Haupthaus eignete sich überhaupt nicht dafür, tageslichtempfindliche Kostbarkeiten auszustellen. Der offene Wettbewerb für ein neues Literaturmuseum der Moderne (LiMo), mit dem der Aufstieg in die internationale Museumsliga gelingen sollte, konnte 2001 aber keinen ersten Preis erbringen. Platz zwei teilten sich Wilford Schupp mit Heinle Wischer und Partner, dahinter lagen Schuster Architekten aus Düsseldorf auf Platz drei und David Chipperfield auf Platz vier. Die funktionalen Stärken in Chipperfields Entwurf veranlassten die Bauherrschaft, schließlich den Engländer, der unter anderem in seinem Berliner Büro an der Museumsinsel arbeitete, zu beauftragen.

Den kleinen Platz vor dem Altbau mit einem bescheidenen, aber feinen Baukörper zu fassen, und zugleich den Ausblick in das Neckartal zu berücksichtigen, ist David Chipperfield Architects mit einem zweigeschossigen Museumsbau klug gelungen. Auf Eingangsniveau steht ein Tempelchen, eine Art transparentes Schatzhaus, rechtwinklig zum Altbau und in akzeptablem Abstand zu diesem – und zwischen beiden Bauten öffnet sich eine fulminante Terrasse. Etwas merkwürdig muten zwar die Höhenversprünge an, die mit Brüstungen zwischen Tempelchen, Terrasse und Rampen am Haus gefasst werden, doch der Weg ins LiMo erschließt sich wie selbstverständlich.

Das Eingangshaus aus spindeldünnen Betonstützen und einer Holz-Glas-Fassade ruft zwar den griechischen Prototyp assoziativ ins Gedächtnis, aber hebt nicht zu einer Nacherzählung in geschwätziger Banalität an. Hier im Erdgeschoss finden sich nur die Kasse, Schließfächer, ein Aufzug und ein kleiner Vortragssaal – alle Ausstellungsräume befinden sich im Untergeschoss. Klassische Baukunst, in der Hierarchien wie Erdgeschoss, Beletage und Mezzanine als unumstößliche Standards gelten, hat es in Hanglagen natürlich sehr schwer – Chipperfield fängt jedoch die topographische Kalamität mit einer zwar formal einheitlichen, aber baukörperlich deutlichen Unterscheidung der Geschosse und ihrer

In 1859, indefatigable admirers of Schiller created a memorial to him in the humble house in Marbach where he was born. But it was felt that a writer of such calibre deserved a more prestigious monument, and so, in 1903, architects Eisenlohr & Weigle built a cross between palace and pantheon high above the river Neckar in what was described as "the architectural style of Schiller's home and era". The harmonious proportions of this building suffered from the addition of three window axes on either side in 1934. Today, Marbach is internationally renowned for its imposing dual institute housing both a literature archive and a Schiller museum with a staff of more than 170 persons. Over the years, the main building, the archive and a guesthouse dating from the 1970s and 1980s have sprawled to become a heterogeneous architectural ensemble of considerable size. The main building itself, however, is entirely unsuited to exhibiting valuable, light-sensitive documents. In 2001, an open competition to design a new Modern Literature Museum (LiMo) that would put Marbach in the premiere league of international museums found no clear winner. Second place was shared by Wilford Schupp and Heinle Wischer & Partners, with Schuster Architekten of Dusseldorf in third place and David Chipperfield in fourth place. However, the functional strengths of Chipperfield's design prompted the client to commission this British architect whose Berlin office was involved in the redevelopment of the Museumsinsel in Berlin. David Chipperfield Architects have succeeded in finding a solution that cleverly brackets the space in front of the historic building with a modest yet subtle structure without detriment to the views over the Neckar valley. At the level of the entrance there is a little temple almost like a transparent treasure chamber, set at right angles to the old building and at a discreet distance from it. Between the two buildings there is a magnificent open terrace. The height differences with their balustrades, terracing and ramps between buildings may seem rather strange, but the path towards the LiMo is easily navigated and works surprisingly well.

The entrance building of slender concrete pillars and wood and glass facade triggers associations of the Greek prototype without succumbing to the banality of mere citation. Here, on the ground floor, we find the ticket desk, lockers and a small lecture hall. All the exhibition spaces are below ground. Classical architecture with its hierarchical structure of ground floor, bel etage and mezzanine, invariably poses problems on a sloping site like this. Chipperfield, however, has overcome the topographical difficulties by making a formally unified yet structurally clear distinction between the levels and their respective functions. While the architects have approached the LiMo in its entirety as an exercise in restraint, there is nothing sterile about this finely structured and sensual architecture. David Chipperfield Architects have demonstrated a

Architekten Architects David Chipperfield Architects, London, www.davidchipperfield.co.uk; Team: Alexander Schwarz, Harald Müller, Martina Betzold, Andrea Hartmann, Christian Helfrich, Franziska Rusch, Tobias Stiller, Vincent Taupitz, Mirjam von Busch, Harald Müller, Martina Betzold, Laura Fogarasi, Barbara Koller, Hannah Jonas **Bauherr** Client Deutsches Literaturarchiv Marbach **Tragwerk** Structure Ingenieurgruppe Bauen: Josef Seiler, Gerhard Eisele, Markus Filian **Wettbewerb** Competition 2002 **Fertigstellung** Completion 2006 **Standort** Location Schillerhöhe, 71672 Marbach am Neckar, www.dla-marbach.de **Abbildungen** Photo Credits Stefan Müller-Naumann

Ansicht Südost
Elevation, south-east

Funktionszuweisung auf. Die Architekten halten das ganze LiMo für eine »Übung zum Thema Zurückhaltung«, aber »cool« möchte man diese feingliedrige, zugleich sinnliche Architektur gewiss nicht nennen. David Chipperfield Architects beweisen ein feines Gespür für Werkstoffe: Muschelkalkplatten auf dem Boden, mit Jurasand und Muschelkalksplitt veredelter Sichtbeton, heller, dicker Filz und dunkles Tropenholz fügen sich zu einer erstaunlich behaglichen Atmosphäre. Das Ipé-Holz stammt von brasilianischen Plantagen, es schimmert nicht so rot wie Teak und wurde für raumhohe Flügeltüren und die komplette, parkettartige Auskleidung der Ausstellungsräume im Untergeschoss verwendet, die halb im Hang liegen.

Tausend Quadratmeter Ausstellungsfläche dienen je zur Hälfte den Dauer- und Wechselausstellungen. Die Holzauskleidung trägt in diesen nahezu tageslichtlosen, aber fast fünf Meter hohen Räumen zu einer ausgesprochen konzentrationsfreundlichen Atmosphäre vergleichbar mucksmäuschenstillen Bibliothekssälen bei. An den Wänden lässt sich natürlich nichts aufhängen; die durchweg kleinen Exponate werden daher in Vitrinen liegen, die das Büro ›elements‹ aus Basel für das LiMo entwarf. Entlang der Fassade legten die Architekten noch Nischen und Wandelgänge an, die auch auf dieser introvertierten Ebene den Ausblick ins Tal genießen lassen und jeder Klaustrophobie vorbeugen. Die gesamten Raumfolgen sind zielorientiert und präzise aufeinander abgestimmt, denn ausnahmsweise hat einmal niemand den Wunsch nach flexiblen Räumen geäußert, in denen alles Mögliche von voluminösen Nanas bis hin zu kulturgeschichtlich bedeutsamen Fingerhüten zu zeigen sein müsse.

Über dem Neckartal thront das fast hundertfünfzig Jahre lang gewachsene Ensemble inzwischen wie eine Akropolis: Die Hügelkante ist markant und in Dimensionen bebaut, die eine kulturelle, institutionelle Bedeutung weithin signalisieren. Kommt man dagegen von oben, über den Schillerhain, dann gibt sich das gesamte Ensemble bescheiden, fast idyllisch beiläufig. Das LiMo darf als Etüde für das von Chipperfield entworfene Eingangshaus zur Berliner Museumsinsel gelten und demonstrieren, wie viel Aufmerksamkeit die Qualität des Unspektakulären verdient.

Ursula Baus

Ansicht West, Eingang
West elevation, entrance

Ausstellungsraum
Exhibition room

delicate sense of material, using shell limestone flooring, fairfaced concrete enhanced with jura sand and shell limestone chippings, heavy-duty felt and dark tropical hardwood to create a remarkably warm and welcoming atmosphere. Ipé wood from Brazilian plantations, which is less red in tone than teak, is used for the floor-to-ceiling double doors and for the parquet flooring of the basement exhibition spaces that are partly set into the slope.

A thousand square metres of exhibition space are used in equal measure for the temporary and permanent exhibitions. In these almost five-metre-high rooms that receive virtually no daylight, the overall effect is one of tranquillity, as conducive to concentration as any quiet library. Nothing can be hung on the walls and so the small exhibits are displayed in glass showcases designed for the LiMo by the Basel-based firm "elements". Along the facade the architects have created secluded niches and walkways with views out across the valley, countering any sense of claustrophobia. The sequence of rooms is clearly defined, this

project being one of the rare occasions on which nobody asked for the kind of spatial flexibility that would allow them to exhibit anything from massive sculptures to tiny thimbles.

This ensemble, which has grown over a period of almost 150 years, stands enthroned above the Neckar valley like an acropolis: The slope of the hill has been developed with a distinctiveness and sense of scale that signals the cultural and institutional importance of the building for miles around. And yet, if you approach it through the wooded Schillerhaim, the place seems almost modest and idyllic. The LiMo might be regarded as a study for the entrance pavilion that Chipperfield designed for the Berlin Museumsinsel, demonstrating how much care and attention the quality of the unspectacular deserves.

Ursula Baus

Ausstellungsraum
Exhibition room

Längsschnitt Longitudinal section

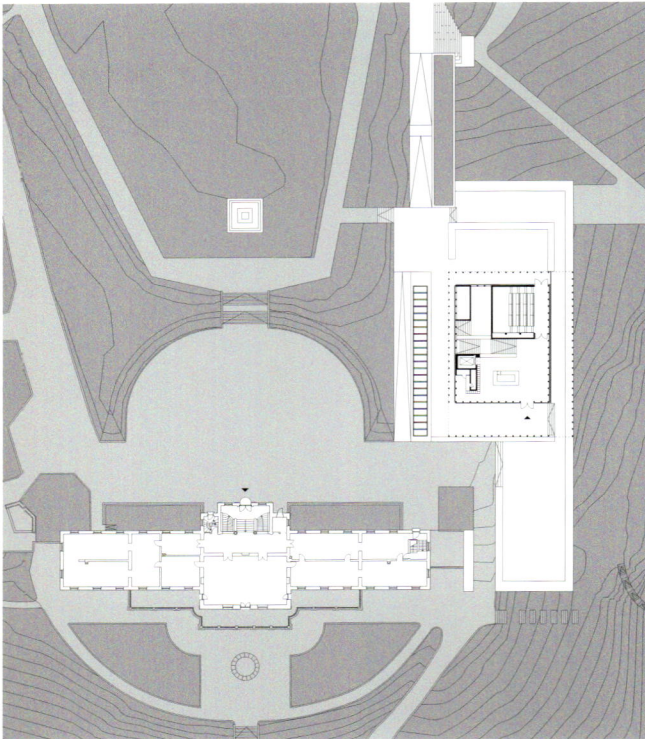

Grundriss Eingangsebene

Floorplan, entrance level

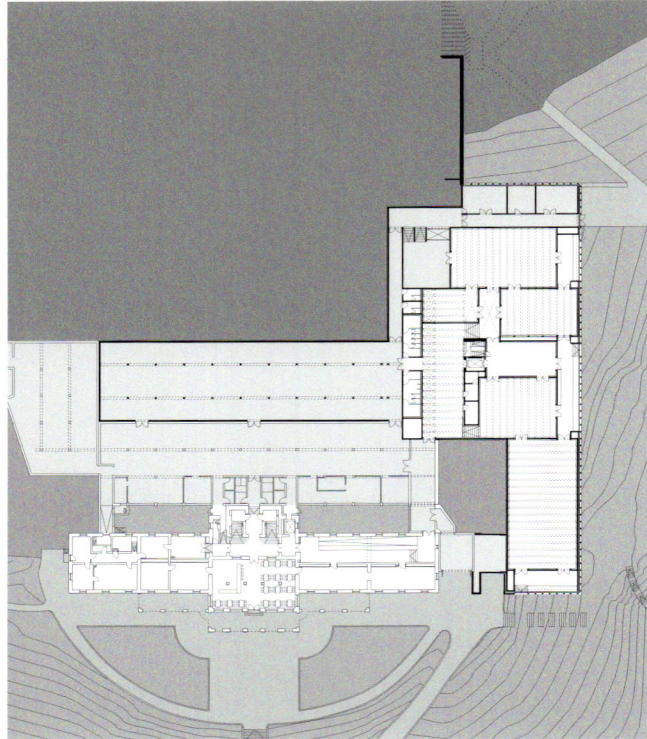

Grundriss Ausstellungsebene

Floorplan, exhibition level

oben und rechts Eingangshalle
top and right Foyer

Seite 92 Wandelgang
Page 92 Colonnade

Seite 93 Blick in Ausstellungsräume
Page 93 View towards exhibition rooms

MUSEUM RITTER, WALDENBUCH
MUSEUM RITTER, WALDENBUCH

Max Dudler

»Ein architektonisches Weltgebäude ist kein Betrieb und keine Fabrik, es ist ein Weltgebäude der Kunst für andere, ungegenständliche Zwecke, in denen das (...) Nervensystem zur Ruhe in Ungegenständlichkeit geführt wird.«
Kasimir Malewitsch[1]

Hier ist Waldenbuch. Ein kleines spätmittelalterliches Städtchen, gekrönt vom historischen Schloss. Streuobstwiesen durchziehen das sich lieblich dahinschlängelnde Aichtal, und überall künden Zäunchen und kleine Schuppen von ordentlich parzelliertem Kleingärtnertum im schwäbischen ›Ländle‹. Direkt an der Schnittstelle zwischen Naturidylle und dem zerfaserten Ortsrand von Waldenbuch erhebt sich seit kurzem ein heller monolithischer Baukörper: das Museum Ritter. Max Dudler hat es für die geometrisch-abstrakte Sammlung Marli Hoppe-Ritter des quadratisch inspirierten Schokoladenimperiums Ritter Sport entworfen. Der Entwurf reagiert auf das Bekenntnis der Sammlung zur reinen Form mit einem subtilen Spiel reduzierter Geometrien: Der Grundriss des zweiteiligen Gebäudes basiert auf dem Quadrat, das Dudler in unterschiedlich große trapezförmige Bauteile untergliedert. Auch die weite Passage, die als Gelenk zwischen den Museumskuben liegt, ist als Trapez konzipiert.

Dem Besucher erschließt sich dieses geometrische Kalkül erst auf den zweiten Blick. Zunächst erfasst das Auge einen mächtigen Korpus aus einem Guss, in dessen helle Muschelkalkhaut dunkel schimmernde Öffnungen eingeschnitten sind. Dieses Fassadenbild der harten geometrischen Schnitte im Kontrast zur ruhig gefügten Fläche des Steins weckt vielerlei Assoziationen: Es erinnert an Arbeiten des ganz jungen Mies van der Rohe, an metaphysische Bilder des italienischen Rationalismus, aber auch an die skulpturalen Objekte von Eduardo Chillida.[2]

Beim Näherkommen öffnet sich dem Betrachter die steinverkleidete Passage wie ein großes Tor: Man tritt ein und wird gleichsam von magischer Hand bis zum Ende des Weges geführt, an dem sich wie in einem gerahmten Bild von Caspar David Friedrich der Ausschnitt weiter Landschaft darbietet: Wiesen und Bäume, Wasser und Himmel – immer neu im Wechsel der Jahreszeiten. Im Winter hemmt eine eingestellte Glaswand den Durchzug der Landluft in der 12 Meter hohen Passage, die auch als Veranstaltungsort dient. Geometrische ›Fenster zum Himmel‹ zaubern in der Passage einen Lichteinfall von oben und zusätzlich reizvolle Schattenspiele.

In der Passage verweilend, hat der Besucher nun die Qual der Wahl zwischen den beiden ganz unterschiedlichen Trakten des Gebäudes: Auf der einen Seite lockt im SchokoLaden der konkrete Konsum mit allen Varianten der quadratischen Leckereien von Ritter Sport. Die zurückhaltend und zweckmäßig gestalteten Räume des Obergeschosses gehören zur didaktischen SchokoWerkstatt

"Architectural world building is neither an enterprise nor a factory; it is the world building of art for other, non-figurative purposes, in which ... the nervous system is led towards calmness in abstraction."
– Kasimir Malevich[1]

So this is Waldenbuch, a small medieval town with a castle, set amidst the lovely orchards of the Aich valley and the neatly tended allotment gardens with the little sheds and fences so typical of rural Swabia. Here, on the boundary between rural idyll and suburban sprawl, stands a brand-new building – bright and monolithic. It is the Museum Ritter, designed by Max Dudler to house the collection of geometric-abstract art accumulated by Marli Hoppe Ritter of the German chocolate manufacturer Ritter, best known for its iconic square bars. The subtle, pared-down geometry of the architecture echoes the collection's focus on pure form: The floor plan of this two-part building is based on the square, which Dudler has subdivided into differently sized trapezoidal elements. Even the broad passageway linking the cubes of the museum is trapezoidal.

Visitors to the building do not immediately notice this carefully calculated geometry. At first, the eye takes in only a massive building that seems to be cast from a single mould, its pale shell-limestone skin perforated by darkly shimmering apertures. This facade of harsh geometric cuts contrasting with the pale expanses of stone triggers many associations. It recalls the work of the young Mies van der Rohe, the metaphysical imagery of Italian Rationalism, and even the sculptural objects of Eduardo Chillida.[2]

On approach, the stone-clad passage seems to open up like a huge gateway. On entering, we feel we are being led by some invisible hand towards the end of the path, where an aperture affords a view out into the surrounding landscape like a framed painting by Caspar David Friedrich. The meadows and trees, water and sky are constantly changing with the seasons. In winter, a glass wall holds back the chill air of the surrounding countryside in the 12-metre-high passageway that also serves as a venue for events. Geometric "windows to the sky" fill the passageway almost magically with light from above, enlivening it with the delightful play of shadows.

As we stand here in the passageway, we are torn between the two very different tracts of the building. On one side of us is the chocolate shop that tempts us to indulge in tasting all the different flavours of the Ritter brand. Above it, the functional, understated upper level houses an informative and educational chocolate workshop with interactive play areas dedicated to that sweet temptation. On the other side of the passageway is the world of art, with a widely varied collection of works from the 1930s to the

Architekten Architects Max Dudler Architekt, Berlin, www.maxdudler.de; Team: Susanne Raupach, Nina Barthélémy, Andreas Enge, Gesine Gummi **Bauherr** Client Marli Hoppe-Ritter-Stiftung zur Förderung der Kunst; Alfred Ritter GmbH & Co. KG, Waldenbuch **Tragwerk** Structure König, Heunisch und Partner, Frankfurt am Main **Entwurf** Design 2003 **Ausführung** Construction März 2004–September 2005 **Standort** Location Alfred-Ritter-Straße 27, 71111 Waldenbuch, www.museum-ritter.de **Abbildungen** Photo Credits Stefan Müller

Abendaufnahme, Passage
Evening exposure, passage

und zu den interaktiven Spielplätzen rund um den süßen Verführer Schokolade. Auf der anderen Seite der Passage winkt die konkrete Kunst in ihren unterschiedlichsten Erscheinungsformen von den dreißiger Jahren bis in die aktuelle Gegenwart. Großzügig verglast, öffnet sich der Haupteingang und lenkt den Besucher durch ein weiträumiges Foyer in einen meditativen, vom milchigen Licht der quadratischen Rasterdecke durchdrungenen Ausstellungsraum. Dieses äußerst ästhetisch gestaltete Kontinuum zitiert den idealen Museumsraum, den Hermann Billing einst in seiner Baden-Badener Kunsthalle entwickelte. Hier darf der Betrachter konzentriert und ungestört in »stiller und schweigender Demut«[3] der Kunst gegenübertreten. Von diesem Raum führt eine schmale, aber dramatisch inszenierte Treppe ins Obergeschoss mit den flexibel unterteilbaren Ausstellungsflächen. Die Kunstbegegnung geschieht hier in Form eines fließenden Erlebnisparcours: Der Besucher durchwandert große, kleine und kleinste Kabinette, bleibt hier und da stehen, um für einen Augenblick von der Kunst zu ›naschen‹ oder den Blick durch die Fenster nach draußen schweifen zu lassen. In einigen Räumen, den so genannten ›Landschaftszimmern‹, gewähren fast raumhoch verglaste Fenster den Panoramablick ins Tal. Es ist ein angenehmes Gefühl, durch Museumsräume zu gehen, in denen die Gratwanderung zwischen Außen- und Innenwelt, zwischen Natur und Kunst so zwanglos gelingt. Auch die Innenraumgestaltung dieses Privatmuseums fördert die synästhetische Raumwahrnehmung: Hier gibt es kein Auftrumpfen mit Effekthascherei, aber auch keinen pathologischen Purismus; hier überzeugt wohl temperiertes Maß bei Materialien und sorgfältigen Details. Das ist auch beim kleinen, dem Foyer vorgelagerten Museumscafé nicht anders. Das Café präsentiert sich als elegante Schwester des ebenfalls von Max Dudler konzipierten ›Schwarzen Cafés‹ in Frankfurt am Main. Auch in Waldenbuch sitzt man wieder auf schwarzen, schrecklich unbequemen Stühlen und zwängt die Beine unter quadratische Tischlein. Aber das tut man gerne – schon wegen der wunderschönen Aussicht ins Naturidyll. Im Sommer wird die gläserne Panorama-Schiebetür offen stehen, es wird nach Wiese und Käsespätzle duften, und alle werden draußen sitzen und die Seele baumeln lassen.

Karin Leydecker

1 Zitiert nach Aaage Hansen-Löve (Hrsg.), Kazimir Malevic, Gott ist nicht gestürzt! Schriften zu Kunst, Kirche, Fabrik, München und Wien 2004, S. 120.
2 »Was mich betrifft, so strebe ich nach dem hohlen Dreidimensionalen, indem ich das volle Dimensionale bestimme – und gleichzeitig eine gewisse Beziehung zwischen beiden entstehen lasse. Auf Grund solcher Beziehungen werden äußere Volumina, die wir einfach umfassen können, unsere untrüglichen Führer, um uns verborgenen Räumen, zumindest im Geiste, zu nähern.« Eduardo Chillida, Elkartu, hrsg. von der Stiftung Museum Schloss Moyland, Ausst.-Kat. Museum Schloss Moyland, Berlin 2001, S. 36.
3 Wilhelm Heinrich Wackenroder, Ludwig Tieck, Herzensergießungen eines kunstliebenden Klosterbruders, Reclam Universal-Bibliothek Nr. 7860, Stuttgart 1994, S. 71f.

present day. The extensively glazed main entrance leads the visitor through a spacious foyer into a meditative exhibition space gently flooded by the milky light of the ceiling. This aesthetically pleasing handling of space cites the notion of the ideal museum space as formulated by Hermann Billing in his design for the Kunsthalle Baden-Baden. This is a place where the art-lover can contemplate works of art in "silent humility".[3] From here, a narrow but dramatically staged stairway leads to the upper level with its flexible exhibition areas, where the encounter with art takes the form of a fluid sequence of experiences: As we stroll through "cabinet" spaces large and small, we are prompted to pause here and there to savour the works of art or to gaze through a window at the surrounding countryside. In some of the rooms – the so-called "landscape rooms" – floor-to-ceiling windows open up panoramic views of the valley. It is a pleasant feeling indeed to wander through a museum whose rooms so easily strike the balance between nature and art, between the outer and the inner world. Even the interior design of this private museum is calibrated to generate a synaesthetic perception of space. There are neither gimmicky effects nor tight-lipped purism – just a well-tempered respect for materials and attention to detail. The same applies to the little café off the foyer of the museum, which is rather like the more elegant sister of Max Dudler's "Schwarzes Café" in Frankfurt/Main. In Waldenbuch, as in Frankfurt, we have to sit on rather uncomfortable black chairs, forcing our knees under square tables. But we do it gladly, if only for the magnificent views of the surrounding countryside. In summer the huge sliding glass door is opened up to let in all the lovely scents of the meadows that mingle with the delicious aroma of the traditional local cuisine, and everyone can just sit outdoors and soak up the atmosphere.

Karin Leydecker

1 Quoted from Aaage Hansen-Löve, ed. Kazimir Malevic. Gott ist nicht gestürzt! Schriften zu Kunst, Kirche, Fabrik. Munich and Vienna, 2004, p. 120.
2 "I, for my part, strive towards hollow three-dimensionality by determining the fully dimensional – while at the same time allowing a certain relationship to build up between the two. Such relationships allow the external volumes that we can quite easily grasp to become our reliable guides, leading us into hidden spaces, at least in the mind." Eduardo Chillida, Elkartu, published by the Stiftung Museum Schloss Moyland, exhib. cat. Museum Schloss Moyland, Berlin 2001, p. 36.
3 Wilhelm Heinrich Wackenroder, Ludwig Tieck, Herzensergießungen eines kunstliebenden Klosterbruders, Reclam Universal-Bibliothek Nr. 7860, Stuttgart 1994, p. 71f.

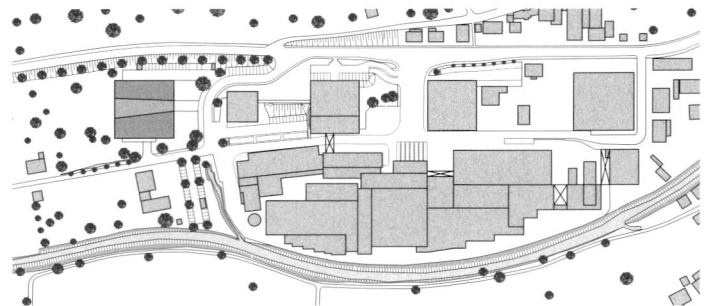

Lageplan Site plan

Ansicht Südosten
South-east elevation

Grundriss Erdgeschoss
Ground-floor plan

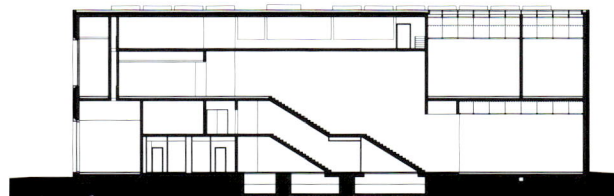

Längsschnitt, Museumstrakt
Longitudinal section, museum wing

Treppenaufgang, Erdgeschoss
Staircase, ground floor

Passage, Blick Richtung Westen
Passage, view westward

Ausstellungsraum, 1. Obergeschoss
Exhibition room, first floor

Foyer und Museums-Shop, Erdgeschoss
Foyer and museum shop, ground floor

Museums-Café, Erdgeschoss
Museum café, ground floor

STUDENTENWOHNANLAGE, GARCHING
STUDENT RESIDENCE, GARCHING

Fink + Jocher

Die Fotos täuschen – wie so oft. Die Bauten sehen darauf ruppig und roh aus, umspannt mit Maschendraht gleich Käfigen. Die Laubengänge kragen unregelmäßig aus wie wellige Käsescheiben auf einem Dreifach-Cheeseburger; die großen Glasscheiben glänzen abweisend. Klar, Studenten sind ungeniert und gehen mit Gemeinschaftseigentum nicht sehr schonend um, aber muss man sie so grob behausen?

Ebenso oft wird man dann durch einen Besuch eines Besseren belehrt. Die beiden Gebäude stehen am Rand einer Neubausiedlung, mit Giebeldachhäuschen bunt wie Ostereier, in der Ferne rauscht die Autobahn. Die Universität liegt etwa zehn Minuten zu Fuß entfernt. Seit 1997 darf sich das nicht sehr hübsche Garching ›Universitätsstadt‹ nennen – damals begann der Umzug des naturwissenschaftlich-technischen Bereichs der TU in den Ort nördlich der Münchner Stadtgrenze. Studentenwohnungen wurden gebraucht, und so entschied sich das Studentenwerk München über ein VOF-Verfahren für das Büro Fink + Jocher.

Geht man auf die beiden Häuser zu, entpuppt sich der ›Maschendraht‹ schon bald als ein filigranes, 3 mm feines Stahlnetz, das zwischen den Geschossen geflochten wurde, glatt und elegant wie Saiten, so dass man es anfassen und die Spannung überprüfen möchte. Das Netz umgibt die Zwillingsbauten wie ein Schleier, sie wirken dadurch leicht. Es ist pro Geschoss bis in Brüstungshöhe dichter gewirkt, während die Maschen hinauf zur nächsten Ebene aufgezogen sind. In Bodennähe werden die Schlingen sogar aufgelöst, damit dort wilder Wein emporranken kann. Schon reicht er in den ersten Stock. Die Wellenlinien der Laubengänge werden mit zweierlei Formen von Fertigteilplatten und ihrer geschossweisen Verschiebung erzeugt, ein scheinbar einfacher Trick, der einen verblüffenden Effekt hat: Das Netz erzielt dadurch eine schillernde Unschärfe, die den Betrachter neugierig macht.

Viel Spielraum hatten die Architekten nicht, das Budget war mit 30 000 Euro Baukosten pro Zimmer knapp. Da half nur minimieren und systematisieren – und vor allem vorab bis ins Detail planen. So musste der Rohbau auch als Ausbau zu gebrauchen sein. In Stahlbeton-Schottenbauweise stapeln sich identische Grundrisse bei beiden Häusern, nur der nördliche Bau ist unterkellert. Es gibt keine interne Erschließung, das heißt, die thermische Hülle umschließt nur den Wohnbereich. Die Laubengänge sind mit 1,40 bis 1,65 Metern breit genug, dass auch Tisch und Stühle Platz haben. An den Stirnseiten der Häuser sind mittels schwarzen Pigments durchgefärbte Betonfertigteile vorgehängt, die eine erstaunlich samtige Oberfläche aufweisen und zudem mit ihrer dunkel gewölbten Textur fast so edel wirken wie Naturstein. Die Stufen der Außentreppen wurden ebenfalls fertig angeliefert, die Brüstungen vor Ort betoniert.

The photos are misleading, as photos so often are. They make the buildings look a bit rough and ready, like cages covered in wire mesh. The covered walkways stick out like wavy cheese slices on a treble cheeseburger. The big panes of glass are like emptily staring eyes. But just because students are not always noted for treating property with respect, is that any reason to put them in such unpleasant accommodation?

And then, as so often happens, a personal visit puts things into perspective. The two buildings are set on the edge of a new development of pitched-roof houses, as bright and colourful as Easter eggs. You can hear the sound of the motorway in the distance. The university itself is about a ten-minute walk away. Since 1997, when Munich University of Technology moved some of its science and engineering departments out here, not-so-lovely Garching to the north of the city has had the privilege of calling itself a university town. Student residences were needed. Designs were invited, and Fink + Jocher were chosen as the architects.

On approaching the two buildings, what appeared at first to be some kind of wire mesh turns out to be a filigree net of fine, three-millimetre steel woven between the storeys, as smoothly and elegantly as the strings of a musical instrument. They make you want to touch them, to test the tension. The net covers the twin buildings like a veil, lending them an air of lightness. On each level of the building, the net is fairly closely woven up to parapet level, with a more open weave strung from there to the next level. At floor level, some of the loops have been left open to act as a trellis for the wild vines that have already grown as high as the first floor. The undulating lines of the covered walkways are created by using two different forms of pre-cast panels, staggered slightly from level to level. This simple device has an astonishing effect: the nets appear to shimmer, and this makes us curious.

With a budget of just 30,000 Euros per room, the architects had very little leeway. So the only way forward was to take a minimalist, systematic approach and, above all, to plan everything in minute detail right from the start. This meant, for instance, that the shell of the building also had to serve as the finished layout. As a result, the floorplans of both buildings are identical on each level, with the floors stacked on top of each other in reinforced concrete cross-wall construction. Only the northern building has a basement. There are no internal corridors, which means that the thermal shell encloses only the living area. The covered walkways are 1.40 to 1.65 metres wide, allowing enough space for table and

Ansicht Laubengänge
Elevation, access balconies

Architekten **Architects** Dietrich Fink + Thomas Jocher, München, www.fink-jocher.de; Team: Stephan Riedel, Florian Braun, Katharina Leuschner, Andreas Matievits, Martin Vaché, Christos Chantzaras, Florian Lünstedt, Andreas Schmid, Jon Steinfeld **Bauherr** **Client** Studentenwerk München **Tragwerk** **Structure** Ingenieurbüro für Baustatik und Tagewerksplanung Joachim Eiermann, München **Fertigstellung** **Completion** 2005 **Standort** **Location** Enzianstraße 1 + 3, 85748 Garching **Abbildungen** **Photo Credits** Michael Heinrich

Möchte man eines der Zimmer besuchen, kann es sein, dass die Tür verschlossen bleibt, denn schon viele Architekten haben ihre Nasen an den Scheiben platt gedrückt und um Einlass gebeten. Manchmal hat man auch Glück. Wie es sich denn da wohnt? Die Studentin kennt sonst nur Wohnheime, wo sich 60 Bewohner eine Küche teilen, und freut sich über die kleinen Wohneinheiten – hier in Garching kann man zwischen Einzelappartements, Zweier-WGs und Vierer-WGs wählen. Auch die Ausstattung der Räume mit Roll-Möbeln findet sie toll.

Jedes der 112 Zimmer hat ein raumhohes, fest verglastes Fenster und eine eigene ›Haustür‹ zum Laubengang. Und die hat es in sich: Ein in das Aluminium-Türblatt eingebauter Fensterflügel lässt sich zur Lüftung öffnen, ist aber einbruchsicher mit einem Musterlochblech geschützt, so kann er im Sommer immer offen stehen. Die großen Scheiben werden durch zweierlei Jalousien ›blickdicht‹: Ein undurchsichtiger Rollo rollt sich von unten nach oben – viele Studenten haben ihn bis zur Schreibtischhöhe hochgezogen. Der zweite, gazeartige Store, der das Licht durchlässt, wird von den meisten bis zur Kante des dichten Rollos heruntergekurbelt. Offenbar mag keiner so recht ganz ohne dasitzen, am ehesten noch diejenigen, die zur Westseite, der Außenseite der Siedlung, wohnen.

Beim Anblick der Wohnhäuser kommt man zu dem Schluss, dass Fink + Jocher bestimmt kein Büro sind, das sich über Marketing-Strategien den Kopf zerbrechen muss. Ihre erfindungsreichen Konzepte sind bis hin zur Realisierung durchgehalten, so dass ihre Bauten selbst die beste Werbung darstellen. Im Fall Garching waren es die geschichteten Plattformen, die den Entwurf von Anfang an bestimmt haben – in der Realität erinnert allerdings nichts an wellige Käsescheiben, da die Plattformen ordentlich in das feine Netz verpackt sind. Außerdem hoffen die Architekten, dass die jungen Leute experimentierfreudig sind und nach einem vielleicht konventionellen Elternhaus mal eine neue Wohnform ausprobieren wollen. Und was sagt die Studentin? »Im Moment muss man schon ein bisschen exhibitionistisch veranlagt sein, aber wird das schön, wenn die Wände grün sind!«

Sabine Schneider

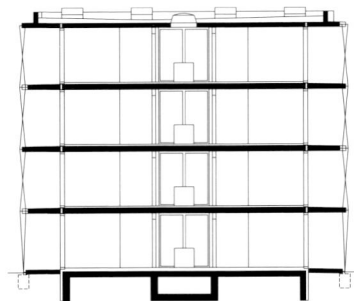

Querschnitt
Cross section

chairs. The pre-cast concrete slabs solid-dyed with black pigment on the narrow ends of the buildings have a remarkably velvety surface and their cloudy, dark texture looks almost as sumptuous as natural stone. The steps of the external stairways were prefabricated and the balustrades cast in situ.

Anyone hoping to visit one of the rooms may well find themselves standing before closed doors. Many an architect has asked to see inside. But sometimes you can get lucky. So what's it like to live here? One student says she had previously only ever seen student residences where up to 60 people had to share a kitchen, and that she likes the small units in Garching, where there is a choice of two-bed and four-bed apartments. She also thinks the furnishings, on rollers, are great.

Each of the 112 rooms has a floor-to-ceiling window with fixed glazing and its own door to the covered walkway. Even the doors themselves have a special design feature: a window fitted in the aluminium door panel can be opened for ventilation. For security purposes, this window has a perforated metal cover so that it can be left open in summer. Two types of blinds on the large windows allow for privacy. One is a non-transparent roller blind that can be pulled up from the floor (many students have this blind pulled up to the level of their desktop). The other is a gauze-like blind, which lets light through, and can be drawn down from the ceiling (most students pull this down to the top of the non-transparent blind). It would seem that nobody really wants to sit there with the window completely uncovered – except perhaps those who live on the west side of the building.

Looking at these buildings, it is easy to conclude that Fink + Jocher are not a team who need to worry about marketing strategies. Their innovative concepts are executed with such consistency from start to finish that the buildings themselves are the best advertisement for their work. In Garching it was the layered platforms that determined the design right from the start – and in reality there is nothing at all like wavy cheese slices about them, for the platforms are so cleverly packed inside the metal net. The architects hope that the young people who live there might enjoy experimenting with their surroundings after the perhaps rather conventional atmosphere of their parental homes. And what does our student have to say about it? "At the moment, you do have to be a bit of an exhibitionist to live here, but it'll be great once the walls are green!"

Sabine Schneider

Lageplan
Site plan

Ansicht Außentreppen
Elevation, exterior stairs

Laubengang Gartenseite
Access balcony, garden side

Ansicht Gesamtanlage
Elevation, entire complex

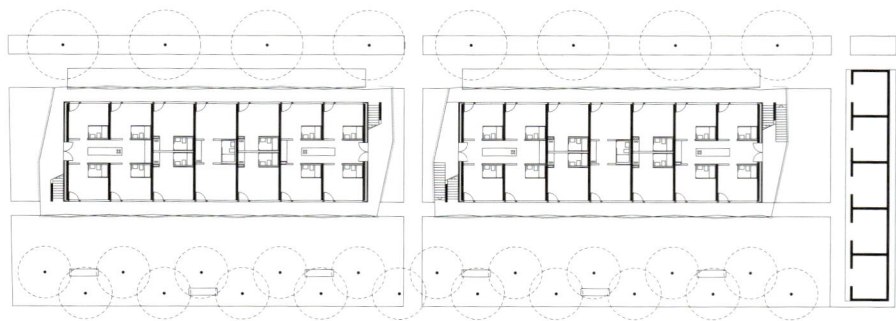

Grundriss Erdgeschoss
Ground-floor plan

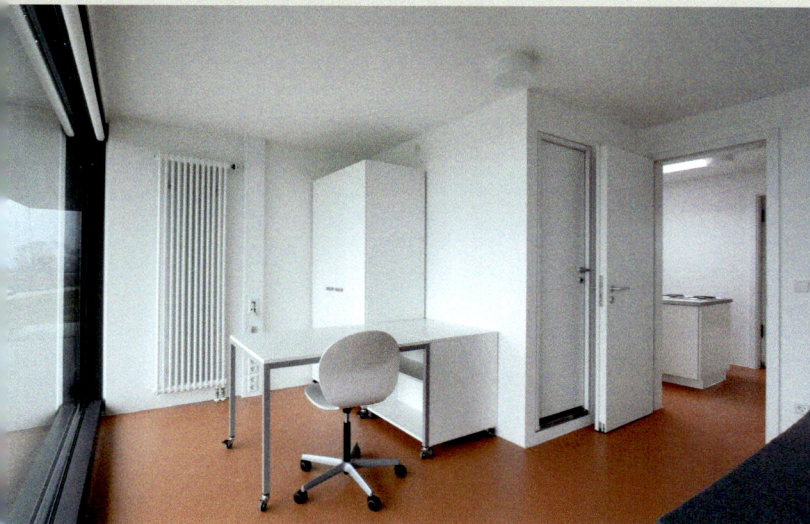

Zimmer mit Nasszelle
Room with bathroom unit

Wohnungstür mit Jalousien
Door of apartment with blinds

Blick in die Küche für vier Bewohner
View in kitchen for four occupants

BIBLIOTHEK DER PHILOLOGISCHEN FAKULTÄT DER FREIEN UNIVERSITÄT BERLIN
LIBRARY FOR THE PHILOLOGIGAL FACULTY OF FREIE UNIVERSITÄT BERLIN

Norman Foster

Die im Volksmund ›Rostlaube‹ genannte Bautengruppe der Freien Universität (FU) von Candilis, Josic, Woods und Schiedhelm mit Jean Prouvé aus den Jahren 1967–1973 ist inzwischen nach dem Konzept von Foster und Partner saniert und um eine neue Bibliothek ergänzt worden. Die entsprechende Baumaßnahme dauerte von 1998–2005 und hat das seinerzeit weltweit aufsehenerregende Konzept des vorhandenen Bauwerks bewahrt und gleichzeitig fortgeschrieben. Um Denkmalpflege im engeren Sinne ging es dabei allerdings nicht, denn für eine Eintragung als Baudenkmal war die Rostlaube noch nicht alt genug.

Die Planung durch das Büro Foster und Partner erfolgte auf der Grundlage eines 1997 gewonnenen Wettbewerbs. Die Architekten hatten damals den zunächst etwas verwegen anmutenden Vorschlag gemacht, die von Prouvé maßgeblich entwickelte und nach über 30 Jahren weitgehend korrodierte Corten-Stahl-Fassade mit ihrer vielschichtigen baukonstruktiven Problematik in ihren ursprünglichen Formen und Details im Wesentlichen zu ersetzen. Einige geringfügige konstruktive Verbesserungen sowie insbesondere eine Ausführung in patinierendem emailliertem Stahl sollten die Fassade regendicht, korrosionssicher und ausreichend wärmedämmend machen.

Für die eher nebenbei geforderte Schaffung von 2500 Quadratmetern zusätzlicher Nutzfläche zur gemeinsamen Unterbringung der Bibliotheken der Philologischen Institute hatten Foster und Partner zu der in der Ausschreibung geforderten Überbauung von zwei Höfen der Rostlaube eine Alternative entwickelt: einen separaten Baukörper auf einem als Parkplatz genutzten Grundstückszwickel. Das Preisgericht favorisierte diese Alternative einhellig, weil sie das Entwurfskonzept des Altbaus mit seinen Straßen und Höfen unangetastet ließ und eine natürliche Belichtung und Belüftung der neuen Bibliothek gestattete. Eine solche Lösung konnte aber nicht näher in Betracht gezogen werden, da nur Mittel zum Umbau des Bestandes, doch keine für einen Neubau zur Verfügung standen.

Die Überarbeitung des Wettbewerbsbeitrags führte dann zu einem Kompromiss: Foster und Partner wurde das mehr oder weniger freistehende Bibliotheksgebäude zugestanden und der Verwaltung ein Umbau, das hieß die Errichtung der neuen Bibliothek innerhalb der vorhandenen Baustruktur. Für diesen Zweck wurde die im architektonischen Konzept der Rostlaube implementierte Transformationsfähigkeit in Anspruch genommen, die es erlaubt, beliebig große Gebäudeteile relativ leicht auseinander zu nehmen und an anderer Stelle nach Belieben wieder zusammenzubauen. Mit diesem Mittel wurden die an den beiden genannten Höfen gelegenen Räume und die dazwischen gelegene Querstraße entfernt, so dass zwischen zwei Hauptstraßen ein großer, annähernd quadratischer Hof entstand.

The architectural ensemble of Berlin's Freie Universität (FU) built by Candilis, Josic, Woods and Schiedhelm together with Jean Prouvé in 1967–1973, and affectionately dubbed the "Rostlaube" (Rust arbour) by locals, has now been refurbished and extended to include a new library on the basis of a design by Foster & Partners. The construction work, which lasted from 1998–2005, has sensitively retained the internationally acclaimed existing building while at the same time creating a sense of continuity in extending it. This is not building conservation in the narrower sense, given that the FU ensemble is not old enough to be a listed historic monument.

The plans drawn up by Foster & Partners were based on their winning competition design of 1997. At that time, the architects had boldly suggested that the complex and structurally problematic Corten steel facade developed by Prouvé, which had largely corroded over the intervening 30 years, should be replaced in its original form and details. A few minor structural improvements, most notably including the use of enamelled steel with a patina, was to make the facade watertight, protect it against corrosion and improve its properties of thermal insulation.

By comparison to this challenge, the creation of an additional 2,500 square metres of floor space to house the library holdings of the university's philological departments was almost a secondary consideration. In response to the brief that called for two courtyards in the "Rostlaube" to be roofed over for this purpose, Foster & Partners came up with an alternative solution in the form of a separate building on a triangular site hitherto used as a parking space. The jury unanimously welcomed this alternative solution, as it left the older building with its streets and courtyards unaltered and permitted natural lighting and ventilation for the new library. However, this proposal could not be accepted because funding was available only for refurbishment but not for a new building.

In the end, the revised competition design was a compromise. Foster & Partner were put in charge of managing the refurbishment project to create a more or less separate new library within the existing ensemble. For this purpose, they took advantage of the versatile concept on which the original "Rostlaube" is based, which allows large sections of the buildings to be dismantled and reassembled elsewhere with relative ease. In this way, it was possible to remove the rooms situated on the two courtyards and the transverse street between them, creating one large and almost perfectly square courtyard.

Luftbild
Aerial photo

Architekten Architects Foster and Partners, London/Berlin, www.fosterandpartners.com; Team: Norman Foster, David Nelson, Stefan Behling, Christian Hallmann, Ulrich Hamann, Ingo Pott, Bettina Bauer, Stefan Baumgart, Mark Braun, Florian Boxberg, Niels Brockenhuus-Schack, Andre Heukamp, Stanley Fuls, Ulrich Goertz, Wendelin Hinsch, Andreas Medinger, Jan Roth, Diana Schaffrannek, David Schröder, Mark Sutcliffe, Hugh Whitehead **Bauherr Client** Senatsverwaltung für Stadtentwicklung, Berlin; Freie Universität Berlin **Tragwerk Structure** Pichler Ingenieure, Berlin **Wettbewerb Competition** 1997 **Fertigstellung Completion** 2005 **Standort Location** Habelschwerdter Allee 45, 14195 Berlin **Abbildungen Photo Credits** Artur, Reinhard Görner, Jürgen Henkelmann

Auf diesen Hof passte nun ein eigenständiges Bibliotheksgebäude. Es erhielt einen annähernd kreisrunden Grundriss und einen elliptischen Querschnitt. Die äußere Hülle hat ein Tragwerk aus einem Mero-System[1], das sich stützenfrei mit einigem Abstand über die in Beton errichteten Geschossflächen spannt. Die Außenhaut besteht aus Metallpaneelen und Isolierglasscheiben, denen sich innen eine weiße Membran anschließt, die den Sonnenschutz bildet; der Zwischenraum dient der Luftzirkulation.

Die Eingänge der neuen Bibliothek befinden sich im Erdgeschoss der jeweils tangierenden Hauptstraße der Rostlaube an der Stelle der ausgebauten Querstraße. Sie sind durch eine neue Straße wieder miteinander verbunden und führen zur mittig gelegenen Treppe. In den oberen Geschossen des Neubaus ist die ehemalige Querstraße als Leerraum angelegt, so dass das natürliche Licht bis weit nach unten fallen kann. Zusammen mit den entsprechend der kuppelförmigen Hülle spielerisch versetzten Geschossflächen ergibt sich so ein subtil differenziertes innenräumliches Kontinuum mit einer hohen Aufenthaltsqualität. Darüber hinaus erzeugen die beschriebenen architektonischen Merkmale in der Form eines menschlichen Gehirns eine der Funktion einer Bibliothek angemessene Zeichensprache.

Über die beschriebene besondere Lichtführung hinaus zeigt die neue Bibliothek auch andere wesentliche Merkmale, für die das Büro Foster und Partner bekannt ist. Dazu gehören unter anderem die elegante und perfekt durchgearbeitete Detaillierung sowie vor allem auch das innovative Energiekonzept. Letzteres sorgt dafür, dass das Gebäude nur an extrem kalten Tagen beheizt und bei sehr großer Hitze künstlich belüftet werden muss.

Bei der Sanierung des Vorhandenen konnten die Architekten demonstrieren, dass die von ihnen als Vorläufer betrachteten Architekten und Konstrukteure der Rostlaube mit ihrem Verständnis einer komplexen, also sensiblen, technologisch fortschrittlichen, kommunikativen und spielerischen Moderne auf dem richtigen Weg waren. Die Gestaltung der neuen Bibliothek entwickelt diese Architekturauffassung weiter ins 21. Jahrhundert. Offensichtlich ist es die gemeinsame Basis einer komplexen Moderne, durch die Alt und Neu trotz deutlicher Unterschiede in der architektonischen Konzeption hier so gut zusammenpassen.

Karl Kiem

1 Mero-System: eine Konstruktionsweise bzw. ein Raumtragwerk aus Knoten und Stäben, die Mitte des 20. Jahrhunderts eine neue und avantgardistische Bauweise besonders in der Industriearchitektur ermöglichte.

Ansicht
Elevation

Anschluss an den Altbau, Hintereingang
Connection to existing building, back entrance

This new, large courtyard was now big enough for a separate library. The library was given an almost perfectly circular floorplan and an elliptical cross section. The outer shell has a MERO-system structure that spans the concrete cast floors without supporting pillars.[1] The outer skin consists of metal panels and insulation glass panes with a white inner membrane as a sunshield, while the space between serves the circulation of air.

The ground-floor entrances to the new library are situated on the main street of the "Rostlaube" at the former crossing points of the transverse streets. A new link is now formed by a street leading to the central stairway. On the upper floors of the new building the former transverse street is now an empty space that allows natural light to fall deep into the building. This, together with the playfully staggered levels that follow the form of the dome-shaped shell, creates a subtly varied internal continuity that enhances the atmosphere within the building. The architectural details in the form of the human brain are an apt metaphor for the library.

Apart from its exceptional natural lighting, the new library has some other important features that are hallmarks of Foster & Partners' architecture. These include the elegant and superbly detailed finishes and, above all, the innovative energy concept that ensures that the building is heated or artificially ventilated only in extreme weather conditions.

In refurbishing the existing building, the architects demonstrated how well their precursors had grasped the spirit of the times in designing and constructing the "Rostlaube" as a complex, sensitive, technologically progressive, communicative and playful modernism. The new library takes this approach to architecture one step further, bringing it into the twenty-first century. Clearly, it is their shared understanding of the basic tenets of a complex modern architecture that allows the old and the new to blend so successfully here.

Karl Kiem

1 MERO-system is a modular structural system or ball-and-node space frame developed in the mid-twentieth century that has enabled the creation of innovative, avant-garde structures, used predominantly in industrial architecture.

Hauptraum, Blick Richtung Haupteingang
Main room, view towards main entrance

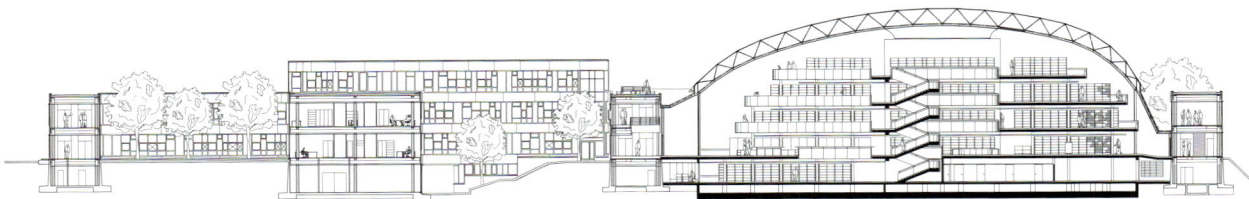

Schnitt
Section

Treppenhaus
Staircase

Galerien
Galleries

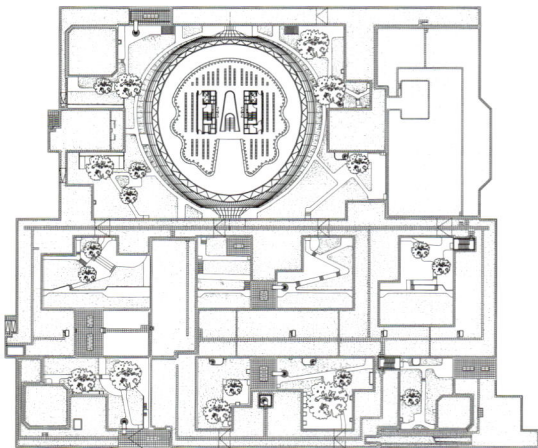

Grundriss Erdgeschoss Ground-floor plan

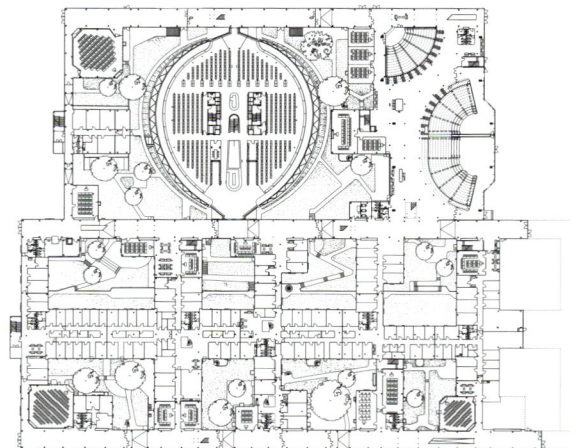

Grundriss 3. Obergeschoss Third-floor plan

Hauptraum mit Servicestation
Main room with service station

Galerie mit Leseplätzen
Gallery with reading spots

Leselounge im dritten Obergeschoss
Reading lounge on third floor

PHÆNO SCIENCE CENTER, WOLFSBURG
PHÆNO SCIENCE CENTER, WOLFSBURG

Zaha Hadid

Am Anfang war das Auto(mobilwerk): 1938 gründeten die Nationalsozialisten die »Stadt des KdF-Wagens«, um inmitten einer nur spärlich besiedelten Landschaft in der niedersächsischen Provinz – aber im Zentrum des damaligen Deutschen Reiches – die größte Automobilfabrik der Welt zu errichten. Erst als das von Peter Koller entworfene Werk Gestalt annahm, entstand vis-à-vis der gigantischen Fabrik, gewissermaßen aus dem Nichts, eine Stadt, zunächst kaum mehr als eine Werksiedlung, die sich schließlich zur kleinen Großstadt Wolfsburg mit heute annähernd 125 000 Einwohnern entwickeln sollte. Als Experimentierfelder einer größtenteils gemäßigten Moderne haben sich sowohl das Volkswagenwerk als auch die Stadt Wolfsburg schon lange einen Namen gemacht. Nun stößt die Stadt mit der »Experimentierlandschaft phæno« an der Schnittstelle zwischen Werk und Stadt in ganz neue, zukunftsweisende Architekturdimensionen vor. Die Strahlkraft dieses in vielerlei Hinsicht ungewöhnlichen Bauwerks lässt allerdings den beklagenswerten Zustand des baulichen Erbes der noch immer jungen Stadt Wolfsburg umso deutlicher hervortreten.

Stadt und Werk sind sich, nicht nur der unterschiedlichen Maßstäbe ihrer Bauwerke wegen, bis heute fremd geblieben – und in den letzten Jahren eher noch weiter voneinander abgerückt. Denn nachdem sich der Autokonzern baulich jahrzehntelang auch jenseits des Mittellandkanals engagiert und unter anderen mit dem Kulturzentrum (Architekt: Alvar Aalto, 1958–62), dem Theater (Hans Scharoun, 1965–73) und dem Kunstmuseum (Schweger & Partner, 1989–94) bedeutende Kulturbauten im städtischen Kontext gefördert hatte, errichtete er ›auf seiner Seite‹ eine autonome künstliche ›AutoStadt‹ (Henn Architekten, 1996–2000), der jegliche Urbanität abgeht, und – mittlerweile mit der Stadt zur so genannten Wolfsburg AG vereint – die »Volkswagen Arena« (HPP, 2001–2002). Diese – vermutlich nicht einmal beabsichtigte – (städte)bauliche Abwendung von der eigentlichen Stadt Wolfsburg wird nun durch das »phæno« (Zaha Hadid, 2001–2005) noch verstärkt, auch wenn in den Werbeprospekten von einem neuen Verbindungsglied zwischen Stadt und AutoStadt die Rede ist: Das phæno ist, wenngleich ein Projekt der Stadt Wolfsburg, ein neuer (stadtseitiger) Brückenkopf der AutoStadt – und ein willkommener Anlass für Besucher, sich mit der Welt der Wissenschaften und der Technik (und anschließend vielleicht auch noch mit jener des Automobils) zu beschäftigen, statt auch nur einen Fuß in die inzwischen unübersehbar desolate Stadt zu setzen.

Das phæno ist aber vor allem eine gewaltige Bauskulptur und ein Manifest heute möglicher Bautechnik. Zaha Hadid hat hier, mit Unterstützung der Lörracher Architekten Mayer Bährle, auf beziehungsweise über einem rund 13 000 Quadratmeter großen Grundstück in Sichtweite des zum ICE-Haltepunkt aufgewerteten Bahnhofs das größte in Europa jemals ausgeführte Bauwerk in

In the beginning was the car (factory). In 1938 the Nazis founded the "City of Strength through Joy" in a sparsely populated region of Lower Saxony (which was then the geographic centre of the Reich) with the aim of creating the world's biggest automobile industry there. It was not until architect Peter Koller's design began to take shape that a town actually started to grow up opposite the vast factory complex. It emerged practically out of nothing and was at first little more than a factory workers' estate, but it expanded into what is now a city of some 125,000 inhabitants. Both the Volkswagen factory itself and the city of Wolfsburg were the blank canvas for a largely temperate form of architectural modernism. Now the city is once again the scene of a bold architectural experiment: the Phæno Science Centre that straddles the boundary between factory and city points the way towards a whole new dimension of future architecture. The new building, unusual in many respects, radiates with a potency that, unfortunately, highlights the deplorable state of this still relatively new town's architectural heritage.

While the town and the factory have always remained separate – and not just because of the different scale of building on either side of the canal that runs between them – that gap seems to have widened still further in recent years. Over the decades, the automobile industry has done much to promote the construction of quality architecture on the "town" side of the canal with such buildings as the cultural centre by Alvar Aalto (1958–62), the theatre by Hans Scharoun (1965–73) and the art museum by Schweger & Partner (1989–94). At the same time, on its "own" side of the canal it has created the "AutoStadt" (Henn Architekten, 1996–2000), an autonomous artificial "city of cars" utterly lacking in even the slightest sense of urbanity and the "Volkswagen Arena" football stadium (HPP, 2001–02), now run as a joint venture between the municipal authorities and Volkswagen in form of the so-called Wolfsburg AG. Though the creation of such an architectural divide between the town and its industry was probably never actually intended, that sense of division has now been further underscored by the Phæno (Zaha Hadid, 2001–05) even though it is touted in the publicity blurb as forging a new link between the city and the "city of cars". In spite of being a municipal project, the Phæno seems to form a new bridgehead for the AutoStadt. It may be located on the "town" side, but visitors are far more likely to be tempted to go on from here to explore the world of technology and science (and, of course cars) in the AutoStadt than to bother even setting foot in the town of Wolfsburg itself, which is now looking so conspicuously bleak.

Spitze Richtung Stadt
Tip towards city

Architekten Architects Zaha Hadid Architects, London, www.zaha-hadid.com und and Mayer Bährle, Lörrach, www.mayer-baehrle.com; Team Zaha Hadid Architects: Christos Passas, Sara Klomps, Gernot Finselbach, Helmut Kinzler, David Salazar, Janne Westermann, Chris Dopheide, Stanley Lau, Eddie Can, Yoash Oster, Jan Hubener, Caroline Voet, Patrik Schumacher, Silvia Forlati, Guenter Barczik, Lida Charsouli, Marcus Liermann, Kenneth Bostock, Enrico Kleinke, Constanze Stinnes, Liam Young, Chris Dopheide, Barbara Kuit, Niki Neerpasch, Markus Dochantschi; Team Mayer Bährle: Rene Keuter, Tim Oldenburg, Sylvia Chiarappa, Stefan Hoppe, Andreas Gaiser, Roman Bockemühl, Annette Finke, Stefanie Lippardt, Marcus Liermann, Jens Hecht, Christoph Volkmar **Bauherr Client** Stadt Wolfsburg **Tragwerk Structure** Adams Kara Taylor, Großbritannien Great Britain und and Tokarz Frerichs Leipold, Deutschland Germany **Wettbewerb Competition** 1999 **Ausführung Construction** 2001–2005 **Standort Location** Willy-Brandt-Platz 1, 38440 Wolfsburg **Abbildungen Photo Credits** Roland Halbe, Werner Huthmacher, Klemens Ortmeyer

selbstverdichtendem Beton errichtet. Dieser extrem flüssige Beton kann – konventionell durch allerdings individuell zugeschnittene Schalungsbretter – in jede beliebige Form gebracht werden, ohne dass er durch Rütteln nachverdichtet werden muss.

Die rund 9 000 Quadratmeter große Aktionsfläche für Besucher, die im phæno spielerisch und experimentell an rund 250 interaktiven Stationen Prinzipien der Naturwissenschaft und der Technik kennen lernen können, lagert auf zehn unterschiedlich geneigten, als ›Cones‹ bezeichneten kegelförmigen Gebäudeteilen, die wiederum spezielle Räume und Nutzungen beherbergen: vom Laden über eine Bar, ein Bistro, ein Auditorium und ein Wissenschaftstheater bis zum recht unspektakulären und nicht gerade leicht auffindbaren Eingangsfoyer. Unter der ›Experimentierlandschaft‹ erstreckt sich eine – durch die zehn Kegelvolumina gegliederte – ruppige Stadtlandschaft, die mit ihren Niveausprüngen wie für Skateboarder gemacht erscheint und Sichtkontakte, sonst aber keinerlei Beziehungen zu den umliegenden Bauwerken gewährleistet.

Der ›Hauptweg‹ vom Bahnhof führt nicht etwa zum phæno-Eingangsfoyer, sondern nahezu direkt zu einer Brücke, die über den Mittellandkanal die AutoStadt erschließt. Wer schließlich doch das Eingangsfoyer findet und über eine Rolltreppe zur eigentlichen Aktionsfläche rund sieben Meter über dem Erdgeschoss gelangt, dem bietet sich ein schier überwältigender, auf der Nordseite (parallel zur Bahntrasse) rund 150 Meter messender Großraum, der in verschiedenen Grautönen gehalten ist: Der Industrieestrich-Fußboden, der sich stellenweise zu ›Hügeln‹ aufschwingt, die bis zu 40 Grad geneigten Sichtbetonwände (mit nur wenigen Öffnungen, die eher dem Lichteinfall als der optischen Bezugnahme auf die bauliche Umgebung dienen) und nicht zuletzt die offene Dachkonstruktion bilden einen neutralen Hintergrund für die vielen interaktiven Stationen, deren gelegentliche optische und akustische Ausreißer dem Raumeindruck insgesamt wenig anhaben können. Die freitragende, nur auf den unregelmäßigen Kegelvolumina aufgelagerte Dachkonstruktion besteht aus einem 4700 Tonnen schweren Stahlrost aus sich in unterschiedlichen Winkeln kreuzenden Hauptträgern.

Farbe haben die Architekten betont zurückhaltend eingesetzt, anders als in den manchmal recht bunten Experimentierstationen: Eine hellgrün verputzte Decke und teilweise ockerrote Wände prägen das zweigeschossige Restaurant an der südöstlichen Spitze des Bauwerks. Außen dominiert das helle Grau des fein gearbeiteten Sichtbetons, dessen Fläche durch feine Fugen zwischen den einzelnen Schalungsabschnitten und markante, kleinformatige Fenster belebt wird.

Die – leicht abgeknickte – nordwestliche Spitze des hier weit auskragenden Bauwerks zielt knapp am Bahnhof vorbei und genau auf das Autowerk: Dort, auf der anderen Seite des Mittellandkanals, spielt die Musik, scheint uns diese bauliche Geste sagen zu wollen.

Oliver G. Hamm

The Phæno is first and foremost a massive architectural sculpture that bears witness to the possibilities of cutting-edge construction techniques. Here, on (or rather above) a 13,000-square-metre site just a stone's throw from the ICE high-speed rail station, Zaha Hadid has joined forces with Lörrach-based architects Mayer Bährle to create the biggest self-compacting concrete structure ever built in Europe. Self-compacting concrete is an extremely fluid concrete that can be moulded and cast into any form using conventional and tailor-made shuttering without any need for subsequent compaction by mechanical vibration.

The 9,000-square-metre main exhibition area where visitors to the Phæno can discover technology and science at some 250 experimental and entertaining interactive stations is propped up on ten cone-shaped columns leaning at different angles. These cones themselves house various facilities such as a shop, bar, bistro, auditorium and science theatre, as well as the rather unspectacular entrance foyer, which is not very easy to find. Beneath this "experimental landscape", structured by the ten cones, is a rough urban landscape with dips and slopes that seem destined to become a skateboarders' paradise. From here there are views of the surrounding buildings, but there is no engagement or dialogue with them.

The main route from the railway station does not lead to the entrance foyer of the Phæno, but almost directly to a bridge crossing the canal to the AutoStadt. Visitors who do manage to find the entrance foyer and take the escalator up to the main exhibition area's "activity zone" some seven metres above the ground floor find themselves in an absolutely overwhelming space measuring 150 metres on the north side (parallel to the railway line). Grey, in all its hues, is the predominant colour here, from the industrial cast flooring which occasionally rises in waves, to the exposed concrete walls tilted 40 degrees (with only a few window apertures to let in light rather than to offer any views of the surroundings) and finally the open roof structure, forming a neutral backdrop for the many interactive stations whose occasional visual and acoustic excesses are completely absorbed into this huge exhibition space. The cantilever roof construction, resting only on the irregular conical columns, consists of a 4,700-ton grid of steel girders that intersect at various angles.

The architects have exercised restraint in the use of colour here, in contrast to the often very brightly coloured activity stations. A pale green ceiling and some ochre-red walls mark the two-storey restaurant at the south-east tip of the building. On the exterior, the pale grey of the fair-faced concrete predominates, its surface enlivened by the fine joints between the individual shuttering sections and by the distinctive small windows.

The slightly angled north-west tip of the building, which sweeps out strongly here, points beyond the railway station towards the car factory. Over there, on the other side of the canal, is where it's all happening. That, at least, is what this architectural gesture appears to be saying.

Oliver G. Hamm

Detail Fassade

Facade detail

Erdgeschoss Kegelhalle
Cone hall, ground floor

Gesamtansicht
Complete elevation

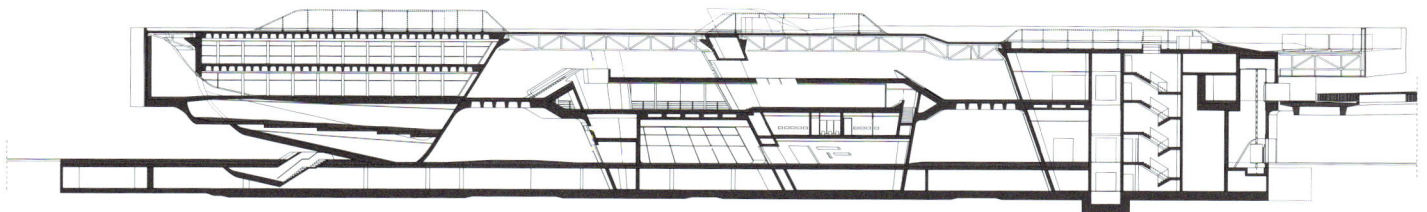

Längsschnitt
Longitudinal section

Ausstellungsraum auf der Pocketebene
Exhibition space on pocket level

Empfang im Erdgeschoss
Reception on ground floor

Schließfächer auf der Hauptebene
Lockers on main level

Durchgang zur Pocketebene
Passageway to pocket level

Laden
Shop

Ausstellungsraum auf der Hauptebene
Exhibition space on main level

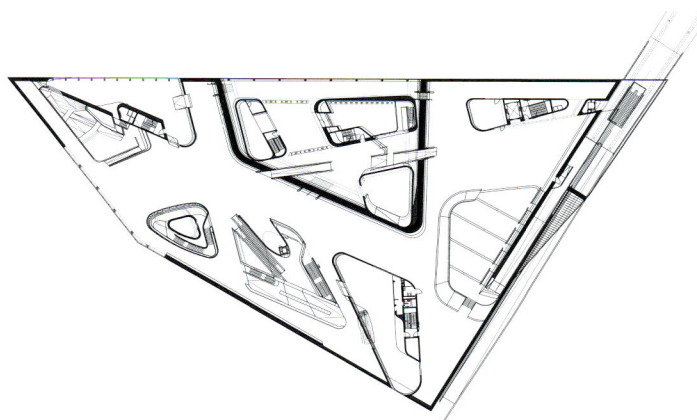

Grundriss Hauptebene und Pocketebene
Mainlevel plan and pocket level

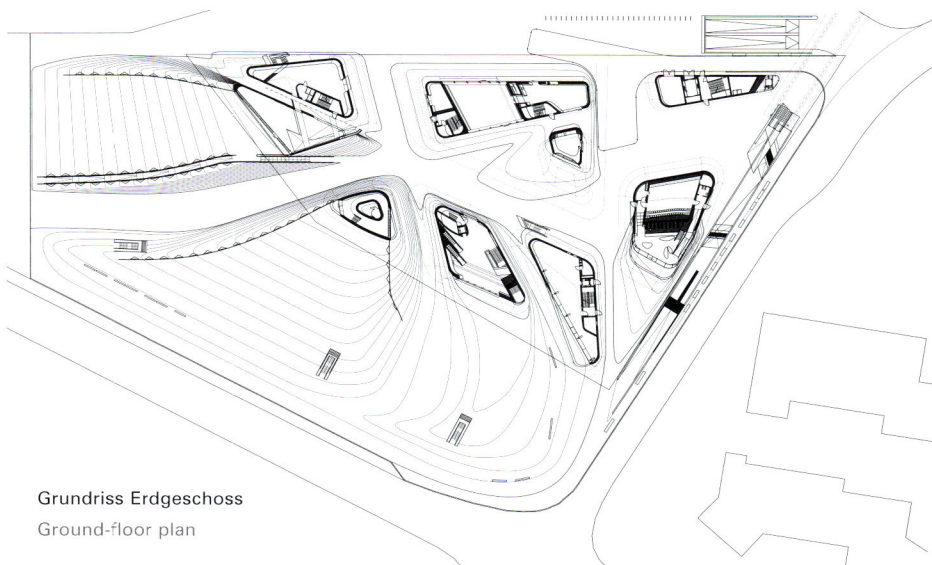

Grundriss Erdgeschoss
Ground-floor plan

INFORMATIONS-, KOMMUNIKATIONS- UND MEDIENZENTRUM IKMZ, COTTBUS
INFORMATION, COMMUNICATION AND MEDIA CENTRE (IKMZ), COTTBUS

Herzog & de Meuron

In die Lausitz der Baukunst wegen? Architekturfreunde machen neuerdings den Abstecher nach Cottbus, um das Castel del Monte des 21. Jahrhunderts zu besuchen. Leicht erhöht auf einem künstlichen Hügel stehend und ähnlich proportioniert, erinnert die neue Universitätsbibliothek unwillkürlich an die Trutzburg Friedrich des Zweiten in Apulien. Die erhabene Wirkung ist nicht nur kontextuell bedingt. Kein herkömmliches Fenster schaut in die Runde, kein Sockel, kein Gesims, kein Dach gibt dem Auge eine Hilfestellung. Nicht einmal eine Eingangstür heißt die Passanten willkommen. Irgendwo eine sechs Meter hohe schwarze Öffnung: Dorthin lenkt der Besucher zwangsläufig seine Schritte. Das Artefakt ohne Maßstab baut keinen Bezug zur Umgebung auf und bleibt unnahbar.

Es wurde verlautbart, das neue Informations-, Kommunikations- und Medienzentrum IKMZ sei bewusst an der Nahtstelle zwischen dem bisher isolierten Campus der Universität und dem Stadtzentrum positioniert worden und verbinde nun beide baulich miteinander. Offenbar will es das aber nicht, oder die Architekten hatten anderes im Sinn; denn genau dies gelingt dem Bauwerk nicht, für das man, gäbe es ihn nicht bereits, den Begriff Solitär eigens hätte erfinden müssen. Vielleicht wird es der Institution IKMZ als solcher gelingen, vielleicht knüpft sie eine virtuelle Verbindung zwischen dem weitläufigen Studiergelände und der kaum lebendigeren Innenstadt, wenn ins Bewusstsein der Bürger eingedrungen sein wird, dass hier nicht nur Studenten der Brandenburgischen Technischen Universität willkommen sind, sondern ein Serviceangebot der Informationsvermittlung und Web-Recherchen für Geschäftsleute und kleine Betriebe geboten wird; dass man hier als Cottbuser die wichtigen Zeitungen und Zeitschriften lesen kann und dass hier Ausstellungen und Veranstaltungen stattfinden, die sich nicht nur an die Alma Mater wenden.

So wird denn der Bau in seiner allenfalls als Alvar-Aalto-Vase schon einmal gesehenen, vielleicht als Zylinder mit amöboidem Grundriss zu beschreibenden Form niemals seinem Quartier zugehöriger Baubestand sein, sondern immer ein eigens anzusteuerndes Ziel darstellen, das man ganz bewusst aufsucht. Es hat allerdings den Anschein, dass die Architekten gut daran taten, den Kontext zu ignorieren und ein autarkes Fanal mit Eigenwert zu entwerfen, das weit über Cottbus hinausweist (was ihnen ohnehin mehr liegt).

Die geradezu unwirkliche Präsenz des Gebäudes, die je nach Witterung und Tageszeit zwischen ephemerer Luzidität und wuchtiger Masse changiert, ist darüber hinaus seiner Fassade geschuldet. Einer Fassade, die alles ist, nur nicht konkrete Wand, einer Fassade auch, die in Opposition zur konkreten Statuarik des Baukörpers steht, die mehrdeutig, vielschichtig, unfassbar, verhüllend und eröffnend ist, nicht Abgrenzung, sondern Grenzraum, zwischen innen und außen vermittelnd. Den Typus des Gebäudes

Why would anyone go to Cottbus for its architecture? Well, recently, architecture lovers have been doing just that to see what has been described as the Castel del Monte of the twenty-first century. Similarly proportioned and standing on an artificial hill, the new university library in Cottbus really is somewhat reminiscent of Emperor Frederick II's stronghold in Puglia. And it is not just its slightly raised setting that gives it such a majestic air. To the eye, it looks impenetrable, with no conventional windows, no basecourse, no sill or cornice, no discernable roof. It doesn't even seem to have an entrance door. Only a six-metre-high black aperture suggests that this is the way in. It stands aloof from its surroundings like an artefact with no quantifiable scale.

It has been said that the new information, communication and media centre (IKMZ) was deliberately positioned on the boundary between the hitherto isolated university campus and the city centre to forge a link between them. But the building itself does not seem to take on that role at all. Perhaps the architects had something else in mind. If it had not been coined already, surely the word "solitaire" would have to have been invented to describe this building. Perhaps the IKMZ as an institution will be able to forge the link itself – a virtual link between the sprawling campus and the inner city – once people begin to realise that this place is not just for the students of Brandenburg University of Technology, but that it is also an information and research facility for business people and entrepreneurs, where anybody can come to read the newspapers and periodicals or to visit the exhibitions and events that are not just aimed at the student population.

The new university library, which has been likened to an Alvar Aalto vase and described as a cylinder on an amoebic floorplan, will never be an integral part of its surroundings. It will always be a place apart; somewhere you actively choose to go. The architects were absolutely right to ignore the surroundings in this way and to create an independent landmark in its own right that makes its mark far beyond the town of Cottbus (fittingly enough for this team of architects).

The building has an almost unreal presence, its appearance changing with the weather and the time of day, between ethereal lightness and solid mass. This effect is due mainly to the facade, which is anything but just another concrete wall. The facade is inscrutable, many-facetted, intangible, concealing and revealing at once. It is not a boundary, but a place of transition, mediating between interior and exterior.

Rarely have Herzog & de Meuron, known for their buildings of spatial fluidity and changing surfaces that capture the essence of our world of interwoven transparency, polyvalence and virtuality, so concisely encapsulated all these factors in a single building.

Yet at the same time – and here's the rub – they have indulged

Architekten Architects Herzog & de Meuron, Basel; Team: Sarosh Anklesaria, Christine Binswanger, Jens Bonnessen, Massimo Corradi, Jaqueline Gäbel, Diana Garay, Harry Gugger, Jaques Herzog, Ana Inacio, Jürgen Johner, Carla Leitão, Yves Macquat, Matei Manaila, Florian Marti, Laura McQuary, Ascan Mergenthaler, Pierre de Meuron, Katharina Reichert, Miquel Rodriguez, Heeri Song, Marco Volpato **Bauherr** Client Liegenschafts- und Bauamt Cottbus
Tragwerk Structure Pahn Ingenieure, Groß-Gaglow **Fassadenplanung** Facade Albert Memmert + Partner, Neuss **Wettbewerb** Competition 1994 **Ausführung** Construction 2001–2004 **Standort** Location Karl-Marx-Straße 53, 03044 Cottbus **Abbildungen** Photo Credits Duccio Malagamba, Margherita Spiluttini

Ansicht Haupteingang
Elevation, main entrance

Ansicht Haupteingang, Abendaufnahme
Elevation, main entrance, evening exposure

mit »temporärer Begrenzung« und veränderlicher Oberfläche, wie ihn Herzog & de Meuron als dem Wesen unserer von Vernetzung und Transparenz, Polyvalenz und Virtualität charakterisierten Welt entsprechend sehen, haben sie selten so konsequent realisiert.

Gleichzeitig jedoch, und das macht die Sache pikant, frönen sie der neuen Lust am Ornament und überholen Robert Venturi, ohne ihn einzuholen. Denn das Haus scheint ohne kommunikatives Anliegen auszukommen, ohne Botschaft, ohne Symbolismus, weil das postmoderne Fabulieren noch immer verpönt ist. Die semantische Aufladung der Architektur ist nicht opportun, auch nicht mit Dedikationen à la ›Guild House‹, wie es Herzog & de Meuron früher hielten. Doch man wird bei der Fassadengestaltung ja wohl spielen dürfen, mit Formen und Strukturen. Und wenn dann eine Art Ornament daraus wird, ist das eben Zufall. Oder wenn man als Spielmaterial Buchstaben nimmt, warum nicht? Ein Schelm, wer zwischen Buchstabensuppe und Bibliothek einen Zusammenhang sieht.

Solcherart eingestimmt, erwarten den Besucher im Inneren frappierende Raumerlebnisse. Zwar haben die sieben Geschosse der Präsenzbibliothek eine nur knapp über den Regalmaßen liegende Deckenhöhe, doch öffnen sich im Gebäude alternierend immer wieder zweigeschossige Lesesäle, die aufatmen lassen. Zwar gehorchen die Möbel, Regale, Teppichböden, Brüstungen und Streckmetalldecken einem ruhigen Farbkanon mit gedeckten Weiß-, Grau- und Silbertönen, und dennoch triumphieren die lackierten Treppenkernwände, Stützen und Kautschukböden in fünf Farben Gelb, Giftgrün, Magenta, Zinnoberrot und Blau, die man nicht anders als schreiend charakterisieren kann. Besonders die dominante, alle Geschosse verbindende Wendeltreppe wird durch die Farborgie zur unvergesslichen Skulptur und ihre Begehung zum Architekturerlebnis. Trotz dieser heftigen Farberuptionen ist das Innere des IKMZ, welches die Architekten einschließlich der Möblierung und Leuchten komplett entwerfen konnten, von einer Leichtigkeit und Selbstverständlichkeit, die sich auf die Arbeitsatmosphäre auswirkt.

Völlig unabhängig vom Kontext ist ein Bau entstanden, der sich die Freiheit nimmt, die Welt neu zu erklären. Deshalb unternehmen Architekturfreunde die Reise in die Lausitz.

Falk Jaeger

in the new love of ornament, outdoing Robert Venturi without embracing him. For the building seems to manage without any communicative aim or message or symbolism, or any of the postmodern fantasies that are still so frowned-upon. Semantically freighted architecture is not the order of the day – not even with the kind of guild house reference that Herzog & de Meuron used to practise. But surely it is acceptable to play with the facade design a little, with forms and structures. And if that in itself turns into a kind of ornament, then surely it is pure coincidence. Why not play with letters of the alphabet? It would be petty to suggest that there is any connection between alphabet soup and library.

Having finally entered the building, visitors are unprepared for the way that space is handled here. Although the seven floors of the reference library have a ceiling height only slightly above the shelving height, the spaces alternate with reading rooms two storeys high that provide a sense of openness. And although the furnishings, shelves, carpeting, handrails and extruded metal ceilings are all in mutes tones of white, grey and silver, the stairwell walls, supports and rubber flooring are defiantly bright in shades of yellow, green, magenta, vermilion and blue that can only be described as lurid. In particular, the spiral staircase linking all the floors is a dominant feature – an orgy of colour that makes it an unforgettable sculpture to look at and an architectural adventure to walk on. For all the brashness of this eruption of colour, the interior of the IKMZ, designed by the architects themselves, right down to the furnishings and lighting, has a clarity, levity and rightness that has a positive effect on the working atmosphere.

Completely detached from its surroundings, this is a building that takes the liberty of looking at the world in a new way. And that is why lovers of architecture are going to the Lausitz.

Falk Jaeger

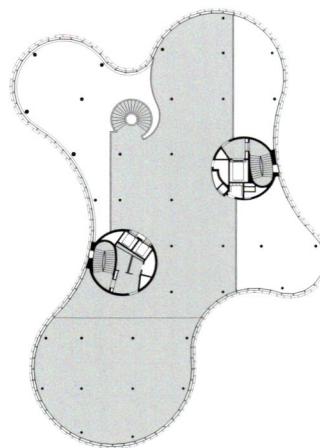

Grundriss Erdgeschoss
Ground-floor plan

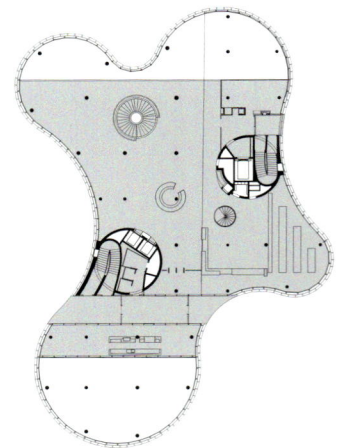

Grundriss 4. Obergeschoss
Fourth-floor plan

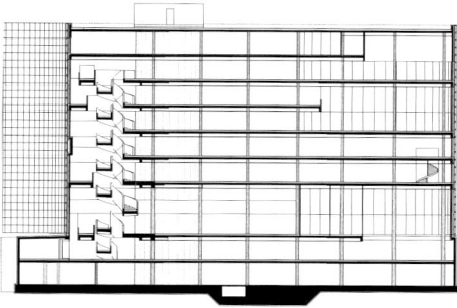

Längsschnitt
Longitudinal section

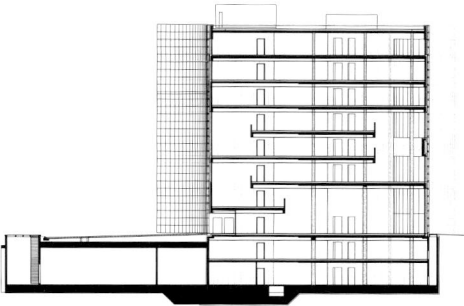

Querschnitt
Cross section

Detail Fassade
Facade, detail

Eingangshalle
Foyer

Eingangshalle
Foyer

Empore
Gallery

Untergeschoss
Basement

Lesesäle
Reading rooms

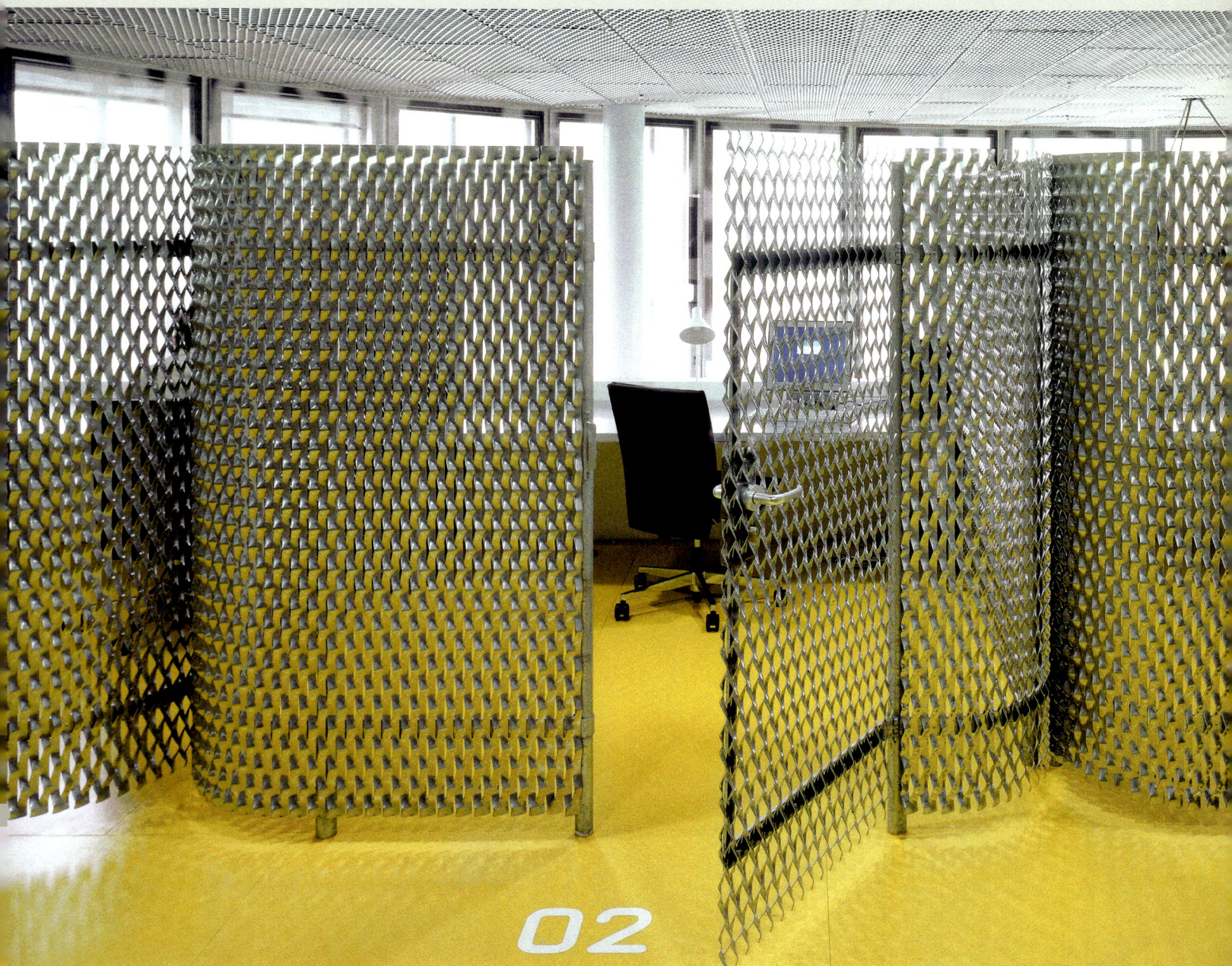

Einzellesekabine
Single reading cabin

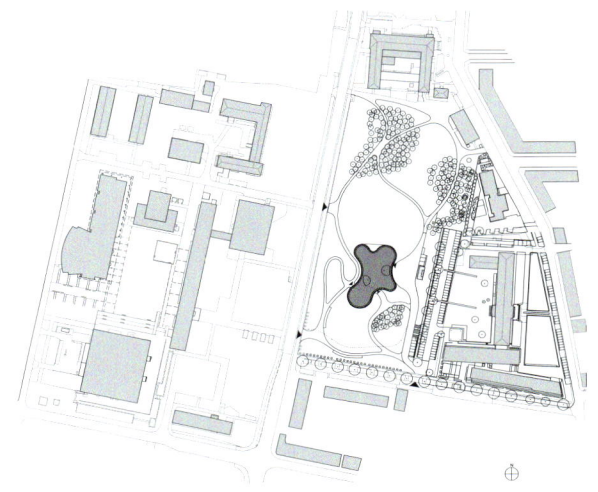

Lageplan
Site plan

MITTELDEUTSCHES MULTIMEDIAZENTRUM, HALLE
MIDDLE GERMAN MULTIMEDIA CENTRE, HALLE

Letzel Freivogel

Es gehört zu den Eigenarten der Medien, dass die Bauwerke ihrer Produktion oft viel weniger spannend sind als ihr Inhalt. Man denke an Filmstudios. Dennoch gibt es die Sehnsucht nach einer Art Medienarchitektur. Solche Visionen münden dann oft in Bildschirmfassaden, wie sie seit ›Blade Runner‹ das kollektive Gedächtnis auch der Architekten bevölkern. Medienzentren sind also latent gefährdet, Versuchslabor für solche Wünsche zu werden.

Das neue Medienzentrum in Halle an der Saale der Architekten Nadja Letzel und Gábor Freivogel enthält sich solcher Oberflächlichkeiten, und das ist gut so. Vielmehr bezieht es seine architektonische Kraft aus dem städtischen Kontext und der schlüssigen Umsetzung des Programms. Die Umgebung des Baus ist ein heterogenes Ensemble von Bruchstücken und Fragmenten der Stadtgeschichte Halles. Er liegt am Rande der historischen Altstadt von Halle, deren Struktur und Bauten nach den Zerstörungen durch Krieg und Nachkriegszeit hier aber nur noch partiell erhalten sind. Sichtbar werden diese Verluste durch das nahe Hallesche ›Loch‹ – eine große Brache am Hallmarkt unterhalb der Türme der Marktkirche. Die nahen Bauten der Händelhalle und des MDR zeigen die Modernisierung nach der Wende, können aber den Verlust an städtebaulicher Ordnung nicht kompensieren.

Zum anderen wird die Lage vor Ort durch die Saale und den Übergang zu Halle-Neustadt geprägt: direkt am Flussufer gelegen, befinden sich gegenüber in der Saaleaue der aus DDR-Zeiten stammende Klotz eines Kaufhauses und die historischen Anlagen der Saline – das historische Herz der ›Salzstadt‹ Halle. Die seltsame Konstellation dreier Brücken verstärkt die Ambivalenz dieser Nahtstelle zwischen den beiden Teilen der Doppelstadt Halle/Halle-Neustadt.

Der Entwurf übersetzt diese vielfältigen Bezüge in eine spannende Typologie. Dabei folgt das Grundkonzept erstaunlich stringent dem Bauprogramms: ein langer straßenbegleitender Riegel nimmt die kleinteilige Bürostruktur von Gründerzentrum und Universitätsinstituten auf, im Sockel werden Fernsehakademie und Studios untergebracht, ein Kubus dient vor allem als Gehäuse für den Kinosaal. An der Nahtstelle zwischen Kubus und dem von den Architekten als »Schwebekörper« bezeichneten Riegel öffnet sich der Kubus durch eine mehrere Geschosse übergreifende Halle, die ein angemessenes Entree schafft. Dieser Schwebekörper wurde bewusst ohne tragende Innenwände konstruiert, so dass der innere Raumzuschnitt variabel bleibt. Alle drei Teile werden durch die offene Gasse zwischen Kubus und Riegel sowie die Verglasung des Erdgeschosses des Schwebekörpers klar voneinander abgesetzt. Verschiedene Oberflächen verstärken die Lesbarkeit: Glas, Bahnen aus nicht oxidiertem Kupferblech und grüne Kunststofftafeln für den langen Riegel, schlichter Putz für den Kubus und einfacher Werkstein für den Sockel.

One of the things about the media is that, as often as not, the buildings in its productions are considerably less substantial than the content. Just think of the film studios. And yet, our unabated hunger for a kind of "media architecture" has spawned visions that often culminate in the screen facades which have been etched on the collective memory, including the minds of architects, ever since *Blade Runner*. Because of this, media centres invariably run the risk of becoming experimental laboratories for wishful thinking.

The new Media Centre in Halle an der Saale by architects Nadja Letzel and Gábor Freivogel does not indulge in any such superficial gimmickry. And that is just as well. Instead, it draws its architectural energy from the surrounding urban fabric and from the inherent integrity of its approach to the purpose for which it is built.

The building is set amongst a heterogeneous ensemble of motley architectural fragments from the history of Halle. It is located on the edge of the historic old town, which has survived the consequences of wartime bombing and post-war redevelopment only piecemeal. Nowhere is the extent of the damage more poignantly evident than in the nearby "Hole of Halle" – a huge urban wasteland on Hallmarkt in the shadow of the Marktkirche church towers. The nearby Händelhalle concert hall and the MDR broadcasting studios bear witness to the town's economic and architectural revival since German reunification, but they cannot compensate for the loss of urban cohesion.

On the other hand, the site is also influenced by its proximity to the river Saale and the transition to the Communist-era new town of Halle-Neustadt. On the banks of the river, on the Saaleaue flood meadows, the gigantic Communist-era department store and the historic salt works that are the very heart of this ancient salt-mining town face each other down. The rather odd constellation of three bridges further underlines the ambiguity of this seam between the two constituent parts of the double city of Halle/Halle-Neustadt.

The architects have designed a building that translates these many semantic references into an extraordinarily interesting typology. Somewhat surprisingly, perhaps, given that the basic concept has adhered so rigorously to the client's brief: an elongated structure following the line of the street contains enterprise agency offices and the offices of various university faculties, while the television academy and studios are housed in the plinth and there is a cuboid structure for the cinema. On the join between the cube and the block that the architects describe as a "floating body" the cube opens up into a hall several storeys high, forming an appropriately grand entrance. This floating body was deliberately constructed without load-bearing interior walls, so that the interior

Architekten Architects letzelfreivogel architekten, Halle, www.letzelfreivogel.de; Team: Gábor Freivogel, Nadja Letzel, Günter Heiß, Jörg Wetzke, Robert Bleschert, Jan Wortmann, Thomas Schumann **Bauherr** Client Mitteldeutsches Multimediazentrum GmbH Halle **Tragwerk** Structure Bollinger + Grohmann, Frankfurt am Main **Wettbewerb** Competition 2000 **Fertigstellung** Completion August 2006 **Standort** Location Mansfelder Straße 56, 06108 Halle **Abbildungen** **Photo Credits** Punctum Leipzig, Bertram Kober

Schwebekörper und Kubus Floating body and cube

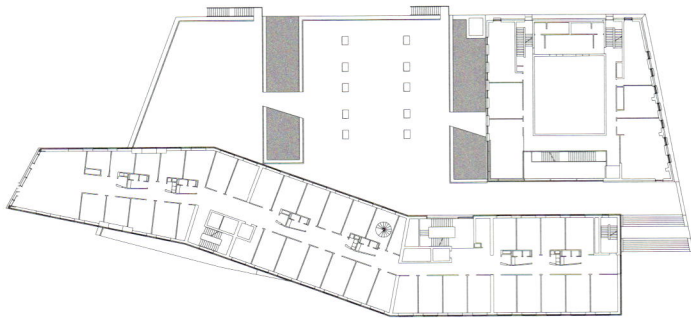

Grundriss Erdgeschoss
Ground-floor plan

Die klassische Orthogonalität moderner Architektur bricht der Entwurf auf subtile Art. Der Sockel, auf dem Riegel und Kubus ruhen, folgt dabei schlicht der Grundstücksgrenze und verlässt an den Ecken den rechten Winkel. Die Brechungen des Schwebekörpers lassen sich als eher freie Reaktionen auf den Verlauf des Straßenraums deuten, die vertikal geneigten Wände des Kubus nehmen diesen sanft zurück und fügen ihn damit geschickt in die hier fast kleinstädtische Umgebung ein. Der freie Umgang mit den Konventionen scheut nicht vor starken Gesten zurück: Der Riegel folgt zunächst dem Profil der als Brückenrampe ansteigenden Mansfelder Straße, löst sich dann frei vom Erdgeschoss, um sich nur von zwei Stützen gehalten der Saale entgegenzustrecken. Die zwei V-förmigen Betonpfeiler sind kein bloßes Revival der 60er-Jahre, sondern vor allem ein dezenter Verweis auf ein Bauwerk, das Halle bis heute prägt, die Hochstraße. Der Abschluss des Schwebekörpers zur Saale erfolgt markant als schräger Schnitt, der das Innere hinter Glas freilegt und Räume mit wunderbarem Blick auf die Saaleaue schafft.

Diese selbstbewusste – nie aufdringliche –, elementare – nie simple – Handschrift der Architekten macht den Bau so sympathisch. Er ist modern, ohne den Dogmen der Neuesten Sachlichkeit oder eines dekonstruktivistischen l'art pour l'art zu folgen. Das neue Medienzentrum in Halle, kaum traut man sich das heute zu schreiben, hat die Lektionen der Postmoderne – darf man an James Stirling erinnern – gelernt und verzichtet auf deren Spielereien und Niedlichkeiten. Die Lektionen heißen Lesbarkeit der Idee, Interpretation und Fortschreibung der Stadt sowie Mut zur eigenen architektonischen Sprache. Die hier aufgerufenen medialen Metaphern machen deutlich, dass Architektur selbst ein Medium sein kann, das zur Selbsterkenntnis und damit zum Selbstverständnis der Stadt beiträgt.

Dieses neue Medienzentrum bereichert die Stadt, auch wenn Halle nun doch nicht Kulturhauptstadt Europas 2010 sein wird, und weite Teile des ehrgeizigen städtebaulichen Programms damit wohl Vision bleiben. Ein Programm, das mit Themen wie ›Balanceakt Doppelstadt‹, ›Museumsufer‹ und ›Stadt am Fluss‹ auch auf den Ort zielte, an dem jetzt das Medienzentrum einen großen Schritt wagt. Es wäre gut für Halle, wenn es so weitergeht.

Jörg Brauns

layout remains flexible. All three areas are clearly separated from one another by the open corridor between the cube and the block and by the ground-floor glazing. Various surface finishes further enhance the legibility of the building: glass, strips of unoxidised sheet copper and green plastic panels for the long block, plain plaster skimming for the cube and simple ashlar for the plinth.

The design subtly breaks with the classical orthogonal design of modern architecture. The plinth on which the long block and the cube are resting simply follows the boundary line of the site, departing from the right angle at the corners. The breaks in the floating body can be seen as free responses to the line of the street, while the vertical walls of the cube gently incorporate this into the almost small-town feel of the surroundings. In taking such a free approach to conventions, neither have the architects shied away from bold gestures: the long block initially follows the line of Mansfelder Strasse as it rises towards the bridge, only to break away from the ground floor and reach out to the river Saale, supported by only two pillars. The two V-shaped concrete pillars are more than just a nod to the 1960s. They are, above all, a subtle reference to the structure of Hochstrasse that continues to dominate Halle to this day: The floating body ends at the Saale with a distinctive angular incision revealing the interior behind a glass facade where the rooms have wonderful views over the flood meadows of the Saaleaue.

The architects have made a statement here that is confident yet never brash, elementary yet never simple. And it is this that makes the building so appealing. It is modern without bowing to minimalist dogma or deconstructivist posturing. I would even be so bold as to assert that the new Media Centre in Halle has actually learned the lessons of postmodernism (James Stirling springs to mind here) and has eschewed all its frivolity and cuteness. Those lessons are: a legible concept, interpretation and continuity of the urban fabric, and the courage to formulate an independent architectural language. The media metaphors that are conjured up here clearly show that architecture itself can be a medium capable of contributing to a city's sense of identity.

Even though Halle has failed in its bid to become European City of Culture 2010 and, as a result, has shelved many of its ambitious visions for urban regeneration, this new Media Centre is undoubtedly an enrichment. The envisaged redevelopment programme based on such notions as the "Dual City Balance", the "Museum Riverbank" and the "Riverside City" was clearly aimed at the overall setting. Now, the Media Centre has taken a step in the right direction. It would be good for Halle to continue in this vein.

Jörg Brauns

Lage an der Saale
Site at the river Saale

Ansicht von der Brücke
View from the bridge

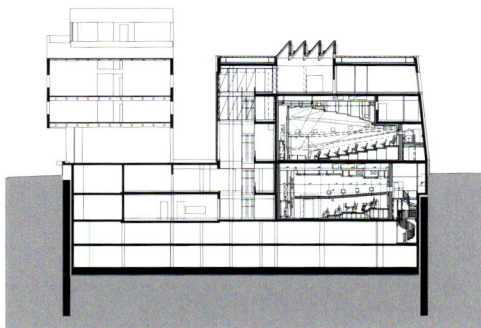

Querschnitt
Cross section

Längsschnitt
Longitudinal section

Multifunktionsraum im Kubus
Multifunctional room in the cube

Besprechungsraum im Schwebekörper
mit Blick auf die Stadt
Meeting room in the floating
body with view towards the city

Treppenhaus im Schwebekörper
Staircase in the floating body

links Fassadendetail Schwebekörper
left Facade detail, floating body

BIBLIOTHEKS- UND HÖRSAALGEBÄUDE, WEIMAR
LIBRARY AND LECTURE HALL, WEIMAR

Andreas Meck und Stephan Köppel

Auf was trifft man in Weimar schon seit geraumer Zeit, wenn nicht auf Schritt und Tritt auf das Gleichmaß und das Geordnete? Wobei die geraume Zeit mittlerweile gut 250 Jahre umfasst, und das Gleichmaß auf Schritt und Tritt ein Ensemble aus spätem Barock, authentischem Klassizismus, Neobestrebungen während der Gründerzeit, denen dann die Bauhausmoderne sezessionistisch aufgepfropft wurde. Unregelmäßige Form genauso wie Jokusarchitekturen waren nichts Rechtes für Weimar, eher die Konvention, und dafür wurde die Stadt in ihrem kleinen Kern wie von einer Eminenz an die Hand genommen und architektonisch gelenkt, jedenfalls was ihre Schauseiten angeht.

Das gilt vordergründig auch an der Steubenstraße. Denn oberflächlich gesehen, handelt es sich bei diesem Areal mit seiner historischen Blockrandbebauung zum Frauenplan hin um etwas Homogenes. Tatsächlich aber hat Andreas Meck aus München sein Bibliotheks- und Hörsaalgebäude in ein überhaupt nicht gleichartiges Gefüge hineingebaut und mit ihm eine klaffende Lücke zwischen dem gelben Backstein einer Gründerzeitbrauerei und einer klassizistischen Bebauung geschlossen, zu der der Neubau mit einem Passstück sowohl die Verbindung aufnimmt als auch Distanz hält.

Vierzehn Jahre dauerte es, um dieses Gebäude fertig zu stellen – und zu dieser Geschichte, mit Planungsworkshops, Kapitulation des Investors und schließlich der Willenslenkung durch die Bauhaus-Universität, gehört es auch, dass doch noch die Vernunft walten konnte, um ein zwischenkeliges Gebäude zu errichten, das in eine Hinterhofumgebung eingestellt werden konnte. Gleich einem Bücherregal steht darin das Gebäude und begründet mit seinen verglasten Fassaden nicht zuletzt ein schmales Forum und einen Kleincampus. Das Hochschulforum, welches durch eine Monumentalplastik aus roter Eiche (Hermann Bigelmayrs »Lehrstuhl – leer Stuhl«) räumlich stark beansprucht wird, öffnet sich dreiseitig: schmal zur Steubenstraße, dagegen breit mit einer Freitreppe zur Schützengasse sowie über recht steile Stufen hin in einen (noch ungenutzten) Hof. Dieser wird in einem spitzen Winkel gerahmt, einerseits von dem Verwaltungstrakt, gegenüber vom Hörsaal im Untergeschoss und darüber von der Bibliothek; kopfseitig spiegelt sich in der Fensterfront die gegenüberliegende Bebauung, darunter das feine Eckermann-Haus neben einigem anderen, was in den letzten Jahrzehnten an Schuppen und Anbauten hier fabriziert worden ist, bloß einen Steinwurf entfernt von Goethes wohl proportioniertem Wohnhaus.

In dieser weniger wunderlichen Mannigfaltigkeit als vielmehr gestrüpppartigen Bebauung bilden die dunkelgrau gestrichenen, bewusst ungleichmäßig behandelten, gelegentlich lehmartig wirkenden Betonflächen und die plan eingesetzten Fenster einen rationalen Kontrast. Durch eine rostrote, zweiflügelige Tür, die

For some time now – that is to say, for about 250 years – Weimar has been a place of order and unity: the order and unity of the late baroque, of classicism, of nineteenth-century neo-movements, and even of Bauhaus modernism with a touch of Secessionism. But Weimar has never really had any truck with irregular forms or gimmicky architecture. It has always embraced the conventional. This town with its compact centre is like a place that has been guided by the hand of a distinguished architectural authority – or so it seems on the surface.

It is certainly true of Steubenstraße. At first glance, anyway, this area with its historic street blocks has a certain homogeneity. In reality, however, Munich-based architect Andreas Meck has built his library and lecture hall into an urban fabric that is nothing like his own design. He has closed a gaping hole between the yellow brickwork of a nineteenth-century brewery with a piece of architecture that keeps its distance from its surroundings while at the same time forging a link. And that in itself is a classicist approach.

It took 14 years to complete this building. For all its planning workshops, conflicts with the investor and the intervention of the Bauhaus University, it has to be said that reason finally prevailed and a dual-tract building was duly inserted into a courtyard setting. Now the building stands there like a bookshelf, its glazed facades creating a narrow forum and mini campus. The forum, dominated by a monumental sculpture in red oak (by Hermann Bigelmayr, entitled *Lehrstuhl – leer Stuhl* as a pun on the university chair) has openings on three sides: a narrow opening to Steubenstraße, a broad entrance with a stairway to Schützengasse and very steep steps down into a (still unused) courtyard. This latter is framed at a sharp angle by the administrative tract on one side and by the basement lecture hall with library above it on the opposite side; at the narrow end the window facade mirrors the lovely Eckermann house and quite a lot of the sheds and extensions that have been created here in the course of the last few decades, just a stone's throw from Goethe's finely proportioned home.

Amid this motley jumble of architecture, the dark grey wash of the deliberately uneven, almost clay-like concrete surfaces and the flush windows set a rational contrast. A rust-red double door high enough to evoke the elegant grandeur of Weimar leads into the foyer. The flooring and walls are raw, the materials minimalist.

This house of books openly embraces all that is tactile. And the first and most obvious distraction for those who open a book here

Blick von der Steubenstraße
View from Steubenstrasse

Architekten Architects Andreas Meck, Meck Architekten, München, www.meck-architekten.de und Stephan Köppel, München; Team: Werner Schad, Bernd Bayer, Susanne Frank, Christoph Engler, Volker Hauth, Maximilian Rimmel, Uli Schwarzburger, Wolfgang Amann, Peter Sarger **Bauherr** Client Freistaat Thüringen, vertreten durch Staatsbauamt Erfurt **Tragwerk** Structure Pabst & Partner Ingenieure, Weimar **Städtebaulicher Ideenwettbewerb** Urban Ideas Competition 1991 **Fertigstellung** Completion 2005 **Standort** Location Steubenstraße 6, 99423 Weimar **Abbildungen** Photo Credits Michael Heinrich

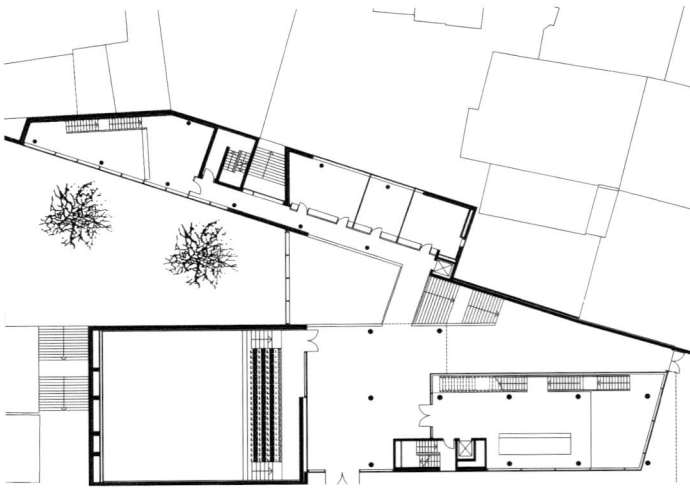

Grundriss Erdgeschoss
Ground-floor plan

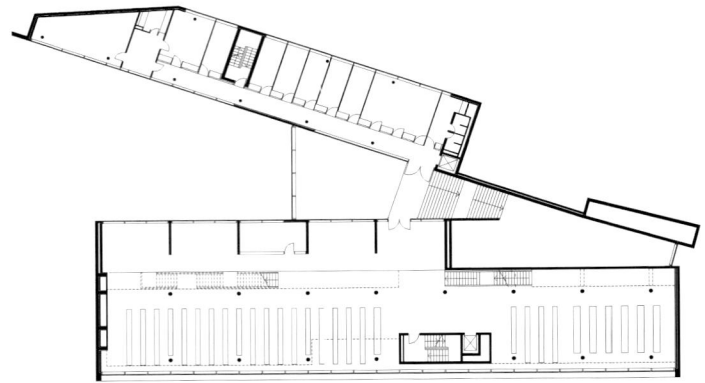

Grundriss Obergeschoss
First-floor plan

hoch genug ist, um etwas Weimaresk-Residenzhaftes zu haben, kann man auch von hier aus das Foyer betreten. Roh sind Boden und Wände behandelt, reduziert die Materialien.

Regelrecht zum Haptischen bekennt sich dieses Haus der Bücher. Und die allererste und beharrlichste Ablenkung für den Nutzer, der ein Buch aufschlägt oder sich ans World Wide Web anschließt, geschieht sicherlich durch das Eichenholz. Der Tresen für die Ausleihe, die Treppen ebenso wie die Podeste, auf denen die Bücherregale stehen, sind aus massiver Eiche. Die zum Lesen eingerichteten Boxen sind es, und die Arbeitstische sind es. Helle Eiche beherrscht das Gebäudeinnere, als Lamellen bis unter die Decken, und als Latten mit schwarzen Fugen und bis zu den Wänden des feinen Hörsaals mit seinen 420 Stadionsitzen. Herrlich ist das Holz gehobelt worden, um seitdem immer wieder mit Lauge gereinigt und in einem edlen Rohzustand belassen zu werden.

Da aber, wie man in Weimar weiß, alles bloß Gleichförmige bald durchschaut ist und die Neugier rasch resignieren lässt, schicken Meck Architekten die Nutzer ihrer Bibliothek auf eine Doppelroute: auf eine funktional klar gegliederte Promenade, bei der man gelegentlich Halt an einem geschmiedeten Handlauf findet, und einen abwechslungsreichen Parcours, der über vier Eingänge möglich ist und insgesamt fünf Bibliotheksgeschosse erschließt. Sie werden nicht allein durch weit gespannte Glasflächen belichtet, sondern auch durch Oberlichte und, etwa über die Länge des Foyers hinweg, durch miteinander korrespondierende Fenster, die auf Weimars Außenwelt gerahmte Blicke eröffnen.

Aus dieser Perspektive wiederum ist schon auf einige Entfernung hin auszumachen, dass die in die Steubenstraße leicht hineinragende Betonwand von Farbbeutelattentaten gezeichnet ist. Wie auch immer man das bewerten mag, so ist es doch am Ende stets so, das Narrenhände noch nie irgendetwas von (Bau-)Kunst begriffen haben, wo auch immer, auch nicht an einem Bauhausstandort, in dessen Stadtraum dieses Haus der Bücher auskragt. Es ist gar nicht falsch, wenn man sagt: in der Art eines Lesezeichens.

Christian Thomas

or surf the web is surely the oak. The countertop at the lending checkout, the stairs, the platforms for the bookshelves – al are of solid oak. So are the reading booths and the desks. Pale oak dominates the interior, in thin strips up to the ceiling, in broad planks jointed in black, even on the walls of the lecture theatre with its 420 seats. The wood has been beautifully planed, repeatedly washed with lye, and left in its lovely natural state.

In Weimar, however, it is well known that mere unity of form alone soon loses its appeal. And so Meck architects have sent the library users on a double route: a clearly structured promenade with a wrought handrail for occasional support, and a varied parcours that has four different entrances and gives access to a total of five different library levels. These are naturally lit not only by the extensive expanses of glass, but also by the skylights and by the corresponding sets of windows that run the length of the foyer, giving views of Weimar.

From this vantage point, even at quite a distance, it is evident that the concrete wall jutting slightly into Steubenstraße has been attacked with paint-bombs. No matter how that is to be interpreted, it is clear that there are fools who never did understand much about the art of architecture – even in Weimar, home of the Bauhaus, where this house of books stands like a landmark Or rather – like a bookmark. Idiots never understood much about the art of architecture.

Christian Thomas

Innenhof
Inner court

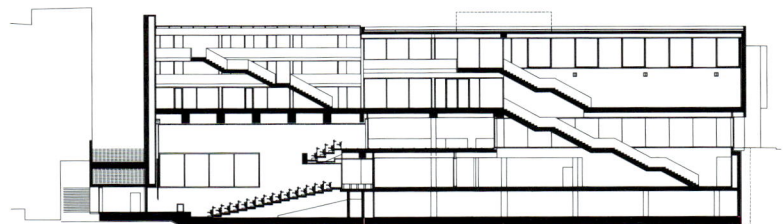

Längsschnitt Bibliothek und Hörsaal
Longitudinal section, library and auditorium

Bibliothek
Library

Treppe aus massiver Eiche in der Bibliothek
Stair of solid oak in library

Hörsaal
Auditorium

Leseräume
Reading rooms

Foyer
Foyer

FIRMENSITZ, NIEDERSTETTEN
HEADQUARTERS, NIEDERSTETTEN

Florian Nagler

Bei der Fahrt auf der Landstraße hinunter ins Tal von Niederstetten ist der Ausblick faszinierend. Auf der Kuppe der gegenüberliegenden Anhöhe zeichnet sich ein flaches, in drei gleiche Teile gegliedertes Gebäudeband ab, das über einem Meer von Einfamilienhäusern zu thronen scheint. Dort oben angekommen, befindet man sich auf einer Hochebene; ein markanter Ort, an dem die Gemeinde das Gewerbegebiet ›Hohe Buche‹ neu erschlossen hat. Der neue Firmensitz der Bass GmbH nimmt den höchsten Punkt ein.

Betrachtet man die klar aufgebauten, bis in die Details sorgsam und ohne Kompromisse durchgearbeiteten Fassaden, liegt die Vermutung nahe, dass der Bauherr ein Gespür für ambitionierte Architektur hat. Ein Gespräch mit den Geschäftsführerinnen Christel und Stefanie Leenen bestätigt dies. Sie zeigen nicht nur eine Passion für ihr neues Werkgebäude, sondern haben auch mit Neugier und Freude das Neubauprojekt entwickelt und begleitet. Es ging ihnen dabei um eine gezielte Verstärkung der Corporate Identity. Vor allem sollten die Präzision und der Anspruch der Erzeugnisse – Hochleistungs-Gewindebohrer aus unterschiedlichen Metallwerkstoffen – mit einer unverkennbar auf das Werk zugeschnittenen Architektur zum Ausdruck gebracht werden. Gleichermaßen wichtig war den Bauherrinnen bei der Konzipierung auch die gemeinsame Arbeit in offenen Raumfolgen, der Zusammenhalt der Belegschaft und damit verbunden der Wunsch einer starken Bindung an das Werk. Nötig wurde das Gebäude, da der Altbau im Ortskern Niederstettens nicht mehr den Anforderungen entsprach.

Bei der Planung ließ man sich beraten und entschied im Jahr 2002, einen eingeladenen Wettbewerb mit sieben Teilnehmern, Routiniers und jungen Architekten, auszuloben. Florian Naglers Entwurf erhielt den 1. Preis. Die Abfolge seiner drei großen Hallen (für die Werkbereiche Weichbearbeitung, Hartbearbeitung und Versand) mit zwei eingefügten Kern- und zwei Randzonen ist extrem einfach und erklärt die Produktionsschritte unmittelbar. Diese Gliederung in sieben Einheiten wird in der Freiraumgestaltung nochmals hervorgehoben. Dabei interpretierte Nagler das Landschaftsbild der umliegenden Hänge, auf denen zwischen vor Wind schützenden ›Steinriegeln‹ Wein angebaut wird, neu. Breite Erdwälle führen die bauliche Gliederung des Gebäudes fort. Auf den Wällen stehen Apfelbäume.

Im Erdgeschoss sind beide Längsseiten nach Westen und Osten nahezu vollständig verglast. Ein direkter Ausblick und gute Tagesbelichtung waren bereits beim Wettbewerb gefordert gewesen. Der Produktionsablauf der Fertigung, der sich in zwölf Schritten vollzieht, wird – mit Ausnahme der Härtung in Öfen und der Sonderbearbeitung – klar ersichtlich. Konzeptionell ist die Erschließung besonders überzeugend gelöst worden. Hinter beiden Längsfassaden verlaufen interne Wege. Im Westen ist es der vier Meter breite Erschließungsweg mit den zwei einläufigen Treppen

Driving along the road that leads down into the valley of Niederstetten, a fascinating sight comes into view. There, on the brow of the hill, enthroned above a sea of one-family houses, is a long, flat band of a building divided into three equal parts. Close up, the building turns out to be set on plateau. On this imposing site, visible from afar, the local community has created the new industrial estate of Hohe Buche, with the recently completed Bass GmbH building occupying the highest point.

This clearly structured building with its painstaking attention to detail and uncompromising facade design suggests that the client has a taste for ambitious architecture – as a conversation with executive directors Christel and Stefanie Leenen confirms. Not only are they passionate about their new building, but they have also been closely involved in its development, which they have followed with interest and enthusiasm. They wanted the architecture to enhance the corporate identity primarily by reflecting the precision and quality of their products as manufacturers of high-performance cutting and drilling tools in carbide, steel and other metals. Equally important to the clients was their wish for an open layout that would promote a sense of community among the workforce and allow them to identify strongly with their place of work. The new building was needed because the old premises in the centre of Niederstetten no longer met the company's requirements.

Following intensive planning consultations, seven architects, including established names and emerging talents, were invited in 2002 to submit their designs. Florian Nagler's design took the first prize. His sequence of three large halls (for machining before and after heat treatment and for dispatch, respectively) with two inserted core zones and two marginal zones gives an extremely simple and easily legible overview of the various stages in the production process. The open plan layout further underlines this structure of seven units. At the same time, Nagler has interpreted the topographical situation of the surrounding hills with their walled vineyards by creating broad embankments of earth as a structural continuation of the building itself and planting them with apple trees.

On the ground floor, both the long sides of the building, facing east and west, are fully glazed. This ensures the open views and natural light that the clients called for in their brief. With the sole exception of furnace hardening and special processing, every phase of the twelve-stage manufacturing process is clearly visible. Access and traffic routes within the building have been particularly

Ostfassade East facade

Architekten Architects Florian Nagler Architekten, München, www.nagler-architekten.de; Team: Matthias Müller, Almut Schwabe, Claudia Tiemann **Bauherr** Client Bass GmbH **Tragwerk** Structure Merz Kaufmann Partner, Dornbirn, Österreich Austria **Wettbewerb** Competition 2002 **Bauzeit** Construction März 2004– Januar 2005 **Standort** Location Bass-Straße 1, 97996 Niederstetten **Abbildungen** Photo Credits Stefan Müller-Naumann

Ansicht Ost East elevation

ns Obergeschoss, im Osten der ebenfalls vier Meter breite Trans-
portweg, der sich durch große Schiebetore von Halle zu Halle öffnen lässt.

Überraschend sind die beiden weitgehend geschlossenen Stirnseiten des Gebäudes, die mit ihren schmalen Rampen und Frei-
treppen nahezu gleich ausschauen. Die Nordseite dient der Anlie-
ferung und als Mitarbeitereingang, die Südseite der Auslieferung
der fertigen Produkte und als Eingang der Geschäftsführung sowie
der Kunden. Zwischen diesen Eingängen spannen sich die inter-
nen Wege entlang der Fassaden. Dieses unscheinbare Entree am
Ende einer Rampe sorgte bei Kunden und Besuchern bereits für
Irritation. Im Vordergrund steht hier ganz bewusst das Werk, die
Produktion, und nicht ein elegant hergerichteter Empfang.

Auch innen erwartet den Gast Ungewohntes: Er tritt in einen
grasgrün gestrichenen Vorraum ein, den ein Schaukasten mit den
Produkten ziert. Von dort wird er abgeholt und über das Foyer des
Haupterschließungsflurs, den nur kleine, drehbare Wandelemente
von der Versandhalle abtrennen, ins Obergeschoss mit den Büros
geleitet. Auf dieser Warte angekommen, wird der Gesamteindruck
vom überwältigenden Blick durch die Panoramafenster hinunter
ins Tal von Niederstetten und dahinter ins weite Land dominiert.
Die Büros gliedern sich entlang einer offenen Flurzone in drei
Blocks (mit den Bereichen Marketing/Vertrieb, Konstruktionsabtei-
lung und Geschäftsführung), die in der Fassade auskragen und mit
Aluminiumblechlamellen verkleidet sind. Dazwischen sind Terrassen angeordnet. Wie bei der Produktion lassen sich auch hier die
Zuordnungen leicht erklären. Nichts geschieht im Verborgenen.
Durch Verglasungen, die eine ganze Wand einnehmen, werden
auch Blicke in alle drei Chefräume gewährt. Außerdem kann vom
Bürotrakt aus durch ein Fensterband in die Werkhallen hinunter-
geschaut werden. Oben und Unten sollen jederzeit miteinander
kommunizieren können. Der hohe konzeptionelle und gestalterische Anspruch wird leider im Pausenraum für die Mitarbeiter nicht
erreicht. Dieser befindet sich in einem der mittleren Kerne. Den
einzigen Ausblick, nach Westen, beeinträchtigt eine der beiden
Treppen ins Obergeschoss. Als Brüstung dient ein Gitter aus
Bewehrungsmatten, das auch weite Teile der Glasfläche einnimmt.

Der Konstruktion der drei Hallendächer gilt eine besondere
Würdigung. Der Dachaufbau entspricht in etwa der gesamten
Höhe des Obergeschosses. Man blickt daher von den Büros in
diese Konstruktion hinein, in der sämtliche Installationen – vom

well designed. Internal corridors run directly behind the two long
facades. The west side has a four-metre wide access corridor with
two stairways leading to the upper level. The east side has a four-
metre wide transport corridor with huge sliding doors between the
halls.

The narrow ends of the building, which are more or less completely closed and almost identical, harbour something of a surprise in the form of their narrow ramps and open stairs. The north
end is used for deliveries and also acts as the main entrance for
the employees, while the south end is used for dispatching the finished products and serves as the entrance for management and
customers. These two entrances are linked by the internal corridors that run the length of the building on either side. The unspectacular entrance at the end of a ramp has already caused some
consternation among customers and visitors. But it was a con-
scious decision to put the main emphasis on the actual production
rather than creating a prestigious reception area.

The interior is unexpected: visitors enter a grass-green
antechamber in which there is a display case showing the company's products. They are met there and taken through the foyer
of the main corridor, separated from the dispatch hall by only a
few small revolving wall elements, to the office floor on the upper
level. Here, the panorama windows afford breathtaking views over
the Niederstetten valley and beyond. The offices are set along an
open corridor in three blocks (housing the sales and marketing
department, the construction department and the managerial
offices) which protrude from the facade and are clad in strips of
sheet aluminium. Between the blocks there are open patios. As on
the production floor, the company structure is easily legible here.
Nothing is hidden. Fully glazed walls permit views into all three
executive offices. What is more, the production halls below can
also be seen through a band of window. This means that communication between the two levels is always possible. Unfortunately,
the otherwise highly ambitious standards of concept and design
have not been met in the staff room, which is located in one of the
central cores. The only view from the staff room is to the west,
and even that is restricted by one of the two stairways leading to
the upper level. The balustrade is made of reinforcement mesh
which covers a considerable area of the glazing.

Finally, the structure of the three hall roofs deserves special
mention. As the roof system itself corresponds to almost the

Wasser-, Heizungs-, Druckluft- und Schmierölrohr bis zum Lüftungselement und Starkstromkabel – gut sichtbar eingefügt sind. Dabei fällt der Aufbau der lasierten Brettschichtholz-Binder ins Auge. Das Tragwerk spannt über die 28 Meter breiten Hallen und endet im Osten in der Technikzone oberhalb des dortigen Transportwegs. Es setzt sich aus drei Teilen zusammen: einem 1,28 Meter hohen Hauptträger, der die eigentliche Last aufnimmt, mit zusätzlich je einem nur 12 Zentimeter hohen Ober- und Untergurt. Die drei Teile mit einer Gesamthöhe von rund 3,50 Metern werden über eine stählerne Zangenkonstruktion zusammengehalten. In den so gewonnenen Freiräumen finden sämtliche Installationen gut Platz, sind leicht erreichbar, und für die Mitarbeiter bleibt das Raumvolumen der gesamten Halle erhalten.

Das mit Tageslicht und mit Ausblicken fast schon verschwenderisch verwöhnte Bauwerk strahlt in seiner exponierten Lage neben sympathischer Offenheit auch atmosphärisch eine große Ruhe und Gelassenheit aus. Es brilliert vor allem durch die Klarheit seiner Entwurfslogik.

Sebastian Redecke

entire height of the upper floor, all the installation pipes for water, heating, compressed air and lubricant, as well as the ventilation system and high-voltage power cables installed within it, can be seen from the offices. The glulam trusses are particularly striking. The load-bearing structure spans the entire 28-metre width of the halls, ending in the technical utilities zone above the transport corridor on the east side of the building. It comprises three separate elements: a 1.28-metre-high main girder that takes the brunt of the load, with top and bottom chords of just 12 centimetres in height. These three elements with an overall height of some 3.5 metres are held together by a steel frame, leaving plenty of space for all technical installations to be easily accessed while at the same time ensuring that the spatial volume of the entire hall can be fully used by the workforce.

This building with its enviable views is flooded with natural light. Set in an exposed position, it has a pleasantly open aspect and a distinctly calm, relaxing atmosphere. Above all, it is the sheer clarity and logic of the design that stand out here.

Sebastian Redecke

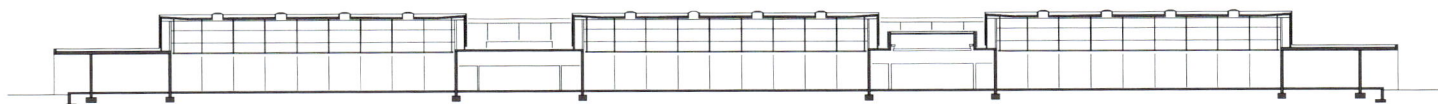

Längsschnitt
Longitudinal section

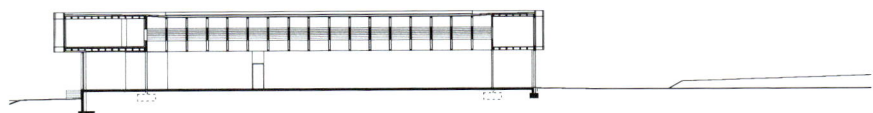

Querschnitt
Cross section

Ansicht West
West elevation

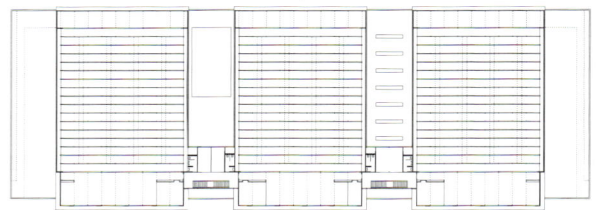

Grundriss Obergeschoss
Top-floor plan

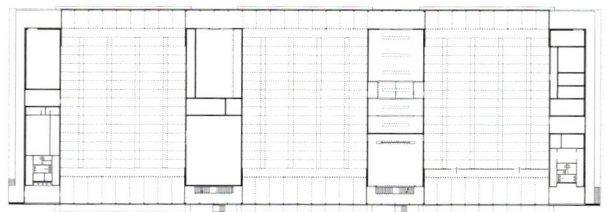

Grundriss Erdgeschoss
Ground-floor plan

Deckenkonstruktion
Ceiling structure

Werkhalle
Workshop

KAUFHAUS, KÖLN
DEPARTMENT STORE, COLOGNE

Renzo Piano

Lange Jahre kam die Kaufhaus-Architektur in Deutschland von der Stange. Erstaunlich, wie bieder sich Kaufhof, Karstadt und andere zumeist heute noch präsentieren, obwohl die Anziehungskraft einer ansprechenden architektonischen Verpackung längst Allgemeingut ist. Die Branche scheint keine Erinnerung mehr an die Prachtentfaltung des frühen 20. Jahrhunderts zu pflegen, als von Kathedralen des Kommerzes und von Wallfahrtsstätten zum Fetisch Ware die Rede war. Selbst die expressionistische Eleganz der Zwischenkriegsmoderne, mit der Erich Mendelsohn für Schocken und andere baute, geriet in Vergessenheit. Ein Kaufhaus ist die Kiste geblieben, deren Fassade mit Rücksicht auf Kunstlichtinszenierung und Regalraumeffizienz im Inneren weitgehend geschlossen ausgeführt wird, allenfalls mit ein paar Deko-Elementen als Reverenz an die Nachbarschaft versehen.

Vor allem Textilkaufhäuser machen neuerdings die seltenen Ausnahmen von der Regel. Das muss am Bewusstsein der Branche für die Bedeutung der Hülle liegen. Mit Jean Nouvels Galeries Lafayette an der Berliner Friedrichstraße fing es Mitte der neunziger Jahre an. Jetzt ist in Köln eines der so genannten Weltstadthäuser von Peek & Cloppenburg hinzugekommen. Wie schon bei den vier anderen Häusern dieses Anspruchs wählte P&C einen renommierten Architekten, in diesem Fall Renzo Piano. Der Italiener hatte zuvor die Teilnahme an einem Wettbewerb abgelehnt und kokett die Direktbeauftragung gefordert. Die Modeunternehmer sind mittlerweile reich dafür belohnt worden, dass sie sich darauf eingelassen haben. Im Rückblick relativiert sich denn auch der Ärger über die langwierige Baugeschichte. Wegen eines Streits zwischen Bauherrn und Generalübernehmer herrschte zwei Jahre lang Stillstand auf der Baustelle. Hinter dem Zwist standen statische Schwierigkeiten mit der anspruchsvollen Konstruktion, die schließlich durch Umplanungen gelöst werden konnten.

Auf einem schwierigen Grundstück hat Piano ein kleines Raum- und Gestaltwunder vollbracht. Über der Tunnelrampe der so genannten Nord-Süd-Fahrt, zwischen einer Hauptverkehrsachse namens Cäcilienstraße und der Schildergasse, einer der wichtigsten Einkaufsmeilen Kölns, hat er einen Bau nach Art der Blobmeister gesetzt – einen 130 Meter langen und bis zu 34 Meter hohen Glaskörper aus 6800 Scheiben, jede von ihnen ein handgefertigtes Unikat. Mag sich Piano mit seinem Entwurf auch am eigenen IBM Travelling Pavillon orientiert haben, hat er dennoch für Köln einen Spannungsbogen maßgeschneidert, der dem bisherigen Unort eine Fassung gibt. Allerdings musste auch Pianos Blob geerdet werden: Der gläserne Lindwurm schmiegt sich an einen Kubus, der entlang der Antonsgasse mit einer monotonen, 30 Meter hohen und 100 Meter langen Natursteinfassade mit wenigen Fenstern aufragt. Darin sind weitere Verkaufsflächen, aber auch Büros und Nebenräume untergebracht.

For years, department stores in Germany were architecturally bland. Even now, in a time when the appeal of good architectural design is universally acknowledged, it is remarkable how run-of-the-mill such chains as Kaufhof, Karstadt and the like still tend to be. This sector seems to have forgotten the heady days of the early twentieth century when department stores were described as cathedrals of commerce, dedicated to the fetish of the commodity. Even the Expressionist elegance of the interwar years, when Erich Mendelsohn designed buildings for Schocken and others, has faded from memory. A department store has become little more than a box with a closed facade on which only the occasional decorative touch pays lip service to its surroundings – all the better to maximise the shelving and display fittings in the artificially lit interior.

Lately, there have been some notable exceptions to this rule, especially in the clothing sector. Perhaps that has something to do with the fashion industry's awareness of the importance of outward appearances. It all began with Jean Nouvel's Galeries Lafayette on Friedrichstrasse in Berlin in the mid 1990s. And now Cologne has its very own flagship Peek & Cloppenburg store – the fifth in a series of prestigious new "Weltstadthaus" outlets for which the company has commissioned high-profile architects. In this case, they chose Renzo Piano. The Italian architect had previously turned down the invitation to take part in a design competition, boldly asserting that he would accept only a direct commission. The fashion company has been richly rewarded for going along with that. In retrospect, even the long and fraught saga of its delayed construction seems to have been worthwhile. Disagreement between the client and the general contractor about the structural challenges posed by the sophisticated design brought the building site grinding to a halt for two years. In the end, with a few amendments, a solution was found.

Piano has achieved something of a miracle of space and design on this difficult site. Straddling a motorway underpass and wedged between the arterial thoroughfare of Cäcilienstrasse and the busy shopping street of Schildergasse, he has created a kind of Blobmeister architecture: a 130-metre-long glass construction, up to 34 metres high in places, whose 6,800 panes are each unique and handmade. Though Piano may have based the design on his own IBM Travelling Pavilion, his Cologne department store is tailor-made to arch its way sinuously into this space, lending real presence to what was previously a drearily non-descript urban area. But even Piano's "blob" has a more conventional side: this glass creature nestles against a cubic tract on the Antonsgasse side whose homogeneous 30-metre-high and 100-metre-long natural stone facade has only a few windows and contains not only additional shop floor space, but also offices and ancillary rooms.

Architekten Architects Renzo Piano Building Workshop, Genova, Italien, www.rpbw.com; Team: B. Plattner, E. Volz, L. Coreth, J. Knaak, J. Ruoff, A. Symietz, R. Baumgarten, A. Belvedere, J. Carter, O. Hempel, J. Paik, M. Prini, J. Wagner; O. Aubert, C. Colson, P. Furnemont, Y. Kyrkos **Tragwerk** Structure Knippers & Helbig **Fassade** Facade Büro Mosbacher **Geometrische Studien** Geometry Studies A. Walz **Ausführung** Construction 1999–2005 **Standort** Location Schildergasse 65–67, 50667 Köln **Abbildungen** Photo Credits Michel Denancé

Lage in der Stadt
Site in the city

Architektonisch eine Ausnahmeerscheinung in der banalen Umgebung schlichter Schachteln der Nachkriegszeit, zeigt sich das Kaufhaus städtebaulich überaus feinfühlig. Der Glasbau dreht vor der spätgotischen Antoniterkirche an der Schildergasse – weit und breit das einzige Überbleibsel des alten Köln – respektvoll bei und fällt auch in der Höhe etwas ab. Indem Pianos P&C die Bedeutung des Nachbarn hervorhebt und mit ihm einen neuen Platz bildet, entsteht eine Art Solidarität der Solitäre gegen die Zumutungen der Zweckbauten.

In der Stadt wird Pianos Orangerie der Mode mit einer Verkaufsfläche von rund 14400 Quadratmetern als »gestrandeter Wal« bezeichnet. Wie bei aller zeichenhaften Architektur von Qualität öffnet sich ein ganzes Assoziationsfeld. Auch von einer Seifenblase ist die Rede und von einem geblähten Spinnaker. Piano selbst soll von einer »magischen Laterne« gesprochen haben, die das ganze Haus in ein Schaufenster verwandele. Dazu gehört auch, dass eine Hierarchie von Vorder- und Rückseite nicht auszumachen ist. Der Cäcilienstraße wendet der Wal seinen markanten, aber türlosen Kopf zu, der Schildergasse die Flosse mit dem Haupteingang.

Die Wunderlampe entfaltet ihre Wirkung auf Passanten vor allem durch die Überlagerung von Transparenz und Spiegelung, die je nach Lichtstand Einblicke gewährt oder verweigert. Die Hülle aus Sonnenschutzglas ist vollständig vom fünfgeschossigen Stahlbeton-Skelettbau im Inneren losgelöst. Ein Abstand von zumeist 1,20 Metern liegt zwischen den Geschossdeckenrändern und der Fassade, die von 66 geschwungenen Holzleimbindern aus sibirischer Lärche getragen wird. Im Atrium an der Schildergasse sind es sogar mehr als fünf Meter. Wer hier den Blick hebt, der sieht die einzelnen Geschosse gestaffelt wie die Decks eines Schiffes.

Im Inneren kann der Bau nicht ganz das halten, was die Hülle verspricht. Die Materialien wie Eichenparkett und Steinfußboden gab P&C vor, ebenso die Multifunktionsdecken. Immerhin: In der Kuppel kommt jene erhebende Stimmung auf, mit der schon die Kaufhaus-Urahnen gearbeitet haben. Es ist eine geniale Raumerfindung, die zu einer paradoxen Raumerfahrung führt: Im obersten Geschoss sorgt Piano für einen Ausblick auf die Stadt und gewährt gleichzeitig einen Einblick in den innersten Zusammenhalt seiner Konstruktion. Denn dort laufen die Holzrippen in einem Stahlfirst zusammen – der Besucher fühlt sich wie im Rumpf eines gekenterten Schiffes. Für ein Warenhaus, das ein Flaggschiff vom Stapel gelassen haben will, ist das eine gefährliche Assoziation. Der Masse der Kunden wird sie nicht in den Sinn kommen, da dieser Raum aus brandschutztechnischen Gründen nicht als Verkaufsfläche nutzbar ist, sondern nur besonderen Veranstaltungen vorbehalten bleibt.

Matthias Alexander

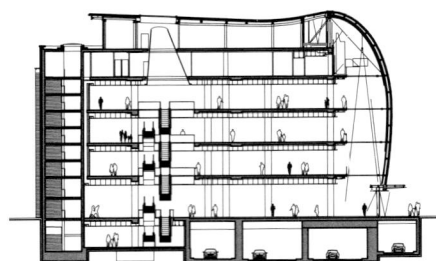

Schnitt Gebäude
Section, building

However radically Piano's design may contrast with the plain, box-like, post-war architecture that surrounds it, his department store fits into the urban fabric with great sensitivity. It turns respectfully and dips its height in deference to the late Gothic Antoniterkirche on Schildergasse. Emphasising the importance of its neighbour in this way and working with it to create a new space is like a statement of solidarity in architectural singularity against the affront of mediocrity.

Locals have already dubbed Piano's 14,400-square-metre orangery of fashion a "stranded whale". Like all iconic architecture of high quality, it triggers many different associations. It has been likened to a soap bubble and to a spinnaker in the wind. Piano himself is said to have spoken of a "magic lantern" that transforms the entire building into a shop window. There is no discernable hierarchy of facades, front or back. The whale turns its distinctive, doorless head towards Cäcilienstrasse, its tail with the main entrance towards Schildergasse.

The lantern works its magic on passers-by through its layered transparency and mirroring that change with the changing light conditions. The skin of solar-control glazing is completely separate from the five-storey steel reinforced concrete skeleton within. There is a gap of mostly 1.20 metres between the edges of each floor and the facade which is supported by 66 curved glue-laminated timber girders of Siberian larch. In the atrium on Schildergasse the gap is wider than five metres. Standing here and looking up into the building reveals the individual floors staggered like the decks of a ship.

The interior does not quite live up to the promise of the exterior. Materials such as oak parquet and stone flooring were stipulated by P&C, as were the multi-functional ceilings. But even so, the cupola has the kind of uplifting effect that the original department store architects had in mind. It is a brilliant spatial invention that creates a strangely paradoxical sense of space. On the top floor, Piano has ensured a view of the city while at the same time allowing a view into the very structure of the building. Here, where the wooden ribs connect with the steel ridge girder, the building feels like an upturned boat. For a department store chain that has just launched a flagship outlet, that may be a rather unfortunate association to make. Not that many customers are likely to notice, since fire regulations do not permit this area to be used as a sales floor. It is used only for special events.

Matthias Alexander

Haupteingang Schildergasse

Main entrance, Schildergasse

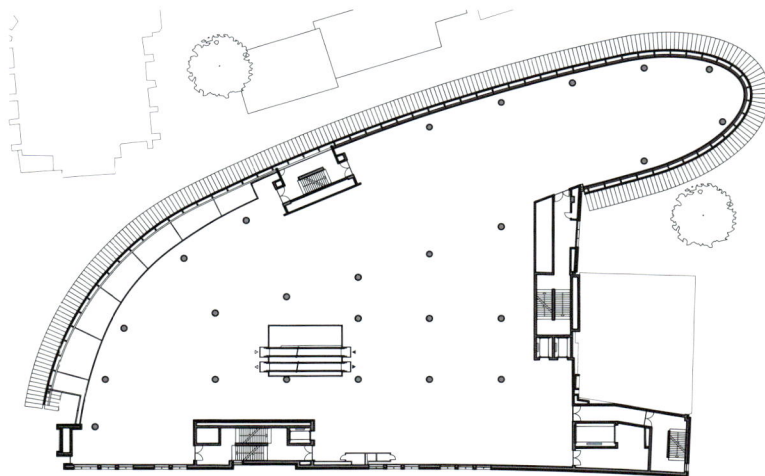

Grundriss Verkaufsgeschoss

Floorplan, shopping level

Kopfbau
Building front

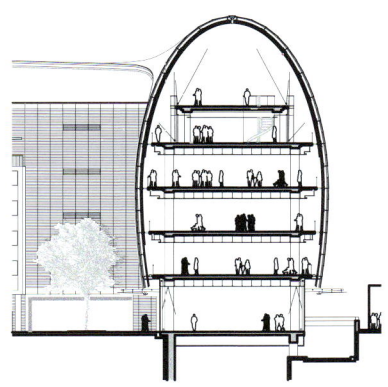

Kuppel, Dachgeschoss
Cupola, top floor

Schnitt Kuppel
Section, cupola

links Blick auf die Antoniterkirche
left View towards Antonite church

Atrium
Atrium

ZOLLVEREIN SCHOOL OF MANAGEMENT AND DESIGN, ESSEN
ZOLLVEREIN SCHOOL OF MANAGEMENT AND DESIGN, ESSEN

SANAA/KAZUYO SEJIMA + RYUE NISHIZAWA

Mitte April kam die Entscheidung aus Brüssel: Im Jahre 2010 darf die Stadt Essen den begehrten Titel der Europäischen Kulturhauptstadt führen – und mit ihr das Ruhrgebiet, das sich schon seit einiger Zeit von der größten Kohlengrube Europas zu einer dichten Kulturlandschaft mit überregionaler Ausstrahlung mausert. Ein zentraler Schauplatz der proklamierten Ruhr-Kulturkapitale wird das Gelände der ehemaligen Zeche Zollverein zwischen Essen und Gelsenkirchen sein. Nicht zuletzt wegen seines einzigartigen Bauensembles, das ein wichtiges Dokument der Industriearchitektur der 1920er-Jahre darstellt, gelangte dieses Areal 2001 auf die Liste des UNESCO-Weltkulturerbes und wird seitdem behutsam auf der Grundlage eines Masterplanes von Rem Koolhaas zum Design- und Kreativstandort ›umprogrammiert‹. Norman Fosters einfühlsamer Umbau des Kesselhauses zum red dot design museum hatte bereits 1997 den Anfang gemacht. Das neue Ruhrmuseum in der alten Kohlenwäsche und ein neu projektierter Design-Gründerpark werden ihm bald folgen. Bereits in diesem Jahr erfolgte die Fertigstellung des Neubaus der »Zollverein Design School« – einer frisch gebackenen Bildungseinrichtung, die Studierende aus den Führungsetagen von Unternehmen und Kreativabteilungen gleichermaßen rekrutiert, um ihnen Schlüsselkompetenzen im interdisziplinären ›Business Design‹ zu vermitteln.

Entworfen wurde das Gebäude von dem japanischen Architekten-Duo Kazuyo Sejima und Ryue Nishizawa (SANAA), denen man Anfang 2003 zum ersten Preis gratulieren durfte. Einstimmig hatte die Jury ihren Entwurf aus über 1 200 Einreichungen in einem zweistufigen Wettbewerb ausgewählt – eine »Sternstunde für die Architektur im Ruhrgebiet« versprach nicht nur Jury-Vorsitzender Thomas Sieverts.

Mit dem ihnen eigenen Sinn für minimalistische Einfachheit plädierten SANAA für einen Kubus mit der Kantenlänge von 35 Metern, der am nordöstlichen Rand des Zollverein-Areals unweit der Schachtanlage 1/2/8 seinen Platz finden sollte. Auf dem Grundstück einer ausgedienten, zur Gelsenkirchener Straße hin orientierten Schraubenfabrik wurde der kompakte Baukörper ganz aus Sichtbeton errichtet. Der Clou sollte dabei die Fassade sein: Statt einer Lochfassade klassischen Zuschnitts ersannen SANAA eine Außenhaut mit einer freien Fensterkomposition. Die über hundertfünfzig viereckigen, in unterschiedlichen Formaten maßkonfektionierten Öffnungen wurden unter Berücksichtigung der vielgestaltigen räumlichen Lichtbedürfnisse zu unregelmäßig über die vier Fassadenseiten verteilten, poetischen Clustern verdichtet. Das wirkt spielerisch, schafft subtile Transparenzen und weckt Assoziationen an Piet Mondrians späte Versuche, der Dynamik des Jazz und dem Rhythmus moderner Metropolen ein visuelles Gesicht zu geben.

In mid-April, the announcement came from Brussels: the city of Essen, representing the Ruhr area, a former coal-mining region that has since become a major player on the international art scene, is to be European Capital of Culture in 2010. One of the most important venues will be the Zollverein Coal Mine Industrial Complex situated between Essen and Gelsenkirchen. An outstanding example of 1920s industrial architecture documenting the evolution and decline of the coal industry, it was added to UNESCO's World Heritage List in 2001 and has since been undergoing careful conversion into a centre of art and design on the basis of a master plan drawn up by Rem Koolhaas. Norman Foster's sensitive transformation of the former boiler house into the red dot design museum already set the tone in 1997. Now the new Ruhr Museum in the former coal washing plant and a projected new Design Park are soon to follow. This year saw the completion of the new Zollverein Design School – a brand new training institute that recruits students from the management and creative sectors alike with a view to providing them with key skills in interdisciplinary business design.

The building was designed by Japanese architects Duo Kazuyo Sejima and Ryue Nishizawa (SANAA), who won the competition in early 2003. The jury unanimously chose their design from more than 1,200 entries in a two-phase competition. Jury chairman Thomas Sieverts was not alone in hailing their design as a golden moment for architecture in the Ruhr area.

With a distinct sense of minimalist simplicity, SANAA called for a 35 x 35 x 35-metre cube to be placed on the north-eastern edge of the Zollverein complex, not far from defunct mine shaft 1/2/8. The compact structure, entirely in fair-faced concrete, was built on the site of a former screw factory facing onto Gelsenkirchener Strasse. The most striking element in the design is the façade. Instead of a conventional perforated facade, SANAA devised an outer skin with a free window composition. More than 150 rectangular apertures of varying sizes and formats are distributed irregularly over the four sides of the building, creating clusters that are both aesthetically lyrical and functionally tailored to the various lighting requirements of the interior. The overall effect is playful and subtly transparent, while at the same time reminiscent of Piet Mondrian's late works in which he sought to transpose the dynamics of jazz and the rhythms of the modern city into a visual mode.

The aluminium profiles of the window apertures are set only a few centimetres into the concrete facade. An unexpectedly innovative solution in thermal insulation has allowed them to be

Gesamtansicht von Südosten
View from south-east

Architekten Architects Kazuyo Sejima + Ryue Nishizawa/SANAA, Tokyo **Generalplaner** General planner Kazuyo Sejima + Ryue Nishizawa/SANAA, Tokyo, Architekturbüro Heinrich Böll, Essen **Tragwerk** Structure SAPS/Sasaki and Partners, Tokyo, B + G Ingenieure/Bollinger + Grohmann GmbH, Frankfurt **Energiekonzept** Energy concept TRANSSOLAR Energietechnik GmbH, Stuttgart **Bauherr** Client Entwicklungsgesellschaft Zollverein mbH **Wettbewerb** Competition 2003 **Fertigstellung** Completion 2006 **Standort** Location Gelsenkirchener Straße 209, 45309 Essen, www.zollverein-school.de **Abbildungen** Photo Credits Christian Richters

Die Aluminiumprofile der Fensteröffnungen sind dabei nur wenige Zentimeter in die Sichtbetonfassade versenkt – ihr Durchmesser konnte dank einer unerwartet innovativen Lösung bei der Wärmeisolierung auf erstaunliche 30 Zentimeter reduziert werden. Statt einer herkömmlichen Dämmstoffisolierung, die eine kostenaufwändige und ästhetisch fragwürdige zweischalige Betonkonstruktion nach sich gezogen hätte, entwickelten SANAA mit ihren Projektpartnern eine aktive Wärmedämmung, die in Form eines eng gewundenen Rohrsystems in die Sichtbetonhaut eingelassen wurde. Seitdem zirkuliert Grubenwasser – auf 27 Grad temperiert und aus tausend Meter tiefen Zollverein-Stollen gepumpt – durch das Gebäude und sorgt nicht nur für die Einhaltung vorgeschriebener Emissionswerte, sondern auch für die schöne Vorstellung, dem Genius Loci des Ortes auch physisch ein kleines Stück näher gekommen zu sein.

Hinter der sichtlich hochwertig ausgeführten Sichtbetonhaut des Würfelsolitärs, der sich übrigens von allen vier Seiten begehen lässt, verbergen sich fünf unterschiedlich hoch ausgebildete Etagen, denen die verschiedenen Funktionsbereiche der Design School zugeordnet sind. Bemerkenswert ist, wie das offene Raumerlebnis des kubischen Baukörpers auf allen Etagen bewahrt werden konnte: Die Anzahl der Stützen wurde auf zwei runde Binnenstützen begrenzt, Raumabtrennungen wurden auf ein Minimum reduziert. Wo wie bei dem Auditorium im EG oder den Büros im 3. OG aus akustischen Gründen räumliche Abtrennungen nicht zu vermeiden waren, wurden sie konsequent in Glas ausgeführt.

Der transparente, offene Innenraum entspricht der Arbeitsweise und dem Selbstverständnis der Bildungsinstitution, die ein Ort der offenen Kommunikation zwischen den Disziplinen sowie ein Kristallisationspunkt vernetzter Arbeitsprozesse sein möchte. Besonders eindringlich zeigt sich die ästhetische Umsetzung dieser Programmatik auf der Werkstattetage im 1. OG. Der mit einer Höhe von über 10 Metern durchaus sakral anmutende, durch die großflächigen Fenster-Cluster vollständig vom Tageslicht ausgeleuchtete Raum ist lediglich zonal differenziert: Zonen des Entwerfens, des Entwickelns und Präsentierens bestehen hier unmittelbar nebeneinander, können gleichzeitig bespielt werden und lassen sich flexibel zu neuen Konfigurationen umorganisieren – eine ›Kathedrale der Arbeit‹, die sich immer wieder neu erfindet und vernetzt. Die vielfältigen Ausblicke, die sich durch die verdichteten Öffnungen der Sichtbetonhaut ergeben, stimulieren diese Atmosphäre des Transitorischen zusätzlich: Kaleidoskopartig lenken sie auf immer wieder neue Aspekte der alten Industrie- und neuen Kulturlandschaft Zollverein.

Dass die historischen, denkmalgeschützten Schachtensembles von Schupp und Kremmer aus den späten 1920er-Jahren durch SANAA's subtilen Eingriff in ihrer physischen und visuellen Integrität nicht gestört werden – sollte ebenfalls positiv hervorgehoben werden. Der monumentale Kubus der beiden Architekten stellt eine Hommage an die sachliche Kubensprache moderner Industriearchitektur dar – und leugnet doch nicht die eigene Zeitgenossenschaft.

Paul Andreas

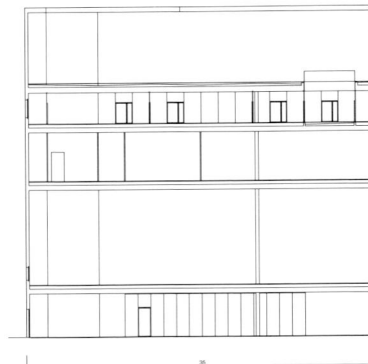

Schnitt
Section

reduced to a mere 30 centimetres. Instead of conventional thermal insulation which would have involved an expensive and aesthetically less satisfactory two-leaf concrete structure, SANAA and their project partners developed an active insulation in the form of a closely wound system of pipes embedded in the concrete skin through which thermal pit water at a temperature of 27 degrees is pumped through the building from a thousand metres down in the old Zollverein mines. While this is in itself a laudable ecological measure, it is also pleasing to think that it brings the genius loci of the Zollverein a little closer, physically.

Behind the beautifully finished fair-faced concrete skin of this cuboid building, which can be entered from all four sides, five levels of differing heights house the various functional zones of the design school. What is truly remarkable here is the way the architects have managed to retain the open sense of space on every floor of the building: There are only two round supporting columns and partitions have been reduced to a minimum. Where spatial divisions are indispensable for acoustic reasons, as in the ground-floor auditorium or the third-floor offices, they are made of glass.

The open and transparent interior reflects the work ethos and aims of this institute as a place of open communication between disciplines and as hub of interrelated processes. The aesthetic approach to this educational programme is particularly evident in the first-floor workshops. With a ceiling height of more than 10 metres, and flooded by daylight from the large clusters of windows, this space has an almost religious feel. It is divided into different zones of design, development and presentation, all juxtaposed in a way that allows interactive use and versatile reconfigurations – a "cathedral of work" marked by constant change and intercommunication. The many and varied views through the apertures in the concrete skin further heighten this atmosphere of fluidity, constantly drawing the eye to different aspects of the old industrial landscape and the new cultural one.

It should also be noted that SANAA's subtle architecture in no way encroaches on the listed historic ensemble designed by Schupp and Kremmer in the late 1920s. The monumental cube by these two architects pays homage to the functional cuboid vocabulary of modern industrial architecture without ever denying its own contemporaneity.

Paul Andreas

Blick von der Kohlenwäsche Schacht 12
View from coal-washing shaft 12

Werkstatt-Etage
Workshop

Werkstatt-Etage Workshop

Seminarräume und Bibliothek Seminar rooms and library

Fassaden-Ausschnitt

Facade detail

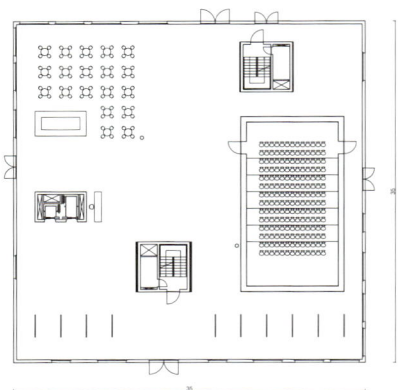

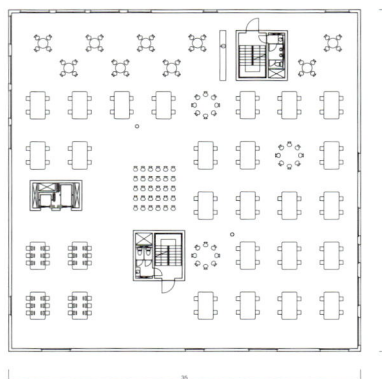

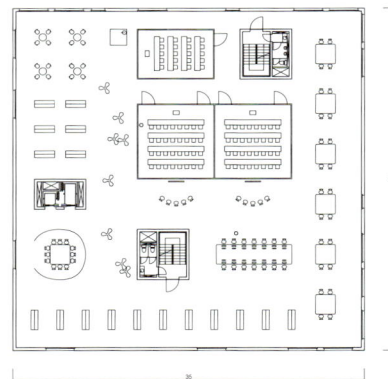

Grundriss Erdgeschoss

Ground-floor plan

Grundriss 1. Obergeschoss

First-floor plan

Grundriss 2. Obergeschoss

Second-floor plan

Werkstatt-Etage
Workshop

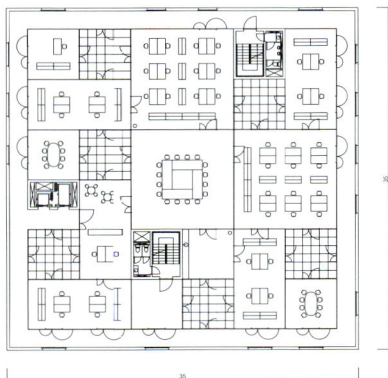

Grundriss 3. Obergeschoss
Third-floor plan

SERVICEZENTRUM AUF DER THERESIENWIESE, MÜNCHEN
SERVICE CENTRE THERESIENWIESE, MUNICH

Volker Staab

Nach 16 Tagen ist alles vorbei. Das Schunkeln, der Rausch, ein letzter Tusch. Achterbahn und Bierzelte werden abgebaut, die Hubtore des Servicezentrums sind geschlossen. Von der Höhe, vor der Ruhmeshalle Klenzes, wacht die Bavaria mit dem Löwen über die leere Festwiese. Kinder lassen Drachen steigen, ein Winterfestival, das Frühlingsfest, dann beginnen im Sommer wieder die Aufbauarbeiten für das Oktoberfest, und Mitte September ziehen Bräurosse die Wirtswagen auf die Theresienwiese.

Auf dem dazumal grünen Gelände vor den Toren Münchens endeten im Oktober 1810 die Hochzeitsfeierlichkeiten von Kronprinz Ludwig und Prinzessin Therese. Der königliche Beschluss, das Fest auf der nach der Braut benannten Wiese alljährlich zu begehen, begründete die Tradition der Oktoberfeste. Jetzt ist das Areal eine immense Schotterfläche im urbanen Kontext, durchfasert von Asphaltbahnen: Wirtsbudenstraße, Schaustellerstraße, Matthias Pschorr-Straße. Der Name Wiesn ist geblieben. Bis heute darf der innerstädtische Ausnahmeort mit den Ausmaßen von ∠20 000 Quadratmetern nicht bebaut werden, im Bebauungsplan gilt § 35, Bauen im Außenbereich.

Dann blieben die Container. Etwa 400 Mitarbeiter von 12 Behörden wie Polizei, technische Dienste, Jugendamt oder Rotes Kreuz waren 30 Jahre lang während der Festtage in 108 Containern stationiert. Weil der Abbau zu teuer und die jährliche Neuinstallation der Technik unmöglich wurden, blieben sie stehen, bis sie marode waren und schließlich der Wettbewerb für ein Servicezentrum als dauerhaftes Gebäude ausgeschrieben wurde. Die Ausnahmebegründung lautet auf einen untergeordneten Bau, der dem Oktoberfest dient. Der Bauplatz am Fuß des Hanges zur Theresienhöhe war vorgegeben, mehr als die Hälfte des Volumens sollte unterirdisch angelegt, und weder das Ensemble von Bavaria und Ruhmeshalle noch der Freiflächencharakter der Theresienwiese durften beeinträchtigt werden.

Pünktlich zur Wiesn 2004 war das neue Servicezentrum des Wettbewerbsgewinners Volker Staab funktionsfähig: 84 Meter lang, 4 Meter hoch, eingeschlagen in ein blankes Kupferkleid. Schmuckstück wurde der Bau genannt, als er so preziös zur Bavaria hinüberglänzte. Zurückhaltung? Die kam mit der Zeit. Heute moniert so mancher Anhänger des Schmuckstückes, es müsse mal wieder ordentlich poliert werden. Die metallene Lade ist so graubraun-scheckig wie der dahinter liegende Hang zur Theresienhöhe, wo sich die Farbe des Blattwerks mit der von Ästen und Erde vermischt; sie wird, ähnlich den Bäumen im Frühjahrslaub, noch mehr ins Grüne patinieren. Dass sich der Bau seinem Hintergrund mimetisch angleicht, war die Intention des Architekten: Das Servicezentrum, dessen Funktion einem Infrastrukturgerät entspreche, solle sich dem Kontext unterordnen und nicht als erste feste Bebauung der seit Jahrhunderten freigehaltenen Theresienwiese

It's all over in just 16 days. Crowds of beer-drinkers linking arms, clinking glasses, and swaying to the music of the brass band. Then the roller coaster rides and the beer tents are dismantled and the roller shutters of the service centre are pulled down and locked. The statue of Bavaria with the lion looks down on the deserted grounds from her vantage point in front of Leo von Klenze's Ruhmeshalle (Hall of Fame). Children come to fly their kites, the winter and springtime festivities come and go – and by summer the beer tents are being set up again in preparation for the Oktoberfest. By mid-September, the procession of horse-drawn beer wagons is wending its way once more through the city to the Theresienwiese.

It was here, on what was once an open field outside the city gates, that the citizens of Munich were invited to celebrate the wedding of Crown Prince Ludwig and Princess Therese in October 1810. The royals decided that the celebration should be held annually on this spot, named Theresienwiese (Therese's meadow) in honour of the bride, and Munich's traditional Oktoberfest was born. Today, what was once a green meadow is now a huge swathe of gravel in the city, criss-crossed by asphalt pathways with changing names – Wirtsbudenstraße, Schaustellerstraße, Matthias Pschorr-Straße. But the name Wiesn, as locals affectionately call both the Theresienwiese and the Oktoberfest itself, remains the same. Municipal building regulations have always stipulated that this unique 420,000-square-metre inner-city site cannot be developed; it still falls under paragraph 35, designating it an area "outside the city boundaries". But then the containers came to stay. For thirty years, the Oktoberfest had 108 containers as stations for some 400 key workers belonging to 12 different departments such as the police, technical services, youth office and Red Cross. Dismantling them every year was prohibitively expensive and re-installing the utilities each October was simply unfeasible. And so they stayed until they became too dilapidated. Eventually, a competition was held to design a permanent service centre. A loophole in the planning regulations allowed the service centre to be built as a "utility" supplying the Oktoberfest. A site at the foot of the slope towards the Theresienhöhe was earmarked. It was stipulated that more than half the volume of the building had to be underground and that neither the ensemble of the Bavaria statue and Ruhmeshalle nor the open space of the Theresienwiese should be adversely affected by it.

The new service centre designed by competition winner Volker Staab was up and running in time for the 2004 Oktoberfest: 84 metres long, 4 metres high, clad in copper. People called it a "gem" because it shone so brightly at the statue of Bavaria. Understatement? Well, that came with time. And now there are those who say the "gem" needs a bit of a repolish. The metal has

Architekten Architects Staab Architekten, Berlin, www.staab-architekten.com; Team: Alfred Nieuwenhuizen, Alexander Böhme, Madina von Arnim, Babette Schumacher, Birgit Knicker, Helga Blocksdorf, Michael Schmid, Manuela Jocheim, Jürgen Rustler, Petra Wäldle **Bauherr** Client Landeshauptstadt München **Tragwerk** Structure Ingenieurbüro CBP Cronauer Beratung und Planung, München **Wettbewerb** Competition 2002 **Fertigstellung** Completion 2004 **Standort** Location Matthias-Pschorr-Straße 4, 80336 München **Abbildungen** Photo Credits Werner Huthmacher

Lage auf der Theresienwiese mit Blick auf die Bavaria
Site on the Theresienwiese, view towards the Bavaria

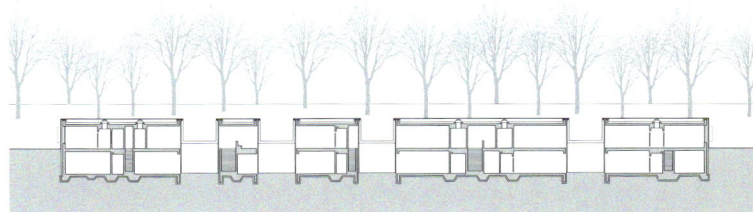

Längsschnitt
Longitudinal section

gelesen werden, so Volker Staab. Das Gehäuse aus Kupferblech-elementen und geflochtenen Streckmetallpaneelen schützt gegen die Exzesse des Bierfestes, die Fenster hinter den Metallgeflechten lassen Tageslicht hinein, aber keinen Einblick. Nur drei Hubtore sind wie bewegliche Visiere als Öffnungen kenntlich, wenn sie während der Festtage hochgezogen werden. Mit den Aufschriften: Polizei, Erste Hilfe, Festleitung ragen sie über die Dachlinie und markieren die Eingänge.

Komplexe Funktions- und Koordinationsanforderungen von zwölf Behörden bedingen die rationale innere Struktur des 22 Meter tiefen Gebäudes. Ein langer Flur entlang der Eingangsfassade ver-klammert alle Funktionsbereiche, die – als Zugeständnis an die Ästhetik oder das Orientierungsvermögen angeheiterter Festbesu-cher – farblich differenziert wurden: Die Sanitätsstation, mit sieben Behandlungskabinen auf etwa 750 Quadratmetern Fläche; Aus-nüchterungsräume für ›Bierleichen‹, die Kinderfundstelle oder die Polizeistation. Das Fremdenverkehrsamt besetzt das ganze Jahr über Büros an den Stirnseiten des Gebäudes; hier lassen sich die Flechtläden vor den Büros auch auffalten. Nur die versteckte Rück-seite zum Hang öffnet sich mit einer grünen, ungeschützten Glas-fassade um vier introvertierte Gärten im Souterrain, die in das Gebäude einschneiden und von außen nicht zugänglich sind. Mit Kupferelementen und Flechtpaneelen über den Oberlichten erscheint die Dachfläche von der Theresienhöhe als fünfte Fas-sade, die sich farblich an den Schotter der Freifläche adaptiert.

Denn das Problem der Erscheinung auf dem Ausnahmedistrikt ist nicht die Zeit der Wiesn, sondern die Monate dazwischen. Dann bleibt ein hermetisches Enigma, dem Naturhaften im Hintergrund zugetan. Mit den Bewegungen seiner Visiere aber, dem Öffnen und Verschließen der Tore, nimmt es den Rhythmus von Fest und Leere auf und verzeichnet wie ein subtiler Taktmesser den Ablauf der Jahreszyklen. Die Theresienwiese bleibt ein anderer Ort.

Michaela Busenkell

become as blotchy and greyish-brown as the Theresienhöhe slope behind it, where the colours of the foliage blend with the branches and the earth. Like the trees in springtime, it will turn greener still as its patina develops. It was the architect's intention that the building should blend into the background like this. The service centre, which, in purely functional terms, is basically an infrastruc-ture-machine, is meant to be subordinated to its context; it is not meant to be read as the first permanent building on a site that has been kept free for centuries, explains Volker Staab. The shell of sheet copper and meshed metal protects against the excesses of the Oktoberfest. The windows behind the mesh let daylight in, while warding off the curious gaze. The only visible apertures are the three lift gates that look like visors when they are pulled up during the festivities. Bearing the inscriptions Police, First Aid, Administration, they jut above the line of the roof, marking the entrances.

The complex operational requirements of twelve separate departments dictate the rational interior structure of this 22-metre-deep building. A corridor running the length of the entrance facade brackets all the different functional zones. Whether in def-erence to aesthetics or as a visual aid to the orientationally chal-lenged reveller, these are colour coded to designate the first aid area with its seven patient cubicles, the sobering-up rooms, the lost kids unit and the police station. Throughout the year, the tourist office operates branches at the two narrow ends of the building. Only the concealed back of the building towards the slope is more open, with a green glass facade set around the four little basement gardens – cut into the building and not accessible from the outside. Seen from the Theresienhöhe, the copper ele-ments and mesh panels over the skylights appear like a fifth facade whose colour blends with the gravel of the Oktoberfest grounds.

It is not so much during the actual Oktoberfest as during the rest of the year that the appearance of the building in this unique spot poses the greatest challenge. In those interim months, it becomes a sealed enigma, merging into the background. By the lifting and closing of the visor-like gates the building echoes the alternating rhythm of crowded festivity and deserted emptiness, marking the passing seasons as subtly as a quietly ticking metronome. Theresienwiese still remains a special place.

Michaela Busenkell

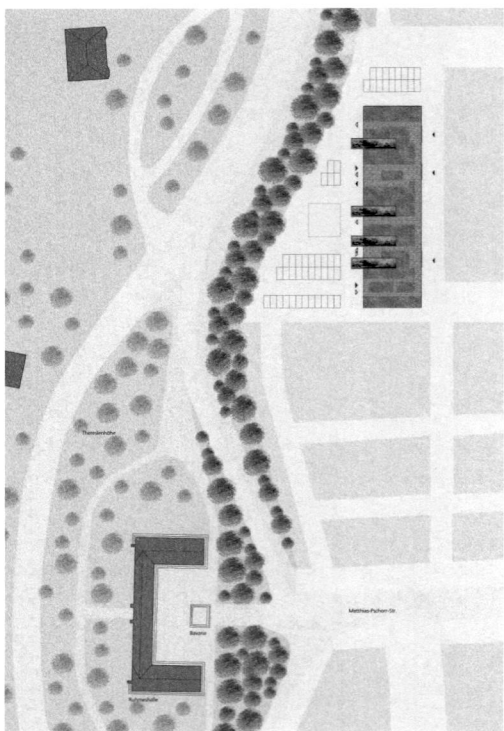

Lageplan
Site plan

Treppe im Innenraum
Staircase in interior

Garten im Souterrain
Garden in basement

Eingangsseite
Entrance side

Faltläden Folding shutters

Fassade Stirnseite Facade, front side

Patinierte Fassade
Patinated facade

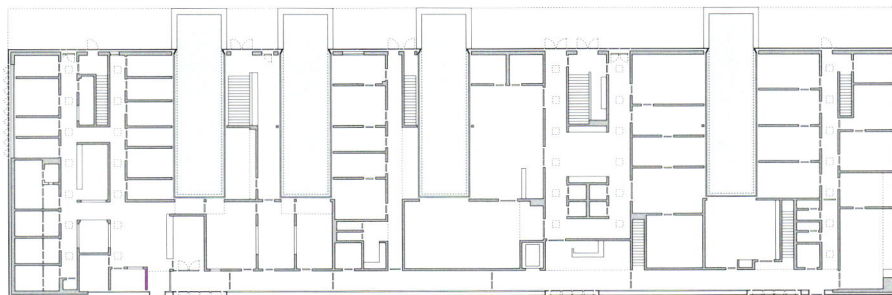

Grundriss Erdgeschoss
Ground-floor plan

NEUES MERCEDES-BENZ-MUSEUM, STUTTGART
NEW MERCEDES-BENZ-MUSEUM, STUTTGART

UN Studio

Böse Zungen behaupten, die Architekten von UN Studio um Ben van Berkel und Caroline Bos bauten einfach ihre Wettbewerbsrenderings. Das stimmt und ist doch erstaunlich. Denn Stuttgarts neues Tor von Osten entlang der B14 entpuppt sich als ein substanzieller Beitrag zur Museumsarchitektur des 21. Jahrhunderts. So ungewöhnlich die kompakte Großform ist – mit fast 50 Metern Höhe und 80 Metern Kantenlänge zeigt sich ein eher breit gelagerter, abgerundeter Körper in Form eines Wankelmotors –, so rätselhaft erscheint auch der innere Aufbau von außen. Silbrig glänzende, geschlossene Aluminiumbänder wechseln sich mit schräg laufenden, kaleidoskopartig geknickten Glasbändern ab, eine klare Geschossigkeit ist nicht ablesbar. Für die Automobilfirma ist es nicht nur ein Museum neben dem Stammwerk, sondern ein Zeichen. Vier Jahre nach Wettbewerbsgewinn wurde dieser markante Silberblock mit dem gigantischen Volumen von einer Viertelmillion Kubikmetern im Mai 2006 eingeweiht. Ben van Berkels UN Studio ist es gelungen, mit diesem Wurf in die Liga der ganz Großen einzutreten, was nicht überrascht, da sein Frühwerk wie etwa die Rotterdamer Erasmusbrücke und das Moebiushaus genau dieses Potenzial erkennen ließen.

Rätselhaft und sogar ein wenig plump: Dieses Bauwerk ist nicht wirklich ›schön‹ im herkömmlichen Sinne. Aufgrund seiner Maßstabslosigkeit, die der digitalen Entstehungsweise geschuldet ist und aus künstlerischen Gründen noch überhöht wurde, ist der Bau schwer zu deuten, macht aber neugierig. Die umgebende Industrelandschaft inmitten sanfter Hügel entlang des Neckars entspricht nicht gerade Arkadien und ist durchsetzt mit flachen Werkhallen, gewundenen Autobahnrampen mit darunter liegenden Parkhäusern und einem Sammelsurium an Zweckbauten. In direkter Nachbarschaft erstreckt sich das elegant geschwungene Oval des Gottlieb-Daimler-Stadions von Schlaich und Bergermann. Hier, wie auch bei den Gasometern im Hintergrund, lassen sich gestalterische Anleihen finden. Eine topografisch ebenso sanft gestaltete, sich sechs Meter hoch wölbende Ebene verbindet das Museum mit einem großen Verkaufshaus. Im Bauch der Ebene befinden sich neben dem Parkhaus Restaurants und Cafés, Ladenzeilen, ein Kindermuseum und sogar eine kreisförmige Openair Arena mit 500 Plätzen. Der Grund für den Hügel: Unter die Erde durfte nicht gebaut werden, läuft doch das Bad Cannstatter Mineralwasser in Form von Grundwasser unter dem Bauplatz hindurch.

Geometrisch weist der Grundriss des Museums die Form eines dreiblättrigen Kleeblatts auf. Die Struktur des Schnitts ist einer verschränkten Doppelhelix nachempfunden und integrativer Teil des Konzepts. Dieses baut maßgeschneidert auf dem schon vor dem Wettbewerb erarbeiteten Museumskonzept von HG Merz auf, so dass Form und Inhalt oder Hülle und Exponate sich gegenseitig entsprechen – was bei Museumsbauten selten der Fall ist.

Wicked tongues have been saying that the architects of UN Studio, headed by Ben van Berkel and Caroline Bos, merely build their competition renderings. Well, funnily enough, there's actually some truth in that – and the result is quite astonishing. Stuttgart's new gateway to the east, along the B14 trunk road, looks set to make a substantial contribution to twenty-first-century museum architecture. This building – almost 50 metres high and 80 metres wide, squat and rounded like a rotary engine – is unusually compact for a structure of its size. No less remarkable is the way the exterior confounds the eye and belies the interior design. Gleaming silver bands of aluminium alternate with kaleidoscopic swirls of glass, thwarting all attempts to discern where the various floors and levels might be. For the famous car company, this is more than just a museum to complement its main production plant. It is an icon. In May 2006, four years after the design competition, this distinctive silver block with a gigantic volume of a quarter million cubic metres opened its doors, catapulting Ben van Berkel's UN Studio straight into the premier league of the architectural world. In retrospect, this should come as no surprise, given the enormous potential that was already evident in his promising earlier designs for the Erasmus Bridge in Rotterdam and the Moebius House in Het Gooi.

The Mercedes-Benz Museum is enigmatic, perhaps even a little ungainly. It is certainly not "beautiful" in any conventional sense of the word. With its loss of proportion – a by-product of the digital design process further exaggerated on artistic grounds – this is a building that is intriguingly difficult to interpret. The surrounding industrial landscape, amid the gently rolling hills of the Neckar valley, can hardly be called idyllic, peppered as it is with flat-roofed workshops, motorway sliproads, multi-storey car parks and a motley array of industrial and commercial buildings. The new museum rubs shoulders with the elegantly sweeping oval of Schlaich & Bergmann's Gottlieb Daimler Stadium, which, like the shape of the gasworks in the background, has clearly provided some inspiration. A gently arching plateau six metres high links the museum with a large car showroom. In the underbelly of this space, there are a car park, restaurants, cafés, shops, a children's museum and even a circular open-air arena seating 500. The reason for this? It was not possible to excavate an underground level because of the Bad Canstatt mineral water springs running beneath the site.

Geometrically, the floorplan of the museum takes the form of a trefoil, or cloverleaf. The sectional structure is based on the shape of the double helix and is an integral part of the design,

Abendaufnahme Haupteingang
Evening exposure, main entrance

Architekten Architects UN Studio, Amsterdam, Niederlande Netherlands, www.unstudio.com; Team: Ben van Berkel, Tobias Wallisser, Caroline Bos & Marco Hemmerling, Hannes Pfau, Wouter de Jonge, Arjan Dingsté, Götz Peter Feldmann, Björn Rimner, Sebastian Schäffer, Andreas Bogenschuetz, Uli Horner, Ivonne Schickler, Dennis Ruarus, Erwin Horstmanshof, Derrick Diporedjo, Nanang Santoso, Robert Brixner, Alexander Jung, Matthew Johnston, Rombout Loman, Arjan van der Bliek, Fabian Evers, Nuno Almeida, Ger Gijzen, Tjago Nunes, Boudewijn Rosman, Ergian Alberg, Gregor Kahlau, Mike Herud, Thomas Klein, Simon Streit, Taehoon Oh, Jenny Weiss, Philipp Dury, Carin Lamm, Anna Carlquist, Jan Debelius, Daniel Kalani, Evert Klinkenberg **Realisierung Realization** UN Studio und and Wenzel + Wenzel, Karlsruhe; Team: Matias Wenzel, Markus Schwarz, Clemens Schulte-Mattler, Ina Karbon, Peter Holzer, Nicola Sibiller, Ingolf Goessel, Walter Ulrich, Christoph Krinn, Christoph Friedrich, Stefan Linder, Thomas Koch, Michael Fischinger, Bendix Pallesen-Mustaky, Stefanie Hertweck, Ulrike Kolb, Marc Schwesinger **Bauherr Client** Daimler Chrysler Immobilien GmbH, Berlin **Tragwerk Structure** Werner Sobek Ingenieure, Stuttgart **Entwurf Design** 2001 **Fertigstellung Completion** 2006 **Standort Location** Mercedesstraße 100, 70372 Stuttgart, www.mercedes-benz.com/museum **Abbildungen Photo Credits** Christian Richters

Die umgebende Industrielandschaft The surrounding industrial landscape

Aufgeteilt in nach innen orientierte und eher dunkel gehaltene Mythosräume und nach außen orientierte und tageslichthelle Sammlungsräume, werden dem Besucher zwei unterschiedliche Rundgänge angeboten, die sich immer wieder verknüpfen lassen. Der Blick ins offene Atrium sorgt dabei für Orientierung. Dort befördern drei Aufzüge die Besucher nach oben, um wie beim New Yorker Guggenheim Museum eine abwärts führende Begehung zu ermöglichen. Um alle Ausstellungsräume stützenfrei zu halten, wurden aufsehenerregende Konstruktionen geschaffen, die den Raumeindruck wesentlich mitprägen. Der ›Twist‹, in letzter Zeit eine Konstante im Werk von UN Studio, findet hier zu seiner Vollendung. Er dient dem sanften Hinübergleiten von einem Raumbereich in den anderen und manifestiert sich in Form schräg stehender Wände, die sich kontinuierlich zu Schaufeln verdrehen, auf deren Oberseiten Treppenrampen die außen liegenden Sammlungsräume verbinden. Hinzu kommen die so genannten Mythosrampen, die sich längs der innen gelegenen Mythosräume von oben nach unten schwingen und diese doppelgeschossigen Räume nach außen hin mit einer Wand abschließen. Über 30 Meter weit spannen die Deckenplatten, die dennoch Exponate mit über vier Tonnen Punktlast (wie den WM-Bus von 1974) abtragen und daher, laut dem Tragwerksplaner Werner Sobek, einen Vergleich mit übereinander gestapelten sechsspurigen Autobahnbrücken nahe legen.

In der Gesamtwirkung bietet die Verbindung der konstruktivräumlichen Elemente Twist und Mythosrampe gemeinsam mit einer Abfolge der beiden Hauptraumtypologien Sammlungsraum und Mythosraum ein räumliches Erlebnis, das schlichtweg ergreifend ist. Der Verlust der Lotrechten, der dynamisch bewegte und sich verdrehende Raum, die riesigen frei spannenden Säle und der stete Wechsel von Licht- und Schatträumen erlauben aufregende Durch- und Einblicke in aufeinander folgende Raumsequenzen – wie sie bei einem Museumsbau so noch nicht zu sehen waren.

Peter Cachola Schmal

tailor-made to accommodate the curatorial concept drawn up prior to the competition by HG Merz, designer of the museum exhibition: that form and content, space and exhibit, should complement each other – which is more than can be said for most museum buildings. Divided into dimly lit, inward-looking "Legend" rooms and bright, light-filled "Collection" rooms, the building offers visitors two different tours which can be combined or alternated at will. The open atrium provides a point of orientation. From there, three elevators transport visitors to the top of the building, allowing them to work their way down through the exhibition spaces, as in the Guggenheim Museum in New York. Extraordinarily complex load-bearing structures have been designed to ensure that all the exhibition spaces are free of columns, creating an exhilarating sense of space. UN Studio's hallmark "twist" truly comes into its own here. It creates a fluidity between the various zones and manifests itself in the sloping walls that continuously switch to shovel-like structures, with narrow stairways on top linking the outer "Collection" rooms. Interlaced ramps connecting the inner "Legend" rooms enclose the two-storey spaces with an outer wall. The floor slabs span more than 30 metres and yet they can carry exhibits weighing more than four tons per wheel (such as the 1974 German World Cup bus), which, according to structural engineer Werner Sobek, makes them comparable to a series of six-lane motorway bridges stacked on top of each other.

All in all, the combination of structural and spatial elements, of twist and ramp, together with the sequence of "Collection" rooms and "Legend" rooms, creates a spatial impression that is absolutely breathtaking. The loss of the plumb line, the dynamic fluidity, the twists and turns, the vast free-spanned spaces and the constant alternation of light and shadow create exciting vistas and views through the sequences of rooms in a way that no other museum building has done before.

Peter Cachola Schmal

Fassade
Facade

Grundriss Ebene 9, Anfang des Rundgangs
Floorplan Level 9, beginning of the tour

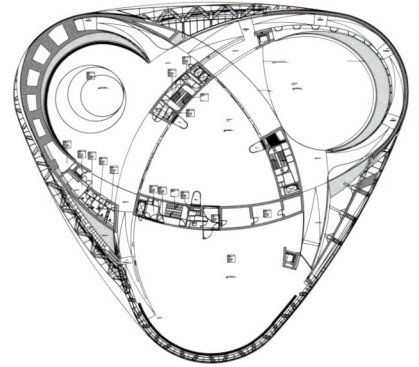

Grundriss Ebene 8, Ausstellungsräume
Floorplan Level 8, exhibition rooms

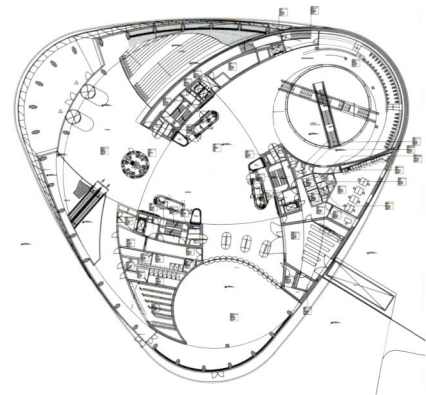

Grundriss Ebene 1, Haupteingang
Floorplan Level 1, main entrance

Restaurant auf Ebene 0
Restaurant on Level 0

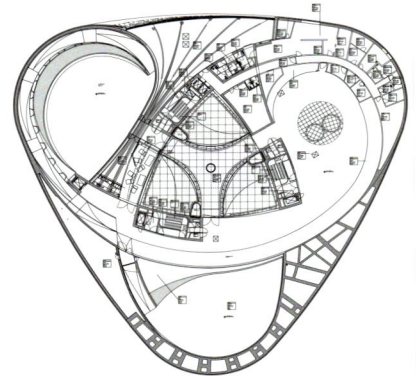

Blick ins offene Atrium
View into the open atrium

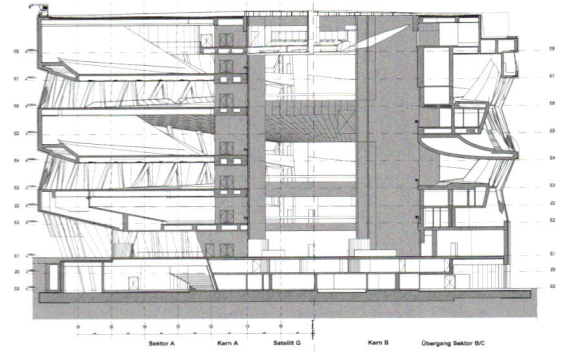

Schnitt
Section

Sammlungsraum
Collection room

Mythosraum
Legend room

Treppenhaus »Faszination Technik«
Staircase "Fascination of Technology"

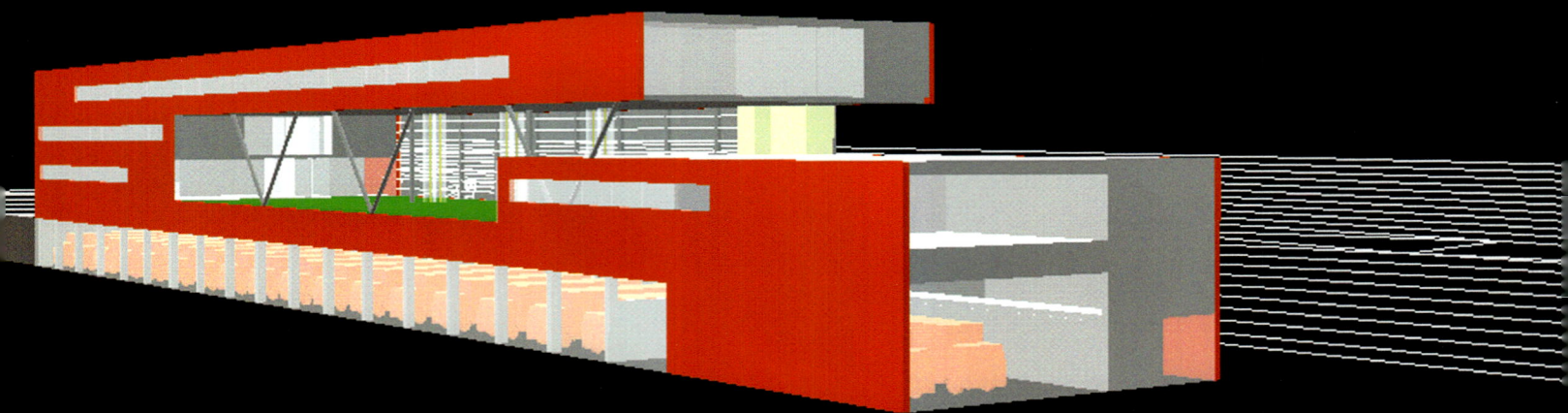

AUS DEM ARCHIV DES DAM
FROM THE ARCHIVES OF THE DAM

MIT GAUDI INS ARCHIV
LANGZEITARCHIVIERUNG VON PIXEL UND BIT
GAUDI IN THE ARCHIVES
LONG-TERM ARCHIVING OF PIXEL AND DATA

Inge Wolf

1

Nicht der Architekt der Sagrada Familia ist gemeint, GAUDI steht hier für *Governance, Architecture and Urbanism as Democratic Interaction* und meint ein Netzwerk, das im Rahmen des Kulturprogramms 2000 von der EU als Forum für europäische Architekturinstitute und -initiativen geschaffen wurde (www.gaudi-programme.net). Im Rahmen des Förderprogramms wird auch eine Arbeitsgruppe von Archivaren und Betreuern europäischer Architektursammlungen unterstützt. Daran beteiligt sind Institute aus Frankreich (IFA, Institut français d'architecture), Großbritannien (RIBA, Royal Institute of British Architects), Italien (Istituto universitario di architettura di Venezia und Ordine degli Architetti di Roma e Provincia), Belgien (CIVA, Centre International pour la Ville, l'Architecture et le Paysage), Finnland (Museum of Finnish architecture), den Niederlanden (NAi, Nederlands Architectuurinstituut), der Schweiz (Fondazione Archivio del Moderno) und Deutschland, das durch das Deutsche Architekturmuseum vertreten ist. 2002 traf sich die Gruppe zum ersten Mal, um sich mit der Problematik und den vielfältigen Auswirkungen der neuen Medien auf die Archive auseinander zu setzen. Ein Ergebnis der Zusammenarbeit ist das Internetportal www.architecturearchives.net, seit 2004 im Netz. Es zeigt Links zu europäischen Architektursammlungen und bietet einen Leitfaden zur Archivierung von Architekturdokumenten.

Archive sollen Kulturgut für Jahrhunderte bewahren und für heutige und kommende Generationen erschließen. Es liegt auf der Hand, dass diese Aufgabe im digitalen Zeitalter neue Lösungen erfordert. Beide Felder – sowohl das Bewahren wie das Erschließen – haben sich mit dem Computer stark gewandelt. Der Karteikasten hat ausgedient und wurde von der Dateneingabe und Recherche am Bildschirm abgelöst. Nutzer wünschen sich umfassenden Zugriff auf Datenbanken – wenn es geht, über alle Instituts- und Ländergrenzen hinweg. Längst sind ganze Bibliotheken digital abrufbar, wurden alte Schriftdokumente oder Bildmaterial in digitale Dokumente umgewandelt. Neues wird oft gar nicht mehr zu Papier gebracht. Leicht lässt sich am Computer alles bearbeiten, abspeichern und versenden; es steht schnell zur Verfügung, doch wie lange bleiben digitale Dokumente erhalten?

Das Problem der Langzeitkonservierung von elektronischem Material ist in den Archiven und Museen angekommen. Weltweit gibt es Initiativen, die sich darum bemühen, Standards für das Sammeln und Bewahren von digitalen Daten festzulegen. Das Interesse von Wissenschaftlern geht dabei naturgemäß weit über das von Industrie und Wirtschaft hinaus. Sind dort einmal Gewährleistungsfristen überschritten, gibt es neuere und bessere Versionen eines Produkts, kann eine alte Fassung für Firmen jede Bedeutung verlieren. Für die Forschung sind auch überholte Entwicklungen oft noch wichtig.

No, this is not about the architect of the Sagrada Familia. GAUDI stands for *Governance, Architecture and Urbanism as Democratic Interaction* – a network set up in 2000 under the EU cultural programme as a forum for European architectural institutions (www.gaudi-programme.net). The programme also supports a steering committee of archivists and librarians of European architectural collections, including institutions from France (IFA, Institut français d'architecture), the UK (RIBA, Royal Institute of British Architects), Italy (Istituto universitario di architettura di Venezia and Ordine degli Architetti di Roma e Provincia), Belgium (CIVA, Centre International pour la Ville, l'Architecture et le Paysage), Finland (Museum of Finnish Architecture), the Netherlands (NAi, Nederlands Architectuurinstituut), Switzerland (Fondazione Archivio del Moderno) and Germany, which is represented by the Deutsches Architekturmuseum. The committee first met in 2002 to discuss the problems, complexities and impact of new media on their archival work. One result of their collaboration is the internet portal www.architecturearchives.net, which has been online since 2004, providing links to European architectural collections and giving guidelines on archiving architectural documents.

Archives preserve documentation of our cultural heritage, making it available to the people of today and future generations. Clearly, this is a task that demands new approaches in the digital age. Computerisation has radically altered the tasks of preserving documents and making them available. The days of the card index are over. Data logging and research are now done at a computer screen. Users want to be able to access data banks quickly and effectively and, if possible, to access them across all institutional and national boundaries. Today, entire libraries can be browsed online, with historic writings and images available in the form of digital documents. Many new documents are never even published on paper these days. It is easy to process, store, send and quickly call up everything by computer. But how long will digital documents last?

Archives and museums are now facing the problem of long-term conservation of electronic material. All over the world, there are efforts to set down standards for collecting and storing digital data. By its very nature, the academic interest in this issue goes far beyond that of industry and commerce. In the business world, once the shelf-life of a product has run out and new and better version has been developed, its forerunners are often of little or no interest to a company. But in the world of academic research, even outdated developments are often of great importance.

Long-term archiving has never been easy. Paper, too, has its problems and requires special treatment. But if digital data is to be saved for posterity, new strategies are needed. Neither hardware nor software have an unlimited lifespan. How long can a disk or

www.gaudi-programme.net

www.architecturearchives.net

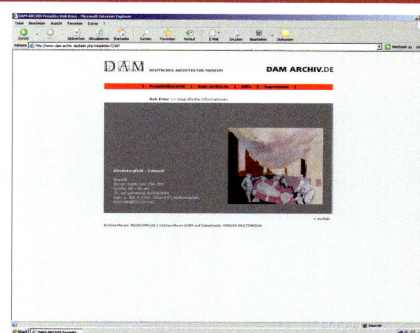

www.dam-archiv.de

Langzeitarchivierung war nie einfach. Auch Papier birgt Probleme und verlangt spezielle Behandlung, doch wenn nun digitale Daten möglichst unbeschadet über die Zeiten gerettet werden sollen, dann sind neue Strategien gefragt. Weder Hard- noch Software sind von unbegrenzter Haltbarkeit. Wie groß ist die Lebensdauer einer Diskette oder CD? Wie lange hält eine Festplatte? Auf welches Format wird man auch in Zukunft gesicherten Zugriff haben? Muss man das, was man bewahren will, ausdrucken? Was macht man dann mit den animierten Bildern? Die Reihe der Fragen ist lang, die richtigen Entscheidungen zu treffen ist vor dem Hintergrund des rasanten Wandels, der mit dem Computer einhergeht, nicht einfach. Maschinen, die gestern noch Räume füllten, haben heute Nachfolgegeräte, die in einer Aktentasche Platz finden. Die erste Software für den Riesen hat mit der für den kleinen Bruder wenig gemeinsam. Der Rhythmus von Austausch und Updates wird immer schneller.

Wie groß ist das Problembewusstsein in den Architekturbüros, dort, wo Zeichengeräte längst durch spezielle Graphikprogramme abgelöst wurden? Welche Strategien gibt es dort zur Verwaltung der Firmenarchive? Die an der GAUDI-Arbeitsgruppe beteiligten Institute haben einen ausführlichen Fragebogen an repräsentativ ausgewählte Büros verschickt. Die Auswertung zeigte Defizite auf, nicht selten wurde ein mangelndes Problembewusstsein deutlich. War in der Vergangenheit meist ›nur‹ der größere Aufwand bei der Bearbeitung zu fürchten, wenn ungeordnete Unterlagen an ein Archiv übergeben wurden, so droht nun die Gefahr, dass ein nicht gepflegter digitaler Bestand schon verloren ist, bevor er in eine Sammlung gelangt. Schadhafte Datenträger und Material, bei dem eine rechtzeitige Konvertierung und Übertragung auf aktuelle Speichermedien versäumt wurde, sind wertlos. Vor Verlusten ist man nie ganz gefeit, aber das Risiko lässt sich minimieren.

Die Weichen für das zukünftige digitale Archiv der Architektur werden in den Büros gestellt. Die Pflege der Daten beginnt bei der Erstellung. Eine systematische Ordnung und gezielte Auswahl für die Ablage, eine Sicherung von notwendigen Zusatzinformationen, die zum Beispiel auch Angaben zur verwendeten Software beinhalten müssen, sind für den späteren Zugriff Voraussetzung. Will man empfindliche Verluste vermeiden, sind eine gute Lagerung, regelmäßige Kontrolle und eine turnusmäßige Übertragung auf neue Datenträger unerlässlich. Nähere Informationen zum Thema bietet die Website www.architecturearchives.net. Dort findet man »Empfehlungen für die Verwaltung und Archivierung von Architekturdokumenten«, nicht zuletzt ein Leitfaden für Architekturbüros, von denen sich die Archive auch in der Zukunft eine Übernahme wertvoller Bestände erhoffen.

CD-ROM last? How long can a hard-disk last? What format can be used to ensure that the data can still be accessed in the future? Should printouts be made of everything that is to be preserved? But what is to be done then with animated images? The list of questions is long and, given the sheer speed of change in the field of computerisation, making the right decisions is no easy task. Only a few years ago, computers were machines that took up entire rooms. Today, they fit into a briefcase. The first generation of software for those giants bears little resemblance to the software that powers their little brothers today. Software is being updated and made obsolete at an ever faster rate.

Just how much awareness of this problem is there in architectural practices where drawing boards have long since been replaced by special design software? What strategies, if any, have they put in place to manage their company archives? The institutes involved in the GAUDI steering committee have issued a detailed questionnaire to a representative number of selected architectural firms. Their responses so far have flagged up a number of problem areas and have also indicated that some firms are not fully aware of the scale of the problem. Whereas, in the past, if an archive received an unsystematic collection of documents, the problem was "only" one of time-consuming filing. Today, we are faced with the possibility that a poorly managed collection of digital data might well be lost forever before it even finds its way into an archive. Damaged disks and material that has not been transferred onto current forms of data storage are useless. There is always a risk of loss – but that risk can be minimised.

It is in the offices of the architecture practices themselves that the ground will be paved for the digital architectural archives of the future. Preservation of data starts with its creation. Systematic filing and clearly defined selection criteria, securing the necessary auxiliary information such as details of the software used – all these are crucial if we are to have access to this data in the future. In order to reduce losses, good storage, regular checks and regular transfer of data onto new storage media are imperative. For more information on this matter, visit www.architecturearchives.net. The website provides recommendations for managing and archiving architectural documents, and sets out guidelines for architectural firms whose valuable collections the archives hope to be able to preserve in future.

1 Animation im Konzerthaus Berlin, Peter Kulka
1 Animation Concert House Berlin, Peter Kulka

DAS ARCHIV PETER KULKA IM DAM
THE PETER KULKA ARCHIVES IN THE DAM

Yorck Förster

Peter Kulka gehört seit eineinhalb Jahrzehnten mit seinen Büros in Köln und Dresden zu den herausragenden Architekten in Deutschland. Das Deutsche Architektur Museum hat sein Werk von November 2005 bis Februar 2006 in der monografischen Ausstellung »Peter Kulka. Minimalismus und Sinnlichkeit« vorgestellt. Kulka hat dem DAM sein Werkarchiv als Schenkung übereignet.

Ausstellungen verdichten ein Œuvre, Archive aber sind das Gedächtnis einer Werkentwicklung mit allen Seitenwegen und Nebenlinien. Bei dem 1937 in Dresden geborenen Peter Kulka ist dieser Entwicklungsweg facettenreich: In der ehemaligen DDR absolviert er zunächst eine Maurerlehre. Ein Ingenieur- und daran anschließend ein Architekturstudium in Berlin-Weißensee folgen. Der Bauhausschüler Selman Selmanagić ist einer seiner Lehrer. Bei Hermann Henselmann arbeitet Kulka 1964 an der Deutschen Bauakademie in Ost-Berlin. Ein Jahr später flieht er in den Westteil der Stadt, dort ist er in den nächsten Jahren für Hans Scharoun tätig. Von 1970 an plant Kulka in einer Arbeitsgemeinschaft mit Köpke, Töpper, Herzog und Siepmann den Neubau der Universität in Bielefeld. Nach sechs Jahren ist das Großprojekt abgeschlossen. Für Kulka beginnt eine Phase kleinteiligerer Planungen. Er gründet ein Büro in Köln. Zeitweilig arbeitet er mit Hans Schilling zusammen. An der RWTH in Aachen erhält er 1986 eine Professur, die er bis 1992 ausübt.

Der Entwurf für den Sächsischen Landtag in Dresden (1991–97) markiert den Beginn der bis in die Gegenwart äußerst produktiven Meisterjahre Kulkas, in denen eine Architektur formal reduzierter Baukörper mit präziser Materialästhetik und einer komplexen räumlichen Fügung entsteht.

Der Archivbestand

Das Herzstück des Archivs Peter Kulka bilden 21 Ordner mit Materialien zu 83 Bauten und Projekten aus den Jahren 1969 bis 2004. Dazu zählen Wettbewerbseinreichungen, Reprovorlagen des Planmaterials und Modellfotografien. Kulka hat zudem konsequent bei den realisierten Bauten renommierte Architekturfotografen mit der begleitenden Dokumentation beauftragt. Teile dieses Bestandes an Mittelformat- und Großdias sind digitalisiert. Die Rezeption der Projekte in Fachpublikationen und Katalogen sowie Aufsätze von und über Peter Kulka sind in einer zweiten Archivgruppe in 29 Stehsammlern zusammengefasst.

Das Werkarchiv ist wortwörtlich als solches zu verstehen. Der überwiegende Teil der Projekte ist in einem knappen Stil ohne zeichnerische Überhöhung dokumentiert. Der Entwurfsgedanke wird nüchtern, fast spröde vorgetragen. Die für Kulkas Bauten charakteristische subtile Bezugnahme auf den Ort, die sinnliche Wirkung der Materialien und das Wechselspiel aus neutralen und kontrastierend gesetzten farbmächtigen monochromen Flächen

With his offices in Cologne and Dresden, Peter Kulka has been one of the biggest movers and shakers on the German architecture scene for almost two decades. From November 2005 to February 2006 the Deutsches Architektur Museum devoted a solo exhibition to him under the title "Peter Kulka: Minimalism and Sensuality", showcasing his oeuvre. Peter Kulka has now donated his archives to the DAM.

Exhibitions condense. They bring a life's work into perspective. But archives trace the memory of an oeuvre's development in all its detours and deviations. In the case of Peter Kulka, born in Dresden in 1937, that development has been richly facetted. In the former GDR he completed an apprenticeship as a bricklayer. He went on to study engineering and then architecture at Berlin-Weißensee. One of his teachers there was former Bauhaus student Selman Selmanagić. In 1964, Kulka worked for the Deutsche Bauakademie in Berlin under Hermann Henselmann. One year later he fled to what was then the "western sector" where he spent several years working for Hans Scharoun. From 1970 onwards, Kulka joined forces with Köpke, Töpper, Herzog and Siepmann to design the new University of Bielefeld. This massive project took six years to complete. What followed was a phase of smaller-scale projects. Kulka established an office in Cologne. For a while, he worked with Hans Schilling. Then, in 1986, he was given a professorship at the RWTH in Aachen – a post he was to hold until 1992.

Kulka's design for the Sächsischer Landtag (Saxon Regional Parliament) in Dresden (1991–97) marked the start of an extremely prolific phase at the height of Kulka's creative powers, during which he produced architecturally pared-down buildings with a keen eye for the aesthetic of the material and a sophisticated handling of space.

The Archives

The core of the Peter Kulka holdings in our archives consists of 21 files containing material on 83 buildings and projects from 1969 to 2004. These include competition designs, repros, plans and photographs of models. Kulka consistently commissioned the finest architectural photographers of the time to document his completed buildings. Some of the photographs are digitalised. A second archival group of 29 files documents the reception of his projects in specialist publications and catalogues, along with essays by and about Peter Kulka.

The "works archive" does exactly what it says on the tin. Most of the projects are documented briefly and factually. The design concept is presented soberly, even laconically. Kulka's characteristically subtle references to the surroundings of a building, the sensual impact of the materials and the alternation of neutral and

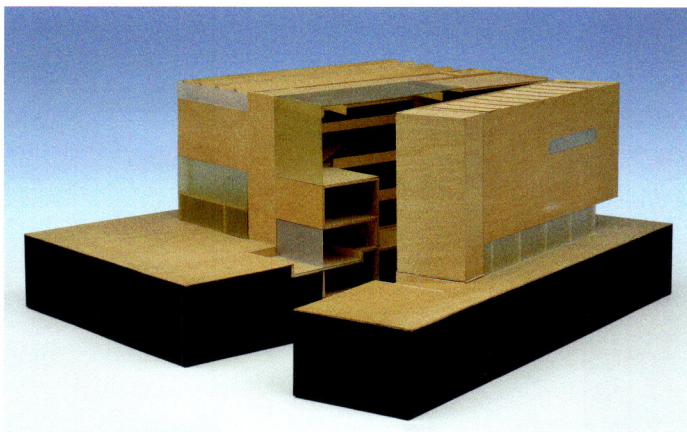

Entwurfsmodell Galerie für zeitgenössische Kunst Leipzig
Design model for Gallery of Contemporary Art Leipzig

sind in dem Protostadium des Entwurfs noch verborgen. Die räumliche Komplexität entfaltet sich für den Betrachter erst dann, wenn er den Plänen in die intendierte Wegführung und Raumkonfiguration folgt.

Anschaulich wird seine Entwurfshaltung durch die 20 Wettbewerbs-, Arbeits- und Präsentationsmodelle in dem Archivbestand. Beispielhaft hierfür ist das zweiteilige Holzspanmodell (1 : 100) des nach Sanierung und Erweiterung der denkmalgeschützten Herfurt'schen Villa (1994–98) in einem zweiten Bauabschnitt vorgesehenen Neubaus der Galerie für Zeitgenössische Kunst Leipzig. Der nicht realisierte Entwurf setzt in seiner Erscheinung den reduzierten, dezidiert modernen Duktus der Villenerweiterung fort. Das Erdgeschoss ist als durchlässiger Bereich konzipiert, der sowohl zur Straße wie zum parkartigen Freiraum geöffnet ist. In den Folgegeschossen entsteht um einen Atriumhof eine differenzierte Verschränkung verschieden proportionierter ›White Cubes‹ mit unterschiedlichen Belichtungssituationen.

Der nüchterne Charakter der Projektdarstellung verändert sich ab dem Ende der 90er-Jahre. Das Büro beginnt auf die Möglichkeiten des Computers zu setzen, um Raumfolgen und vor allem Elemente der sinnlichen Wirkung des Bauobjekts zu veranschaulichen. Ein frühes Beispiel ist eine Animation zum Entwurf der Feuer- und Rettungswache in Leverkusen (2000–02). Elementar, in kräftigen Farben ist das Gebäude dargestellt, nicht aber als Bestand vorgetäuscht. Der Bildraum ist schwarz, weiße Höhenlinien markieren das Terrain. Deutlich hebt sich das leuchtende Rot der Außenfassade davon ab.

Um die Nutzungsmöglichkeiten des als veränderbare Black Box konzipierten Werner-Otto-Saals im Konzerthaus Berlin (2001–03) zu veranschaulichen, ist eine Serie an Raumanimationen entstanden.

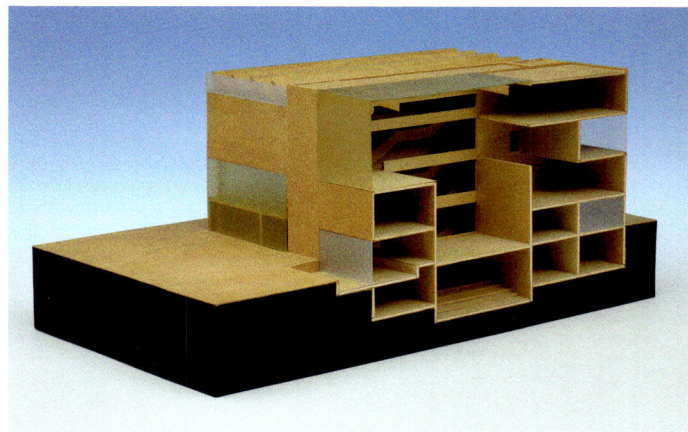

contrasting monochromatic surfaces are not immediately evident in the proto-stage of the design. The spatial complexity evolves more clearly in the pathways and spatial configurations of the design.

The 20 competition, design and presentation models in the archives give a fascinating insight into his design approach. One particularly fine example of this is the two-part plywood model (1:100) of the planned extension for the Galerie für Zeitgenössische Kunst in Leipzig following the refurbishment and extension of the historically listed Herfurt'sche Villa (1994–98). This design, though never actually built, is a continuation of Kulka's reduced and decidedly modern approach to extending a villa of historic importance. The ground floor is designed as an open space, giving onto the park-like gardens and the street. The upper floors, with their dovetailed white cubes of differing proportions and varied lighting, are set around an atrium.

From the late 1990s, there is a change in the sobriety of Kulka's project presentations. From here on in, the team starts to exploit the possibilities offered by computer software in their presentation of spatial sequences and, most importantly, the sensual impact of the finished building. One early example of this is an animation of the fire station in Leverkusen (2000–02). The building is portrayed in an elementary way, using strong colours, without suggesting that it is already real. The screen is black. White highlights define the terrain. The brilliant red of the facade stands out clearly.

Later, an entire series of spatial and room animations is used to illustrate the flexibility of the Werner-Otto Auditorium in the Berlin Concert House (2001–03), designed as a "black box" that can be modified. There is something almost pop-art about the brightly

Geradezu in Pop-Manier wird in kräftigen Farbüberzeichnungen ein Spektrum von Pressekonferenz, Kammerkonzert, Rockereignis bis hin zum Stehempfang durchgespielt.

Einen eher romantischen Charakter vermittelt die Bildcollage für den Wiederaufbau der auf Pöppelmann zurückgehenden Muldebrücke bei Grimma (2003). Der Vorschlag für die neue Konstruktion aus verschränkten Brettschichtholz-Bögen rahmt und steigert die Wirkung der Ruinen des bei dem Jahrhunderthochwasser 2002 zerstörten Bauwerks.

Der Umstand, dass ein guter Teil des Archivs Kulka digital vorliegt, unterstreicht auch den Wandel in der Sammlung des DAM. Die Herausforderung liegt in der für museale Maßstäbe schnellen Veränderung der Speichermedien und vor allem in der Notwendigkeit, konforme Software zu archivieren, um zu einem späteren Zeitpunkt die Projektdaten überhaupt weiter erschließen zu können.

coloured drawings of press conference, chamber concert, rock gig and buffet reception.

By contrast, the collage illustrating the reconstruction of Pöppelmann's Mulde Bridge at Grimma (2003) is almost romantic in tone. The proposal for a new construction of plywood arches frames and at the same time enhances the effect of the ruins of this historic bridge, which was swept away by the catastrophic floodwaters of 2002.

The very fact that a large proportion of the Kulka archives is available in digital form underlines the changes already taking place in the DAM collection. For the museum, the greatest challenge now lies in the rapid development of new recording and storage media and, above all, in ensuring that appropriate software is also archived to allow the project data to be called up in future.

Entwurfsmodell Brücke bei Grimma
Design model bridge near Grimma

Animation Brücke bei Grimma
Animation bridge near Grimma

DAM JAHRESBERICHT 2006
DAM ANNUAL REPORT 2006

Das Deutsche Architekturmuseum (DAM)
zeigte 2006 folgende große Ausstellungen:
In 2006 the Deutsche Architekturmuseum (DAM)
hosted the following major exhibitions:

Peter Kulka. Minimalismus und Sinnlichkeit
Peter Kulka. Minimalism and Sensuality
12.11.2005–05.02.2006

Friedensreich Hundertwasser
Ein Sonntagsarchitekt. Gebaute Träume und Sehnsüchte
A Sunday Architect of Dreams and Longings
19.11.2005–05.02.2006

Engelbert Kremser. Anstiftung zum Raum
Engelbert Kremser. Incitement to Space
18.02.2006–30.04.2006

UN Studio: Entwicklung des Raums
UN Studio: Evolution of Space
25.02.2006–30.04.2006

Jean Prouvé. Die Poetik des technischen Objekts
Jean Prouvé. The Poetics of the Technical Object
13.05.2006–30.07.2006

Felsen aus Beton und Glas. Die Architektur von Gottfried Böhm
Rocks of Concrete and Glass. The Architecture of Gottfried Böhm
26.08.2006–05.11.2006

High-Society. Aktuelle Hochhausarchitektur
und der Internationale Hochhaus Preis 2006
High Society. Contemporary Highrise Architecture
and the International Highrise Award 2006
19.11.2006–11.02.2007

Original Resopal. Die Ästhetik der Oberfläche
Original Resopal. The Aesthetics of the Surface
25.11.2006–11.02.2007

Kleinere Ausstellungen im DAM:
Smaller exhibitions at the DAM:

Ein Leben für die Architektur: Der Fotograf Julius Shulman
A Lifetime for Architecture: The Photographer Julius Shulman
04.10.2005–11.12.2005

Licht Architektur Preis 2005
The Light in Architecture Award 2005
17.12. 2005–05.02.2006

Max 40. BDA-Auszeichnung Junge Architekten in Hessen 2006
Max 40. BDA Architecture Award Young Architects in Hessen 2006
11.02.2006–02.04.2006

Personen und Possen. Architektenporträts
und Collagen von Manfred Sack
People and Pranks. Portraits of Architects
and Collages by Manfred Sack
12.04.2006–21.05.2006

Architecture + Technology Award
09.05.2006–04.06.2006

Caparol »Architekturpreis Farbe – Struktur – Oberfläche«
Caparol "Architecture Award Colour – Structure – Surface"
31.05.2006–09.07.2006

Vom Stadion im Stadtwald zur Fifa WM-Arena Frankfurt
From the Stadium in the City Forest to the Fifa World Cup
Arena Frankfurt
08.06.2006–09.07.2006

End of Year Review. Städelschule Architecture Class
14.07.2006–23.07.2006

WeinArchitektur. Vom Keller zum Kult
(Eine Ausstellung des Architekturzentrums Wien
anlässlich der KULTURTAGE der EZB – Österreich 2006)
WineArchitecture. From Cellar to Cult. (An exhibition
by the Architekturzentrum Wien as part of the
ECB Cultural Days Austria 2006)
05.09.2006–26.11.2006

Frankfurter Wohnungsbau
Housing Construction in Frankfurt
07.09.2006–01.10.2006

Verena Dietrich. Eine Architektin
Verena Dietrich. Architect
06.12.2006–28.01.2007

Dauerausstellung:
Permanent Exhibition:
Von der Urhütte zum Wolkenkratzer
From Primordial Hut to Skyscraper

Kataloge und Veröffentlichungen entstanden zu allen
großen Ausstellungen im DAM sowie zu den meisten
kleineren.
Catalogues and publications have been issued for
all major exhibitions and for most of the smaller ones.

Zu den großen Ausstellungen gab es jeweils ein umfangreiches
museumspädagogisches Programm mit Führungen und
Workshops für Kinder und Jugendliche.
Each of the major exhibitions also included a wide range of
educational events with guided tours and workshops for children
and young people.

Von der Baustelle: Eine Diskussionsreihe vor Ort
From the Building Site: An On-Site Discussion Event
Moderation chaired by Peter Cachola Schmal, Wolfgang Voigt

Eschborn Plaza. Neubau Europazentrale Ernst & Young: 09.09.2005
Jo. Franzke Architekten BDA in Kooperation mit Roger Bundschuh

Generalkonsulat der Islamischen Republik Iran: 02.11.2005
Naghshe Jahan Pars mit with Architekturbüro Möller

Kunsthalle Portikus: 17.11.2005
Prof. Christoph Mäckler Architekten

Haus am Dom: 29.03.2006
Jourdan & Müller PAS

Uniklinik: 25.07.2006
Nickl & Partner Architekten

Vortragsreihen:
Lecture Series:

Junge Architekten in Deutschland
Young Architects in Germany
Andreas Hild, Hild und K, München: 06.10.2005
Hans-Peter Maria Kissler & Roland Gert Effgen,
Kissler+Effgen, Wiesbaden: 20.10.2005
Carsten Roth, Carsten Roth Architekt, Hamburg: 27.10.2005
Nadja Letzel & Gábor Freivogel, letzelfreivogel architekten,
Halle: 03.11.2005

Neue Urbanität
New Urbanity

Hamburg The Hafencity Masterplan
Kees Christiaanse, Zürich: 16.03.2006

London. Zentrumsumbau am Südufer der Themse
Cordelia Polinna, Berlin: 06.04.2006

Städtische Transformationsprozesse – Planwerk
»Stadtraum Leipzig 2015+«
Engelbert Lütke Daldrup, Berlin: 26.09.2006

München
Christiane Thalgott, München: 31.10.2006

Barcelona
Josep A. Acebillo, Barcelona: 21.11.2006

Symposien:
Symposia:

Public Space Forum Korea Germany
Klaus Klemp, Bart Lootsma, Muck Petzet, Nikolaus Hirsch,
Marie-Theres Deutsch, KIM Sung Hong, JOO Daekahn,
KIM Jong Kyu, KIM Kwang Soo: 14.10.2005

Die Berliner Rostlaube und die neue Bibliothek von Foster
and Partners
The Berlin Free University and the New Library
by Foster and Partners
Bernd Dugall, Manfred Schiedhelm, Klaus Ulrich Werner,
Christian Hallmann: 28.06.2006

Ungers-Kolloquium
Ungers Colloquium
»Das ›Haus im Haus‹. Zur Wirkungsgeschichte einer Entwurfsidee«
"The 'House within a House'. On the Impact of a Design Idea"
Jasper Cepl, Andres Lepik, Jörg H. Gleiter, Carsten Ruhl, Romana
Schneider: 04.09.2006

Böhm-Kolloquium
Böhm Colloquium
»Bewundert und bedroht: Gottfried Böhms Kirchen im Kontext«
"Admired and at Risk: Gottfried Böhm's Churches in Context"
Gabriele Wiesemann, Manfred Speidel, Wolfgang Pehnt,
Pfarrer Jörg Dantscher SJ: 13.10.2006

Vorträge:
Lectures:
Julius Shulman, Los Angeles: 04.10.2005
Rob Krier, Luxembourg: 13.10.2005
Rainer Kilb, Frankfurt: 09.11.2005
Ulrike Brandi, Ulrike Brandi Licht, Hamburg: 15.11.2005
Massimiliano Fuksas, Rom: 24.11.2005
Peter Kulka, Köln: 26.01.2006
Layla Dawson, Hamburg: 08.02.2006
Ben van Berkel, Amsterdam: 15.03.2006
Armand Grüntuch & Almut Ernst, Grüntuch Ernst Architekten,
Berlin: 30.03.2006
Wolfgang Förster, Wien: 25.04.2006
Ulrike Brandi, Ulrike Brandi Licht, Hamburg: 26.04.2006
Michael Hensel, Achim Menges, Michael Weinstock, London:
19.05.2006
Catherine Prouvé, Paris & Peter Sulzer, Stuttgart: 12.07.2006
Mark Wigley, Frankfurt: 13.07.2006
Robert Rubin, New York: 23.07.2006
Peter Böhm, Köln: 15.09.2006
Reinhard Hübsch, Berlin: 11.10.2006
Werner Nachtigall, Saarbrücken: 29.11.2006

**Zu den wichtigsten Neuerwerbungen für das Archiv
des DAM zählen:**
The DAM archives' most important new acquisitions include:
Ernst Kasper, Köln: Pläne und Zeichnungen zu 73 Projekten;
Engelbert Kremser, Berlin: freie Arbeiten (Ölbilder, Aquarelle),
4 Modelle, Fotomaterial; Helge Bofinger, Wiesbaden: Zeich-
nungen, Fotomaterial, Haus S., Kronberg/Ts.; UN Studio, Amster-
dam: Rapid Prototyping Model, Neues Mercedes-Benz Museum,
Stuttgart; Gottfried Böhm, Köln: Verwaltungsgebäude der Züblin
AG, Stuttgart, 1982–84 (Modellbau 2001: M. Hornung, C. Neu-
mann, Ph. Neumann), Dauerleihgabe des IFA-Inst. für
Auslandsbeziehungen e.V.; Tezuka Architects, Tokyo: Stahlmodell,
Matsunoyama Natural Science Museum
Ernst Kasper, Cologne: plans and drawings relating to 73 projects;
Engelbert Kremser, Berlin: artworks (oil paintings, watercolours),
4 models, photographs; Helge Bofinger, Wiesbaden: drawings,
photographs, Haus S., Kronberg/Ts.; UN Studio, Amsterdam:
Rapid Prototyping Model, New Mercedes-Benz Museum, Stuttgart;
Gottfried Böhm, Cologne, administrative building for Züblin AG,
Stuttgart, 1982–84 (model constructed in 2001: M. Hornung,
C. Neumann, Ph. Neumann), on permanent loan from the Institute
of Foreign Affairs (IFA); Tezuka Architects, Tokyo: Steel Model,
Matsunoyama Natural Science Museum

Architekturpreise:
Architecture Awards:

Das DAM ist an der Auslobung dreier wichtiger Architekturpreise beteiligt: an dem alle zwei Jahre auszulobenden »Licht Architektur Preis«, der auch 2005 wieder prämiert wurde, dazu an dem von der Messe Frankfurt gestifteten »Architecture + Technology Award. Europäischer Architekturpreis für Architektur und Technik«, der Anfang 2006 vergeben wurde. Dazu kommt der von der Stadt Frankfurt und der DekaBank im Mai 2006 ausgelobte »Internationale Hochhaus Preis«.

The DAM is involved in the presentation of three major architectural awards: the biannual "Light in Architecture Award" that was awarded again in 2005; the "Architecture + Technology Award. European Architecture Award for Architecture and Technology" founded by Messe Frankfurt, which was announced at the beginning of 2006; and finally, in May 2006, the biannual "International Highrise Award" by the City of Frankfurt and the DekaBank.

Mäzene und Sponsoren:
Patrons and Sponsors:

Alle unsere Aktivitäten im vergangenen Jahr wären ohne die großzügige Unterstützung zahlreicher Sponsoren nicht möglich gewesen. Auch im Jahr 2006 ist Ernst & Young AG Wirtschaftsprüfungsgesellschaft der wichtigste Sponsor des DAM. Zu den weiteren Sponsoren, die das Museum durch Geld- und Sachzuwendungen unterstützt haben, zählen:

The museum's activities in the course of the last year would not have been possible without the generous support of our many sponsors. In 2006, the accounting and auditing firm of Ernst & Young AG Wirtschaftsprüfungsgesellschaft has been the foremost sponsor of the DAM. Other sponsors who have kindly provided their financial and material support are:

AES Ingenieurgesellschaft mbH; Akademie der Architekten- und Stadtplanerkammer Hessen; Autodesk GmbH; Bilfinger Berger Projektentwicklung GmbH; Botschaft der Niederlande in Deutschland; Caparol Farben Lacke Bautenschutz GmbH & Co. Vertriebs KG; DekaBank; Deutsche Werkstätten Hellerau GmbH; Dutch Architecture Fund; Frankfurter Allgemeine Zeitung; Frankfurt Holding Wohnungsbau- und Beteiligungsgesellschaft mbH; Frankfurter Sparkasse 1822; von Gerkan, Marg und Partner; Gesellschaft der Freunde des Deutschen Architektur Museums e.V.; Harms & Partner Bauingenieure; Hessische Kulturstiftung; Hochtief Construction AG; Johann Wolfgang Goethe Universität Frankfurt am Main; Alfried Krupp von Bohlen und Halbach-Stiftung; Kulturstiftung der Länder; Messe Frankfurt GmbH; Ministère de la Culture de l'Enseignement Supérieur et de la Recherche/Luxembourg; Nassauische Heimstätte; Resopal GmbH; Röhm Plexiglas; SOKA-Bau Zusatzversorgungskasse des Baugewerbes VVaG; Georg und Franziska Speyer'sche Hochschulstiftung; Stadt Frankfurt am Main; Vitra; Wiemer & Trachte AG; Züblin AG; Zumtobel Staff Deutschland Vertriebs-GmbH.

All diesen Förderern, aber auch manchem Mäzen, der ungenannt bleiben möchte, gilt unser herzlichster Dank.
We wish to express our sincerest gratitude to all our sponsors as well as to those patrons who wish to remain anonymous.

Gesellschaft der Freunde des DAM:
The Society of Friends of the DAM:

Die Gesellschaft der Freunde des Deutschen Architektur Museums e. V. wurde 1985 als eingetragener Verein ins Leben gerufen. Ihr Hauptanliegen ist es, das DAM in der Verwirklichung seiner öffentlichen Aufgaben ideell und materiell zu unterstützen.

Zu den Zielen und Aufgaben des Vereins gehören:
· Vermittlung, Ankauf oder Überlassung von Plänen, Zeichnungen und Modellen internationaler Architekturprojekte und von Architektennachlässen
· Personelle und materielle Unterstützung bei Veranstaltungen, Ausstellungen und der Jugendarbeit
· Bereitstellung einer Wohnung für Praktikanten des DAM
· Beratung und Anregung des DAM.

So wurde im Jahr 2005 anlässlich des 20jährigen Bestehens des DAM vom Freundeskreis ein Museumsführer initiiert und herausgegeben. Im September 2005 hat der Freundeskreis eine Auktion zugunsten des DAM mit Originalzeichnungen, -skizzen und -modellen durch das Auktionshaus Döbritz in Zusammenarbeit mit der Frankfurter Allgemeinen Zeitung durchgeführt, die einen Gesamterlös von € 17.595 erbrachte (www.dam-auktion.de). Mitglieder in diesem Verein sind Personen, Institutionen und Firmen, deren Anliegen es ist, einen Beitrag zur Förderung der Qualität der gebauten Umwelt zu leisten. Der Mitgliedsbeitrag beträgt jährlich € 95,00 für Einzelmitglieder, € 50,00 für Studenten und € 920,00 für juristische Personen und Personenvereinigungen.

The Gesellschaft der Freunde des Deutschen Architektur Museums e. V. [Friends of the Deutsches Architektur Museum] was founded in 1985 as a registered association. Its main purpose is to support the museum both financially and otherwise in its public engagements and cultural work. The aims and duties of the Society of Friends include:
· the procurement, acquisition or bequest of plans, drawings and models of international architectural projects and from the estates of architects
· assisting with the staffing and funding of events, exhibitions and youth work
· providing accommodation for interns and trainees at the DAM
· advice and consultancy for the DAM.

In 2005, to mark the 20th anniversary of the founding of the DAM, the Society of Friends initiated and published a museum guide. In September 2005 the Society of Friends held an auction of original drawings, sketches and models at the Döbritz auction house in collaboration with the Frankfurter Allgemeine Zeitung, which raised a total of € 17.595,– for the DAM (www.dam-auktion.de). Members of the Society are individuals, institutions and firms with an interest in making a contribution to promoting the quality of the built environment. The annual membership fee is € 95 for individuals, € 50 for students and € 920 for corporate bodies and groups.

Gesellschaft der Freunde des DAM
Deutsches Architektur Museum
Schaumainkai 43
60596 Frankfurt am Main
Telefon: +49 (0)69 / 97 20 33 66
Fax: +49 (0)69 / 97 20 33 66
E-Mail: freundeskreis.dam@stadt-frankfurt.de

DIE AUTOREN
THE AUTHORS

Hubertus Adam

*1965 in Hannover. Studium der Kunstgeschichte, Archäologie und Philosophie in Heidelberg. 1996–1998 Redakteur der Zeitschrift *Bauwelt* in Berlin. Seit 1998 Redakteur der Zeitschrift *archithese* in Zürich; freier Architekturkritiker für die *Neue Zürcher Zeitung*. Zahlreiche Zeitschriften- und Buchbeiträge sowie Bücher zur Architekturgeschichte des 20. Jahrhunderts und zur Architektur der Gegenwart.

*1965 in Hanover. Studied art history, archaeology and philosophy at Heidelberg. 1996–1998 editor of *Bauwelt* periodical in Berlin. Since 1998 editor of *archithese* periodical in Zurich; freelance architecture critic for *Neue Zürcher Zeitung*. Has published widely on twentieth-century architectural history and contemporary architecture.

Matthias Alexander

*1968 in Hannover. Studium der Geschichte in Bonn, Bologna, Jena und München; Promotion 1998. Seit 1999 Redakteur der *Frankfurter Allgemeinen Zeitung*. Er berichtet vorwiegend für den Regionalteil, die *Rhein-Main-Zeitung*, über Architektur und Stadtplanung.

*1968 in Hanover. Studied history at Bonn, Bologna, Jena and Munich; doctorate 1998. Since 1999 editor of *Frankfurter Allgemeine Zeitung*, reporting primarily on architecture and urban planning for the *Rhein-Main-Zeitung* regional section.

Paul Andreas

*1973 in Wolfsburg. Studium Kultur- und Kunstwissenschaft in Berlin und Paris; 2000 M. A.; 2001 Japanisch-Studium in Tübingen/Kyoto; 2003 Kurator Oscar Niemeyer-Ausstellung im DAM; 2003–2005 wissenschaftlicher Mitarbeiter für Designgeschichte/ BU Wuppertal. Lebt als freier Journalist und Kurator in Düsseldorf.

*1973 in Wolfsburg. Art and cultural studies at Berlin and Paris, graduating in 2000. Studied Japanese at Tübingen and Kyoto. 2003 curated the Oscar Niemeyer exhibition at the DAM; 2003–05 research assistant for design history at BU Wuppertal. Freelance journalist and curator living in Dusseldorf.

Ursula Baus

*1959 in Kaiserslautern. Studium der Kunstgeschichte, Archäologie und Philosophie in Saarbrücken. Studium der Architektur in Stuttgart und Paris, Stipendien und Promotion. Bis 2003 Redakteurin der *db – deutsche bauzeitung*. Lehraufträge an der Uni Stuttgart und der FH Biberach. Freie Kritikerin, Partnerin bei frei04-publizistik in Stuttgart. Mitglied im Kuratorium der Erich-Schelling-Architektur-Stiftung.

*1959 in Kaiserslautern. Studied art history, archaeology and philosophy at Saarbrücken. Studied architecture at Stuttgart and Paris; fellowships and doctorate. Until 2003 editor of *db – deutsche bauzeitung*. Teaching assignments at Uni Stuttgart and FH Biberach. Freelance critic, partner of frei04-publizistik in Stuttgart. Member of the board of the Erich Schelling Architecture Foun-dation.

Jörg Brauns

*1966. Studium der Architektur in Weimar; 1992–1994 wissenschaftlicher Mitarbeiter bei Prof. Salzmann in Weimar. 1994–1996 Mitarbeiter im Büro Schettler & Wittenberg, Weimar. 1996–1999 Leiter der Ideenwerkstatt 99 der Bauhaus-Universität Weimar. 2004 Promotion (Dr. phil.) zum Thema *Schauplätze. Zur Architektur visueller Medien*. Seit 2002 Leiter des Rektoramts der Bauhaus-Universität.

*1966. Studied architecture at Weimar; 1992–1994 research assistant under Prof. Salzmann at Weimar. 1994–1996 employed in the firm of Schettler & Wittenberg, Weimar. 1996–1999 Head of *Ideenwerkstatt 99* at the Bauhaus University Weimar. 2004 doctoral thesis on architecture and visual media (*Schauplätze. Zur Architektur visueller Medien*). Since 2002 head of the Rector's Office at the Bauhaus University.

Hans-Jürgen Breuning

*1963 in Stuttgart. Studium der Architektur in Karlsruhe, Stuttgart und Florenz; Diplom 1992, Promotion 1999. Seit 1990 freie journalistische Tätigkeit. 1992–1999 wissenschaftlicher Mitarbeiter an der Universität Stuttgart. 1999–2001 Assistent an der TU Graz. Seit 2002 Lehrtätigkeit an der Universität Karlsruhe und der Hochschule für Technik in Stuttgart. Seit 2001 Kurator in der Architekturgalerie am Weißenhof in Stuttgart.

*1963 in Stuttgart. Studied architecture at Karlsruhe, Stuttgart and Florence; Graduated 1992, doctorate 1999. Since 1990 freelance journalist. 1992–1999 research assistant at the University of Stuttgart. 1999–2001 assistant at TU Graz. Since 2002 teaching assignments at the University of Karlsruhe and the Hochschule für Technik in Stuttgart. Since 2001 curator at the Architekturgalerie am Weißenhof in Stuttgart.

Sabine Brinitzer

*1958 in Heidelberg. Studium der Architektur an der TH Darmstadt und Kunstgeschichte an der Universität Frankfurt/M. Promotion über H. B. Reichow. Lehrbeauftragte an der TU Kaiserslautern: 1999–2004 für Kunstgeschichte, ab 2005 für Stadtbaugeschichte. Habilitation über organische Architektur. Seit 2004 Privatdozentin für Baugeschichte an der TU Kaiserslautern.

*1958 in Heidelberg. Studied architecture at TH Darmstadt and art history at the University of Frankfurt/Main. Doctoral thesis on H. B. Reichow. Teaching assignments at TU Kaiserslautern for art history in 1999–2004 and since 2005 for urban development history. Post-doctoral thesis on organic architecture. Since 2004 reader in architectural history at TU Kaiserslautern.

Michaela Busenkell

*1962 in Schleswig. 1992 Diplom Architektur an der TU München, Döllgastpreis. 1992–1996 Mitarbeit in Architekturbüros. 1996–1999 Redakteurin der Zeitschrift *AIT*. 1999–2004 Editorial Director bei *www.a-matter.com*; Kuratorische Beraterin der Ausstellung *Deutschlandschaft* bei der Architektur-Biennale Venedig 2004. Seit 2005 freie Journalistin.

*1962 in Silesia. 1992 graduated in architecture from TU München as Döllgast Laureate. 1992–1996 employed in architectural practices. 1996–1999 editor of *AIT* periodical. 1999–2004 editorial director at *www.a-matter.com*; curatorial advisor to the *Deutschlandschaft* exhibition at the 2004 Venice Architecture Biennale. Freelance journalist since 2005.

Yorck Förster
*1964 in Hannover. Studium der Philosophie, Soziologie und Kunstpädagogik in Frankfurt am Main. Als freier Kurator für das Deutsche Architektur Museum tätig.
*1964 in Hanover. Studied philosophy, sociology and art education at Frankfurt/Main. Freelance curator for the Deutsches Architektur Museum.

Christina Gräwe
*1965 in Idar-Oberstein. Studium von Spanisch und Kunstgeschichte an der FU Berlin und Architektur an der TU Berlin. Mitarbeit in verschiedenen Architekturbüros. 2003–2005 Volontariat im Deutschen Architekturmuseum in Frankfurt/Main; seit Mai 2005 dort als Kuratorin tätig.
*1965 in Idar-Oberstein. Studied Spanish and art history at FU Berlin and architecture at TU Berlin. Employed in various architectural practices. 2003–2005 trainee at the Deutsches Architekturmuseum in Frankfurt/Main, where she has been a curator since May 2005.

Oliver G. Hamm
*1963 in Limburg/Lahn. 1984–1989 Studium der Architektur an der FH Darmstadt. 1989–1992 Redakteur der Zeitschrift *db – deutsche bauzeitung*, 1992–1998 der Zeitschrift *Bauwelt*, seit 2000 Chefredakteur der Zeitschrift *Deutsches Architektenblatt*; freier Autor und Kurator. Deutscher Preis für Denkmalschutz 2003. Lebt in Berlin.
*1963 in Limburg/Lahn. 1984–1989 studied architecture at FH Darmstadt. 1989–1992 editor of *db – deutsche bauzeitung*, 1992–1998 editor of *Bauwelt*, since 2000 editor-in-chief of *Deutsches Architektenblatt*; freelance writer and curator. German Prize for Architectural Conservation 2003. Lives in Berlin.

Anna Hesse
*1977 in Lahn-Gießen, 1997–2004 Studium der Architektur an der TU Darmstadt und am Tec de Monterrey in Querétaro, Mexiko. Studentische Ausstellungen. 2004–2005 Mitarbeit in Architekturbüros. 2005–2006 Volontariat im Deutschen Architekturmuseum in Frankfurt/Main; seit 2006 als freie Kuratorin tätig.
*1977 in Lahn-Gießen, 1997–2004 studied architecture at TU Darmstadt and at Tec de Monterrey in Querétaro Mexico. Student exhibitions. 2004–2005 employed in architectural practices. 2005–2006 trainee at the Deutsches Architekturmuseum in Frankfurt/Main, where she has been a freelance curator since 2006.

Ulrich Höhns
*1954 in Niedersachsen. Studium der Architektur an der Hochschule für bildende Künste in Hamburg. Seit 1983 freier Architekturhistoriker und -kritiker. Forschung, Lehre und Publikationen zur Architektur und Stadtbaugeschichte des 19.–21. Jahrhunderts. Seit 1992 wissenschaftlicher Leiter des Schleswig-Holsteinischen Archivs für Architektur und Ingenieurbaukunst (AAI). Lebt in Schleswig-Holstein.

*1954 in Lower Saxony. Studied architecture at the Hochschule für bildende Künste in Hamburg. Since 1983 freelance architecture historian and critic. Research, teaching assignments and publications in the field of nineteenth- to twenty-first-century architecture and urban development history. Since 1992 head of the Schleswig-Holstein Archives for Architecture and Structural Engineering (AAI). Lives in Schleswig-Holstein.

Falk Jaeger
*1950 in Ottweiler/Saar. Studium der Architektur und Kunstgeschichte in Braunschweig, Stuttgart und Tübingen. Promotion an der TU Hannover. Apl. Professor für Architekturtheorie und -kritik an der TU Dresden. Freier Publizist, Kurator und Architekturkritiker bei Tages- und Fachpresse, Hörfunk und Fernsehen. Lebt in Berlin.
*1950 in Ottweiler/Saar. Studied architecture and art history at Brunswick, Stuttgart and Tübingen. Doctorate from TU Hanover. Professorship in architectural theory and criticism at TU Dresden. Freelance writer, curator and architecture critic for newspapers and specialist periodicals, radio and TV. Lives in Berlin.

Claus Käpplinger
*1963. Lebt als freier Architektur- und Stadtkritiker in Berlin. Zahlreiche Publikationen in *Architektur Aktuell*/Wien, *De Architect*/Den Haag, *DBZ, DB, Der Architekt*. Organisiert seit 1998 den interdisziplinären Diskussionskreis »Stadtsalon« zu Fragen der Stadt, Architektur und Wahrnehmung.
*1963. Lives in Berlin. Freelance architecture and urban critic. Has published widely in *Architektur Aktuell* (Vienna), *De Architect* (Den Haag), *DBZ*, *DB*, *Der Architekt*. Organiser of the interdisciplinary discussion group "Stadtsalon" on issues of urban life, architecture and perception since 1998.

Karl Kiem
* 1953, Architekturstudium (u. a. TU u. HdK Berlin), Promotion in Baugeschichte (TU Berlin) und Kunstgeschichte (Universität von Amsterdam), Habilitation in Baugeschichte (TU Hamburg-Harburg). Seit 1999 Professur für Baugeschichte und Denkmalpflege (Universität Siegen).
*1953. Studied architecture at TU Berlin, HdK Berlin and elsewhere. Doctorate in architectural history (TU Berlin) and art history (University of Amsterdam), post-doctoral thesis on architectural history (TU Hamburg-Harburg). Since 1999 professor of architectural history and conservation at the University of Siegen.

Ursula Kleefisch-Jobst
*1956 in Stuttgart. Studium der Kunstgeschichte, Archäologie und Germanistik in Bonn, München und Rom; Promotion 1986. 1985–1988 Forschungsprojekt an der Biblioteca Hertziana in Rom. 1989–1990 Mitarbeiterin am Landesdenkmalamt in Berlin. Seit 2001 freie Kuratorin am Deutschen Architektur Museum in Frankfurt/Main.
*1956 in Stuttgart. Studied art history, archaeology and German literature at Bonn, Munich and Rome; doctorate 1986. 1985–1988 research project at the Biblioteca Hertziana in Rome. 1989–1990 employed in the Berlin regional conservation office. Since 2001 freelance curator for the Deutsches Architektur Museum in Frankfurt/Main.

Karin Leydecker

*1956 in Speyer. Studium der Germanistik, Psychologie, Kunstge-
schichte und evangelischen Theologie in Mainz, Heidelberg und
Karlsruhe; Promotion 1988. Forschung und Lehraufträge zur
Architekturwahrnehmung an der Universität und der PH in Karlsruhe. Publikationen zur Kunst und Architektur insbesondere des
19. und 20. Jahrhunderts. Lebt als freie Kritikerin in Neustadt an
der Weinstraße.

*1956 in Speyer. Studied German literature, psychology, art his-
tory and Protestant theology at Mainz, Heidelberg and Karlsruhe;
doctorate 1988. Research and teaching assignments on architectural reception at the University of Karlsruhe. Publications on
art and architecture, mostly nineteenth and twentieth century.
Freelance critic. Lives in Neustadt an der Weinstraße.

Hanno Rauterberg,

*1967 in Celle. Studium der Kunstgeschichte; Promotion. Ab-
solvent der Henri-Nannen-Journalisten-Schule. Redakteur im
Feuilleton der ZEIT, schreibt vor allem über Themen der zeitgenössischen Kunst, der Architektur und des Städtebaus.

*1967 in Celle. Studied art history; doctorate. Graduate of the
Henri Nannen School of Journalism. Editor of the arts section in
Die ZEIT, writing mainly on contemporary art, architecture and
urban development.

Sebastian Redecke

*1957 in Osnabrück. Studium der Architektur an der Technischen
Universität Braunschweig und an der Università »La Sapienza«
Rom. Dipl.-Ing. Architekt. Seit 1990 Redakteur bei der Bauwelt in
Berlin. Herausgeber mehrerer Bücher zur aktuellen Architektur
in Berlin und Paris

*1957 in Osnabrück. Studied architecture at TU Brunswick and
University of Rome La Sapienza. Qualified architect. Since 1990
editor of Bauwelt in Berlin. Several books on contemporary architecture in Berlin and Paris.

Peter Cachola Schmal

*1960 in Altötting, 1981–1989 Studium der Architektur TU Darm-
stadt. Mitarbeit in Architekturbüros. 1992–1997 Assistent am Fach-
gebiet Baugestaltung Prof. Eisele TUD. 1997–2000 Lehrbeauftragter
für Entwerfen FH Frankfurt. Seit 2000 Kurator am Deutschen
Architektur Museum in Frankfurt/Main; seit 2006 dessen Direktor.
Seit 1992 freier Architekturkritiker und -publizist.

*1960 in Altötting. 1981–1989 studied architecture at TU Darm-
stadt. Employed in architectural practices. 1992–1997 assistant in
the architectural design department of TU Darmstadt under Prof.
Eisele. 1997–2000 teaching assignments in design at FH Frankfurt.
Since 2000 curator at the DAM in Frankfurt/Main; since 2006
director of the Museum. Since1992 freelance architecture critic
and writer.

Sabine Schneider

*1960 in Schwäbisch Hall. Architekturstudium in Stuttgart, Vo-
lontariat bei der Deutschen Bauzeitung in Stuttgart. Postgraduate-
Studium »History and Theory« an der Architectural Association in
London, Mitarbeit bei The Architects' Journal in London. Seit 1990
Redakteurin der Zeitschrift Baumeister in München.

*1960 in Schwäbisch Hall. Studied architecture at Stuttgart. Intern-
ship at Deutsche Bauzeitung in Stuttgart. Postgraduate studies
in history and theory at the Architectural Association in London,
worked for The Architects' Journal in London. Since 1990 editor
of Baumeister in Munich.

Christian Thomas

*1955 in Lüdenscheid. Studium der Germanistik, Philosophie und
Kunstgeschichte. Seit 1993 Redakteur im Feuilleton der Frankfurter
Rundschau, verantwortlich für Architektur und Städtebau; seit
2003 stellvertretender Ressortleiter. Lebt in Frankfurt/Main.

*1955 in Lüdenscheid. Studied German literature, philosophy and
art history. Since 1993 architecture and urban development editor
for the arts section of Frankfurter Rundschau; deputy chief editor
since 2003. Lives in Frankfurt/Main.

Inge Wolf

*1955 in Kilianstädten. Studium der Kunstgeschichte in Frank-
furt/Main. Seit 1994 wissenschaftliche Mitarbeiterin des Deutschen
Architektur Museums; seit 1996 Leiterin des Archivs.

*1955 in Kilianstädten. Studied art history at Frankfurt/Main.
From 1994 research assistant at Deutsches Architektur Museum
in Frankfurt/Main; director of the archive since 1996.

ABBILDUNGSNACHWEIS
ILLUSTRATION CREDITS

Umschlag Cover
SANAA, Zollverein School of Management and Design, Essen
Foto Photo: Christian Richter

Frontispiz Frontispiece
Herzog & de Meuron
Informations-, Kommunikations- und Medienzentrum, Cottbus
Information, Communication and Media Centre, Cottbus
Foto Photo: Margherita Spiluttini, Wien

8/9 Baumschlager Eberle, Geschosswohnungen Falkenried, Hamburg
Apartment House Falkenried
Foto Photo: Eduard Hueber, Arch Photo Inc., New York

11 Christian Richters, Münster
12 oben top Eduard Hueber, Arch Photo Inc., New York
12 unten bottom Oliver Heissner / artur, Köln
13 oben top René Menges / artur, Köln
13 unten bottom artur, Köln
14 Oliver Heissner / artur, Köln
15 Karl Johaentges, Hannover
17 Oliver Heissner / artur, Köln
19 Maria Bozzo Costa
20 oben top Frank-Heinrich Müller, Leipzig
20 unten bottom Lukas Roth, Köln
21 Andreas Kaufmann
22 Hans-Christian Schink / Punctum, Leipzig
23 U. Kielstein
24 C. Schumann
25 Hans-Christian Schink / Punctum, Leipzig
26 oben top Frank-Heinrich Müller, Leipzig
26 unten bottom Henchion, Reuter und Partner
27 Hans-Jürgen Landes
29 Florian Bolk / Stadtwandel-Verlag, Berlin
30 Lukas Roth, Köln
31 Tomas Riehle, Köln
32 Michael Heinrich, München
33 Stefan Müller, Berlin
34 Reinhard Görner
35 Groth Gruppe
36 Reinhard Görner / artur, Köln
37 Beisheim Center / Idris Kolodziej

38/39 Roedig Schop, Wohnhaus, Berlin
Apartment House
Foto Photo: Andrea Kroth, Berlin

41–47 Florian Holzherr, München
49, 52, 53 oben top Dominik Reipka, Hamburg
50, 51, 53 unten bottom Christian Schaulin, Hamburg
55–59 Linus Lintner, Berlin
61–65 Christoph Kraneburg, Köln
67 Stefan Müller, Berlin
68, 69, 71 Andrea Kroth, Berlin
70 Peter Gruchot
72, 73, 75, 76 oben top, Mitte rechts centre right,
unten bottom Frank Müller
76 Mitte links centre left 77 Christoph Eckelt

78/79 Volker Staab, Servicezentrum, München
Service Centre
Foto Photo Werner Huthmacher, Berlin

81, 82, 84, 85 Christian Richters, Münster
83 Titus Bernhard
87–93 Stefan Müller-Naumann, München
95–99 Stefan Müller, Berlin
101–105 Michael Heinrich, München
107, 113 oben rechts top right artur, Köln
108–110, 113 oben links top left Reinhard Görner / artur, Köln
111, 112, 113 unten bottom Jürgen Henkelmann / artur, Köln
115–119 Werner Huthmacher, Berlin
120 oben links top left, 120 unten bottom, 121 Roland Halbe
120 oben rechts top right, Mitte centre Klemens Ortmeyer
123–126, 127 oben links top left, 127 unten bottom, 128 oben top,
129 Duccio Malagamba, Barcelona
127 oben rechts top right, 128 unten bottom Margherita Spiluttini, Wien
131, 133–135 Bertram Kober / Punctum, Leipzig
137–141 Michael Heinrich, München
143–147 Stefan Müller-Naumann, München
149–153 Michel Denancé, Paris
155–159 Christian Richters, Münster
161–165 Werner Huthmacher, Berlin
167–173 Christian Richters, Münster

174/175 Peter Kulka, Feuer- und Rettungswache, Leverkusen
Fire and Rescue Station
© Deutsches Architektur Museum, Archiv. Foto Photo: Peter Kulka

176 © Deutsches Architektur Museum, Archiv
177 Internet
179 © Deutsches Architektur Museum, Archiv.
Foto Photo Uwe Dettmar
180 oben top © Deutsches Architektur Museum, Archiv.
Foto Photo Uwe Dettmar
180 unten bottom © Deutsches Architektur Museum, Archiv.
Foto Photo Peter Kulka

189 David Chipperfield, Literaturmuseum der Moderne, Marbach
Moderne Literature Museum
Foto Photo Stefan Müller-Naumann, München

Eingangshalle, Literaturmuseum der Moderne, Marbach
Foyer, Modern Literature Museum, Marbach

ARCHITEKTENREGISTER DER JAHRBÜCHER 1992–2006
INDEX OF ARCHITECTS IN THE ANNUALS 1992–2006

Kaag, Werner 1995
Kahlfeldt Architekten 1997
Keim + Sill 1999
Kiessler, Uwe 1994, 1995, 1998
Kissler + Effgen 2005
Kister, Scheithauer, Gross 1993, 1995, 2003
Kleihues, Josef Paul 1993, 1995, 1997, 2005
Knoche Architekten 2001
Koch, Panse, Hühn 1997
Königs Architekten 2003
Köppel, Stephan 2006
Kollhoff und Timmermann 1993, 1994, 1995, 1996, 1997, 2000, 2002
Krahn, Johannes 1998
Krause, Lutz 1999
Krischanitz, Adolf 2006
Kristmundsson, Pálmar 2000
KSP Engel und Zimmermann 1998
Kücker, Wilhelm 1992, 1998
Kulka, Peter 1993, 1996, 1997, 1998, 2001, 2003, 2006

Lamott und Lamott 1998, 2001
Landes, Michael A. 2001
Lederer, Ragnarsdóttir, Oei 2001
Lehtinen, Mäki, Peltola 2000
Léon, Wohlhage, Wernik 1994
Letzel Freivogel architekten 2006
Libeskind, Daniel 1998

Mäckler, Christoph 1993, 1994
Mayer H., Jürgen 2002
Mecanoo 1994
Meck, Andreas 2004, 2006
Meier, Richard 2005
Meier-Scupin & Petzet 1997, 2001
Meixner Schlüter Wendt 2006
Mies van der Rohe, Ludwig 1994
Miralles Tagliabue 2000
Müller und Reimann 2000

Nagler, Florian 2006
Natalini, Adolfo 2004
Navarro Baldeweg, Juan 1997
Nielsen + Nielsen 2000
Noebel, Walter Arno 1998
Nouvel, Jean 1996

Offenberg, Gerd 1993
Olgiati, Valerio 1992
OMA 2004
Ortner + Ortner 1998, 2003
Otto, Frei 2001

Pahl + Weber-Pahl 1995, 1998, 2000, 2001
Pei, Cobb, Freed & Partners 1996
Peichl, Gustav 1992
Pfeifer, Günter 1993, 1994, 1995
Piano, Renzo 2006
Poelzig, Hans 1996
Poitiers, André 2003

Rabenschlag, Anne 1994, 1996
Rasch, Heinz 2000
Rhode, Kellermann, Wawrosky 1999
Roedig Schop Architekten 2006
Roth, Carsten 2004

SANAA 2006
Santos, José Paulo dos 1998
Sauerbruch Hutton 2000, 2002, 2004, 2005
Sawade, Jürgen 1997
Scharoun, Hans 1993, 2000
Schattner, Karljosef 1993, 1994, 1995, 1998
Schelling, Erich 1998
Schmitz, Karl-Heinz 1997
Schmitz Barz-Malfatti 2005
Schneider + Schumacher 1996, 1998, 1999, 2000, 2001, 2003
Schomers, Schürmann, Stridde 1994
Schürmann und Schürmann 1992
Schultes Axel 1992, 1993, 1999, 2001, 2002
Schulz & Schulz 2004
Schweger und Partner 1993, 1994
Schwitzke und Partner 1993
Seidlein, Peter C. von 1997
Seiffert, Stoeckmann – Formalhaut 2002
Simon, Hans 1997
Snøhetta 2000
Snozzi, Luigi 2006
Sobek, Werner 2002
Speer und Partner, AS&P 1994, 1996
Spycher, Ernst 1998
Staab, Volker 2000, 2003, 2006
Staib, Gerald 2003
Steffann, Emil 2003
Steidle und Partner 2005
Stich und Stich 1997
Stirling, Wilford and Associates 1992
Stirling and Gowan 1995
Störmer, Jan 2002
Storch und Ehlers 1995
Studio Granda 1993
Sudau, Rüdiger 1995

Tonon, Benedict 1993, 1994, 1995, 1997, 1999
Turkali Architekten 1995, 1996

Ungers, Oswald Mathias 1993, 1995, 1996
UN Studio 2006

Valentyn, Thomas van den 1993, 2004
Volz, Michael 2000

Waechter, Hans 2003
Wandelt, Angela 2005
Wandel, Hoefer, Lorch + Hirsch 1996, 1998, 2002
Weber, Martin 1992
Weinmiller, Gesine 1996, 1999
Wingårdh, Gert 2000

Zach und Zünd 1997
Zamp Kelp, Günter 1997

IMPRESSUM
IMPRINT

Herausgegeben von **Edited by**
Annette Becker, Anna Hesse, Peter Cachola Schmal
im Auftrag des **on behalf of** Dezernats für Kultur und Freizeit,
Amt für Wissenschaft und Kunst der Stadt Frankfurt am Main

© Prestel Verlag, München · Berlin · London · New York, 2006
© Deutsches Architektur Museum, Frankfurt am Main, 2006
© für die abgebildeten Werke bei den Architekten und Künstlern,
ihren Erben oder Rechtsnachfolgern; Fotonachweis siehe Seite 188
**For the artworks with the architects and artists, their heirs or assigns;
picture credits see page 188**

Urhebernennungen stammen von den beteiligten Architekten selbst.
Für die Richtigkeit dieser Angaben übernehmen das Deutsche Architektur
Museum und der Prestel Verlag keine Gewähr.
**Names of copyright holders of the material used have been supplied by
the architects themselves. Neither the Deutsches Architektur Museum nor
Prestel Verlag shall be held responsible for any omissions or inaccuracies.**

Die Deutsche Nationalbibliothek verzeichnet diese Publikation
in der Deutschen Nationalbibliografie; detaillierte bibliografische
Daten sind im Internet über http://dnb.ddb.de abrufbar.

Library of Congress Control Number: 2006930754
**British Library Cataloguing-in-Publication Data: a catalogue record for this
book is available from the British Library; Deutsche Nationalbibliothek
holds a record of this publication in the Deutsche Nationalbibliografie;
detailed bibliographical data can be found under: http://dnb.ddb.de**

Prestel Verlag
Königinstraße 9
80539 München
Telefon +49 (0)89 3817 09-0
Telefax +49 (0)89 3817 09-35
www.prestel.de

Prestel Publishing Ltd.
4, Bloomsbury Place
London, WC1A 2Qa
Tel.: +44 (0)20 7323 5004
Fax.: +44 (0) 20 7636 8004

Prestel Publishing
900 Broadway, Suite 603
New York, NY 10003
Tel.: +1 (212) 995 27 20
Fax.: +1 (212) 995 27 33
www.prestel.com

Deutsches Architekturmuseum
Schaumainkai 43
60596 Frankfurt am Main
Telefon +49 (0)69 21 23 88 44
Telefax +49 (0)69 21 23 63 86
info.DAM@stadt-frankfurt.de
www.DAM-online.de

Koordination **Coordination**: Anja Besserer
Übersetzung aus dem Deutschen **Translation from the German**:
Ishbel Flett, Edinburgh
Lektorat **Copyediting**: Andrea Hölzl, München (deutsch **German**)
Cynthia Hall, Stephanskirchen (englisch **English**)
Gestaltung und Herstellung **Design and Production**: Cilly Klotz
Satz **Typesetting**: Vornehm, München
Lithografie **Lithography**: Reproline mediateam GmbH & Co. KG, München
Druck und Bindung **Printing and Binding**: Appl, Wemding

Gedruckt in Deutschland auf chlorfrei gebleichtem Papier
Printed in Germany on acid-free paper

ISBN 978-3-7913-3690-9 / 3-7913-3690-8